IS THIS ANY WAY TO RUN A DEMOCRATIC ELECTION?

Debating American Electoral Politics

SECOND EDITION

Stephen J. Wayne

GEORGETOWN UNIVERSITY

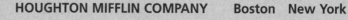

HOUGHTON MIFFLIN COMPANY   Boston New York

To my son, Jared
May you and your generation keep the flame
of American democracy burning brightly.

Editor-in-Chief: *Jean L. Woy*
Sponsoring Editor: *Katherine Meisenheimer*
Editorial Associate: *Tonya Lobato*
Project Editor: *Ylang Nguyen*
Editorial Assistant: *Wendy Thayer*
Senior Production/Design Coordinator: *Carol Merrigan*
Senior Manufacturing Coordinator: *Priscilla Bailey*

Printed in the U.S.A.

Library of Congress Catalog Card Number: 2001133364
ISBN: 0-618-21423-2

123456789-FFG-06 05 04 03 02

Contents

Preface

We are a nation of critics, self-critics. As we laud our democratic system, we also complain about it. The election process in particular has been the source of much lament and critical commentary.

WHAT'S WRONG WITH AMERICAN ELECTORAL POLITICS?

The complaints are legion. The election cycle is too long, too complex, and too costly. The system is controlled by and for the few, the special interests, not the public's interest. Election laws are biased in favor of those who enacted them, the major parties and their candidates and sometimes have been implemented in a discriminatory manner. Money drives the process, and wealthy contributors exercise disproportionate influence over the candidates, parties, their campaigns, and on what follows from this election activity, public policymaking. The news media are more interested in a good scandal than in discussing substantive policy issues and their consequences for society. Politicians are not to be trusted; they will say and do almost anything to get elected, and once elected, they are beholden to their large contributors and the special interest groups that aided their campaign. Moreover, incumbents have stacked the deck in favor of their own reelection, thereby undercutting two of the basic goals of a democratic electoral process—to keep public officials responsive to the people and to hold them accountable for their public policy decisions and actions. And as if these allegations were not enough, there is the charge that election returns today do not result in winners who are compatible with one another, who are willing to compromise on policy issues, and who put the public's interest ahead of their own self-interest. Nor does the outcome of the vote easily translate into a governing agenda and a majority coalition for achieving it. All of these charges have produced negative perceptions of the electoral process today and undoubtedly have contributed to public cynicism, apathy, and mistrust of politicians and the politics in which they engage. Something is very wrong with American electoral politics, or so its critics allege.

Are these charges correct? Is the current way the best way to run a democratic election? Have we drifted from the ideals and goals of the American political tradition? If so, how and when did we do so, and what, if anything, can be done about it? If not, why are there so many persistent complaints, and why do so many people not vote? These are some of the questions that concerned citizens should be asking about our electoral system and that public officials, party leaders, political scientists, and others should be attempting to answer.

GOALS AND STRUCTURE OF THIS BOOK

This book is intended to help its readers participate in the debate on American electoral politics. It aims to explore critical and controversial issues that confront our political system today, and to do so in a reader-friendly way. *Is This Any Way to Run a Democratic Election?* looks at American democracy in theory and practice, notes where and why practices deviate from theory, and then proposes reforms to close the gap.

The book's first chapter discusses democratic theory in general and the democratic electoral process in particular. The next five chapters (Chapters 2–6) examine key aspects of electoral politics: suffrage and turnout, representation, partisanship, money, and the mass media. Each of these factors shapes the contest, affects the outcome, and has consequences for governing. From the environment in which elections occur, we turn in the last three chapters (Chapters 7–9) to the electoral process itself: the nomination, campaigns, and election of public officials.

SPECIAL FEATURES OF THIS BOOK

Each chapter of the book includes useful features intended to pique readers' interest in electoral issues and foster critical thinking and participation. Each chapter begins with "Did You Know That . . . ," an opening feature that presents interesting and sometimes disturbing facts about democratic election practices, processes, and outcomes that may not be widely known. After a discussion of the electoral dilemmas and ways to overcome them, each chapter concludes with a short summary, followed by a critical thinking section, "Now It's Your Turn." Included in this section are Discussion Questions, Topics for Debate, research-oriented exercises that encourage use of the Internet, and a listing of Internet Resources and Selected Readings.

NEW TO THE SECOND EDITION

The Second Edition of *Is This Any Way to Run a Democratic Election?* is thoroughly updated to consider the many controversies resulting from the 2000 elections, including low voter turnout, representational bias, fraud and voting irregularities, the electoral college/popular vote discrepancy, disproportionate contributions and expenditures, soft money, the McCain-Feingold/Shays-Meehan debate, and much more. In addition to the new pedagogical feature, Discussion Questions, the internet exercises have been expanded and web links updated.

IMPROVING THE SYSTEM

The aim of *Is This Any Way to Run a Democratic Election?* is to familiarize readers with crucial issues in American electoral politics. This book is also intended to encourage the reader to make the system better by becoming more involved in politics and government and, at the very least, by taking the responsibilities of citizenship seriously. After all, it is every citizen's system. And it is up to all of us to improve it.

The first step is to understand how electoral politics works, to be informed, to get involved, and to vote; the second is to encourage others to do so. By improving the electoral system, by making it more responsive, and by holding elected officials—individually and collectively—responsible for their decisions and actions in office, we build support for democratic institutions and move closer to the ideal of a government of, by, and for the people. This book is your invitation to begin or accelerate the process of becoming a responsible citizen.

S. J. W.

Democratic Elections: What's the Problem?

Did you know that . . .

- only about half of the voting-age population voted in the last two presidential elections, and only a little more than a third did so in recent midterm elections?
- Bill Clinton and George W. Bush, when elected president, received the votes of less than one quarter of those eligible to vote?
- most members of Congress have no effective opposition in running for renomination? Only three House incumbents and no Senate incumbents who sought renomination by their parties were defeated in 2000?
- nine members of Congress ran unopposed in the general election? One out of four House members won his or her election in 2000 with 75 percent or more of the vote; more than half had 65 percent or more of the vote?
- the incumbency reelection rate has been consistently higher for the House than for the Senate?
- third-party presidential candidate H. Ross Perot received 19 percent of the popular vote in 1992 and 8.5 percent in 1996 but no electoral votes in either election?
- there were more ballots discarded or undercounted in New York City and Chicago than there were in the entire state of Florida in the 2000 election?
- about $3 billion was spent on federal elections in 2000? Of that amount, 40 percent was not subject to federal contribution limits?
- the average length of time that 2000 presidential candidates appeared on the major broadcast networks' evening news shows was about 7 seconds? The anchors and correspondents on those same shows had six times the airtime of the candidates?

- more than 50 percent of candidate advertising in recent federal elections contained some negative reference to an opponent's character or policy positions?
- only about one-third of the people can name their member of Congress during nonelectoral periods?
- since 1968 there have been only six years and four months during which the same political party controlled the White House and both houses of Congress?

Is this any way to run a democratic election?

T HESE FACTS suggest that something is terribly wrong with our electoral process. They raise serious questions about how democratic the American political system really is. They also point to the major problems within that system: low voter turnout; fraudulent, error-prone, and discriminatory voting practices; high costs and unequal resources for those running for office; short, compartmentalized, and negative media coverage; and contradictory, often inconclusive results. Let's take a look at some examples of these problems.

CONTEMPORARY ELECTION ISSUES

Low Voter Turnout

People fight for the right to vote when they don't have it. We certainly did. In 1776 American colonists, protesting British taxation without representation, declared their independence with a rhetorical flourish that underscored the people's right to alter or abolish a government that wasn't fulfilling the purpose for which it was established.

Now, more than 225 years later, in a country that prides itself on its long and successful political tradition and on its fundamental democratic values, a majority of the electorate didn't vote in 1996 and 1998 and only a bare majority did in 2000. What's wrong? Why do so many people not vote? Does it have to do with the candidates running for office, the ways they conduct their campaigns, the declining appeal of the major parties, or a basic mistrust of politicians and elected officials?

Congress considers low turnout to be a problem, a sign that the democracy isn't as vigorous as it could or should be. During the last several decades, it has enacted legislation to encourage more people to vote. At the end of the 1970s, an amendment to the Federal Election Campaign Act was passed to permit parties to raise and spend unlimited amounts of money on building their grassroots base and getting out the vote. Yet turnout continued to decline.

During the 1980s, amendments were added to the Voting Rights Act to broaden its applicability and facilitate minority participation in the electoral process. Yet the turnout of most population groups has continued to decline.

In 1993 a "motor voter" bill, designed to make it easier for people in all fifty states to register to vote, was enacted into law. Since that law went into effect, more than 7 million people have been added to the voter registration rolls.[1] Yet turnout continues at or near its lowest levels. In most contemporary elections in the United States, more people who are eligible do not vote than do so.

The issue of nonvoting raises serious questions about the vibrancy of America's civic culture and democratic political institutions. With so many people not voting, do elections reflect the judgment of the people or, rather, of a small and unrepresentative proportion of them? Similarly, to whom are elected officials responsive—the entire population or those who elected them? Do elections with low participation rates still provide an agenda for government and legitimacy for its actions? If they do not, then what does?

Fraudulent, Error-Prone, and Discriminatory Voting Practices

The Florida voting controversy in the 2000 election highlighted many of the voting problems that have plagued the U.S. electoral system since its creation. For most of the first one hundred years, parties ran American elections. They designed the ballots, rallied their supporters, got them to the polls, and made sure they voted "correctly" by distributing color-coded ballots on which only the names of their candidates appeared. Allegations of fraudulent practices, including voting by those who were ineligible to so do—such as noncitizens and the deceased—casting multiple ballots in the same election, and under- and over-counting the votes, was rampant. The adoption of the secret ballot, the administration of elections by state officials, the expansion of suffrage, and eventually the development of machines to tabulate the vote were responses to these unfair, underhanded, and undemocratic election practices. But problems persisted.

In most states, legislatures designed election laws and legislative districts to benefit those in power. Registration and residence requirements limited the size of the electorate. Geographic representation in one of the two legislative bodies gave rural areas disproportionate advantage and, in some cases, the ability to negate policies that addressed urban and suburban concerns. Moreover, in some states the laws were administered in a discriminatory fashion, making it more difficult for racial and other minorities to vote.

Not until the 1960s did the Supreme Court and Congress address some of these issues.[2] The Court ruled that population and population alone had to be the criterion by which representation was determined: one person–one vote. The Voting Rights Act of 1965 was intended to end discriminatory practices and effectively extend the vote to all eligible citizens. Registration requirements were also eased, voting hours were extended, absentee voting was facilitated, and money for party-building and get-out-the-vote activities was exempted from federal contribution requirements.

These laws and judicial decisions went a long way toward extending the franchise, encouraging turnout, and ending the fraudulent and discriminatory practices that have undercut the democratic character of U.S. elections. But they have not eliminated these problems, as the low turnout (only 51.2 percent in the 2000 presidential election), alleged discrimination, and controversies over the Florida vote reveal. After the 2000 election, the U.S. Commission on Civil Rights issued a report that concluded that African Americans were much more likely than white voters to be turned away from the polls in Florida.[3] Researchers at Massachusetts Institute of Technology (MIT) and California Institute of Technology (Cal Tech) deduced that between 4 million and 6 million votes for president in the 2000 election were not counted, some because of registration foul-ups, some because of voter confusion and error, and some because of faulty equipment.[4] In close elections, such as in 2000, these undercounted voters could have made a difference, even changing the outcome.

Can an election be considered democratic if eligible voters are prevented from voting? Can the results be regarded as legitimate if the votes of a sizable proportion of a state's population, enough to have changed the outcome of the election, are not correctly counted? Can the election be said to represent the will of the people if the ballots are confusing to many voters and if some of the votes were not properly cast or included in the total? Can the winner claim to be legitimate if the true outcome of the election remains in doubt? Six months following the Supreme Court's decision that effectively determined Bush's victory in Florida, 26 percent of the American people indicated that they still did not regard him as the legitimate president.[5]

High Costs and Unequal Resources

Despite the Florida vote controversy, campaign finance is the number one electoral issue and has been for the last two decades. The federal election campaign finance system has broken down. In the last three presidential elections, both major parties used a loophole in the Federal Election Campaign Act to raise and spend hundreds of millions of dollars on behalf of their candidates for federal office.

In the case of the presidential elections, this loophole circumvented limits on federal spending for candidates who accepted government funds. To make matters worse, each party used its access to and the facilities of its party's officeholders as inducements and rewards for obtaining larger donations. Private telephone numbers of cabinet secretaries and .congressional committee heads were regularly made available to top contributors. As president, Clinton held numerous coffee hours in the White House to facilitate the solicitation of money for the Democratic party. He rewarded those who gave the most money with trips on Air Force One, trade missions with the commerce secretary, and sleepovers in the Lincoln bedroom. Not to be outdone by his Democratic predecessors, Vice President Dick Cheney lavishly entertained the most generous GOP contributors at a gala at his official residence.

Even without the illegal solicitations and legal circumvention of the campaign finance legislation, the amount of money required to mount an effective campaign for federal office has become a major issue. Expenditures for mass media advertising have gone sky high, with no end in sight. Moreover, the advertising itself has raised concerns that it distorts rather than enhances the political debate.

Is too much money being raised for and spent on election campaigns? Do the wealthy buy access and influence by virtue of their contributions? Have huge expenditures by nonparty groups, under the guise of free speech, perverted the democratic character of the system?

Compartmentalized and Negative Media Coverage

Closely related to the issue of money is that of news coverage. For better or worse, the mass media have become the principal vehicle through which candidates for national office communicate to voters. Political parties have become much less effective intermediaries between their candidates and the electorate. Dependence on the news media wouldn't be so bad if the goals of the press were similar to those of the parties and the candidates—but they aren't.

The mass media are not oblivious to the need to energize and educate the public, thereby providing the information necessary for an informed vote. But as a business, they are also interested in the bottom line: making money—the more, the better. They get money through advertising that is priced according to the size of the audience. To enhance audience size, the news media present the news that is most interesting to most people most of the time. In campaigns, the most newsworthy items are the dramatic ones—the horserace, with all its color and drama; the unexpected occurrences, the screwups, and the confrontations, as well as the human dimensions of a candidate's personal character and family. These subjects engage readers, viewers, and listeners but don't necessarily educate, energize, or motivate them to participate in the campaign and to vote. In fact, press compartmentalism, negativism, and interpretive "spin" are often blamed for lower turnout and for the public's cynical attitude toward candidates, parties, and the political system.[6]

How to square the interests of largely private media with the needs of an informed and involved electorate is no easy task, nor one that Congress wishes to tackle. Not only must First Amendment protections for the press be considered, but the desires of the public for the news it wants, not necessarily the news it needs, must be weighed in the balance.

Contradictory, Often Inconclusive Results

Another problem, less obvious but equally dangerous for a democratic political system, is that often elections not only do not contribute to governing, but actually make governing more difficult. Candidates make promises, parties present their platforms, and groups promote their own issues. But in a hetero-geneous society, policy priorities and positions are likely to be diverse and even inconsistent. American elections reflect this diversity far better than they mirror a popular consensus. Elections regularly produce mixed and incompatible re-sults, with unclear meanings and undefined mandates. Parties share power, thereby making the institutional divisions that much greater and more difficult to overcome.

Each of these problems has become a contemporary political issue. Each points to shortcomings in the democratic electoral process in the United States, to gaps between theory and practice. One goal of this book is to examine those gaps; another is to discuss ways they could be narrowed or, perhaps, eliminated. Finally, the book aims to stimulate thinking about elections in general and pos-sible improvements in particular.

To answer the central question, "Is this any way to run a democratic elec-tion?" in this chapter, we first examine the nature of democracy and some of the ways in which such a political system may be structured. Then we turn to the role of elections in a democracy and the criteria that these elections must meet to be considered democratic. Finally, we look at the inevitable tensions within a democratic electoral system between political liberty and equality, between majority rule and minority rights, and between a free press and an informed electorate.

THE NATURE OF DEMOCRACY

A **democracy** is, simply put, a government of the people. Initially used in an-cient Greece, where democracy was first practiced, the term itself comes from the Greek words *demos,* meaning "people," and *kratos,* meaning "rule." In a democracy, the people rule.[7]

But *which* people? Everyone? Everyone who is a citizen? Every citizen over eighteen years old? Every eighteen-year-old citizen who is literate and mentally competent? Every eighteen-year-old literate and mentally competent citizen who has knowledge of the issues and can apply that knowledge to make an in-telligent judgment? The list of qualifications could go on indefinitely. Naturally, an informed electorate is desirable, but the more people who are excluded be-cause they lack certain characteristics, the less likely is it that the electorate will reflect the general population.

And *how* do the people rule? By themselves? By selecting others and hold-ing them accountable? By agreeing to a set of rules and procedures by which some will be selected to perform certain public tasks, such as teaching school, maintaining law and order, or protecting against foreign attack?

There is no single right answer to these questions. There are many types of democracies, distinguished by *who* and *how*: by who makes the decisions and by how power is distributed.[8]

TYPES OF DEMOCRACIES

Who Makes Public Policy Decisions?

When the people themselves make public policy decisions, the democracy is said to be a **direct democracy**. A New England town meeting in which all residents participate on matters of local interest, such as where to build a new town hall or whether to recycle disposable waste, is an example of direct democracy at work. A state ballot initiative on which voters indicate their preferences on a range of issues, such as legalized gambling, affirmative action, or public benefits for illegal immigrants or new residents, is another example of direct democracy. When George W. Bush, as a managing partner of the Texas Rangers, convinced voters of Arlington, Texas, to support a special tax to pay for a new baseball stadium, he was engaging in direct democracy.

In a direct democracy there is true collective decision making. Obviously, in a country as large and diverse as the United States, such a system would be impractical and undesirable for the nation as a whole. There would be too many people participating in too many decisions with limited information and understanding of the issues. As a consequence, most democracies are by necessity **representative democracies,** in which people choose others to represent them in government, to formulate and implement public policy, and sometimes even to adjudicate it.[9]

A basic goal of representative government is to be responsive to the needs and interests of the people who elected that government. How can these needs and interests be identified? One way is through elections. Although elections aren't the only way that public views find expression and can influence public policy, they are the most decisive means for doing so. That's why they are such a critical component of a democratic political system. Elections are a mechanism through which the citizenry expresses its desires and by which it can evaluate the performance of those in office. Elections link the government to the governed.

How Is Power Distributed?

Another way to categorize democracies is according to how they distribute power. In a **popular,** or **plebiscitary, democracy,** the people exercise considerable influence over the selection of government officials and the policies they pursue. Such a system provides opportunities for the populace to initiate policy issues and vote on them directly as well as to elect candidates and, if necessary, to remove them from office. Ballot access is easy, there are few impediments to voting, and the people have the last word.

In a **pluralistic democracy,** a wide variety of groups—from political parties to groups with economic interests (such as business, labor, and the professions) to those motivated by social and political (ideological and issue-oriented) beliefs—all compete for influence. They do so in line with their own interests and beliefs, using their own resources to gain and maintain public support. James Madison argued in *The Federalist,* No. 10, that such factions in society were inevitable and that one of the merits of the Constitution being debated for ratification was that it prevented any one of them from dominating the government.[10]

A third model is an **elitist democracy,** in which power is concentrated in fewer hands than in a pluralistic system. There is more hierarchy, and more discretion is exercised by those in power. However, because it is a democracy, there is still competition between elites to gain election to government and to exercise influence within it.

In all three systems, government officials remain accountable to those who elected them. Whatever the form of democratic government, it rests on popular consent. Elections anchor that government to its popular base. Without elections, a democratic political system cannot exist.

ELECTIONS AND DEMOCRACY

Elections tie citizens to their government. They are essential for several reasons. They provide a mechanism by which the people can choose those government officials—legislators, top executives, and, in some cases, judges—who make, implement, and adjudicate public policy. Elections are also a means by which the public can hold these officials accountable for their actions and keep them responsive to the people's needs, interests, and desires.

In order to make decisions on who should be selected to lead the government and to make judgments on the performance of those in government, voters need information. A free press is a conduit for that information. Without a free press reporting the election news, the electorate would be either dependent on gathering and analyzing its own information or dependent on those with a vested interest in doing so, such as the candidates, parties, and interest groups. Naturally, those with an interest in the election might be inclined to release only information that put them in the best possible light. The public needs alternative sources that are credible and objective—free and unbiased media.

In choosing the people who will run the government, elections—directly or indirectly—provide direction to that government. They establish the agenda that guides public officials, and they help build coalitions that will facilitate governing.

Elections also confer legitimacy on government and what it does. By giving citizens an opportunity to select public officials and influence their policy agendas, elections contribute to the ongoing support for the policy decisions and administrative actions of government as well as for those who make or take them. Whether people agree with a particular policy, they are more likely to accept that policy as valid and lawful if those who made it were selected in a fair and honest way. And they will also be more likely to accept policy if they know that they will have other opportunities down the road to express their opinions, participate in a political campaign, or vote for the candidates of their choice. Similarly, people will respect and abide by the decisions of elected officials, even approving their performance in office when they do not like them personally, as long as they consider their election legitimate. Take President Clinton, for example. His job approval exceeded his personal favorability throughout his second term and especially during his impeachment trial.[11]

Criteria for Democratic Elections

For elections to be consistent with the basic tenets of a democratic political system, they must meet four operational criteria: political equality, universal suffrage, meaningful choice, and the free flow of information and ideas.[12]

Political equality is the basic situation in which everyone is considered of equal worth. If there is political equality, there can be no classes or ranks, no individual or group whose position elevates it to a higher status. As Thomas Jefferson put it in the Declaration of Independence, "All men are created equal."

If everyone is equal, then all should be able to exercise an equal voice in the running of the political system. At the very least, this means that the principle of one person–one vote must apply to all elections unless otherwise specified in the Constitution. It also means that all votes count equally, that no individual, group, region, or jurisdiction should gain extra representation or exercise extra influence. Translated into election terminology, equality requires **universal suffrage,** the right of all adult citizens to be able to vote.

Unless all adult citizens have an opportunity to participate in the electoral process, the resulting electoral decisions cannot be said to reflect the views of the entire country. The exclusion of any group of citizens because of any characteristic other than characteristics directly related to their capacity to exercise an informed and intelligent vote (such as being literate, being an adult, and having normal mental capabilities) naturally weakens the representative nature of the system. The more people who are excluded for whatever reason, the less the government can be said to rest on the consent of the governed.

Not only must all adult citizens capable of making a voting decision be given the opportunity to do so, but the voting decision itself also must be meaningful. If there were only one candidate for an office or if all the candidates had equal qualifications and shared essentially the same views, then there would be grounds for claiming that the voters had no **meaningful choice.**

To choose is to select from among diverse alternatives. But how diverse should they be? A choice among candidates who differ widely in their beliefs, particularly if the views of one of them is extreme, may amount to no real choice at all. If the major parties were to agree on the same candidate and the only other candidate was unknown to most voters, that would probably not constitute a meaningful choice. To be meaningful for most of the people, the choices should lie within the broad parameters of public acceptability yet be distinctive enough for voters to weigh them on the basis of their own values, attitudes, and opinions.

Related to making a meaningful choice is the **free flow of information and ideas.** Unless there is ample information and discussion within the public arena, people will have difficulty understanding the issues—much less determining which candidates best represent their positions, are most qualified, and merit their support. We normally think of a free press as essential to the operation of such a marketplace of ideas.

Democratic Electoral Systems

The number of people who are elected, the way winners are determined, and the size and shape of electoral districts may vary within the country as well as among countries. In the United States, the United Kingdom, and some other democratic nations, public officials are elected on the basis of **plurality rule in single-member districts.** Simply put, this means that the candidate who receives the most votes for a particular office within an electoral district wins. Unless rules specify otherwise, the winner need not receive a majority of the vote; a simple plurality is usually sufficient. If there is a majority requirement, however, and no candidate receives more than half the votes in the initial balloting, there will be a runoff election between the top two vote getters in the first round of voting.[13]

The U.S. Supreme Court has also ruled that all legislative districts must be equal in population to ensure that the one person–one vote principle prevails—except, of course, for the Senate, in which each state, regardless of its population, is entitled to two senators.

The main advantage of a plurality voting system is that it is simple and direct. The winner is easily and usually quickly determined, and the elected representative is accountable to the entire district. Responsibility, in other words, can be pinpointed.

The principal disadvantage of a plurality system is that those in the minority are less likely to be represented by a candidate of their choice. Their views and interests may not be adequately considered when public policy decisions are made. Moreover, plurality voting systems tend to enlarge the advantage of the majority if that majority is equally dispersed across the entire electoral area.[14] What happens is that those in the majority tend to vote for candidates who have similar demographic and attitudinal characteristics, except in those situations in which a minority group constitutes a majority within an electoral district.

To improve minority representation in Congress, the U.S. Department of Justice, citing the 1982 Voting Rights Act and several Supreme Court decisions, pushed states to create legislative districts in which minority groups, such as African Americans or Latinos, constituted the voting majority. However, the Supreme Court subsequently declared that race could not be the primary factor for determining the boundaries of these districts, once again putting minorities at a disadvantage in the U.S. system of plurality voting in single-member districts.

There is another way, however, to achieve broader representation: by instituting a system of **proportional voting,** in which the winners are determined in proportion to the vote that they or their party receives. In some democratic countries, such as Canada and Israel, parties run slates of candidates in districts. Similarly, in the presidential nomination process in the United States, there may be proportional voting. Democratic party rules require and Republican rules permit, on a state-by-state basis, the election of delegates pledged to their party's national convention in proportion to the vote they receive.

The principal advantage of proportional voting is that it provides a fairer and more accurate representation of minorities in the government. A principal disadvantage is that majoritarian sentiment is more difficult to discern. Such sentiment, often referred to as political or policy consensus, must be constructed after the election by those who have been selected rather than by the electorate in the votes they have cast.

Proportional voting also increases the likelihood of a splintered government in which coalitions among competing parties may be necessary to achieve a working majority. Such coalitions in turn are likely to be more fragile and less able to agree on public policy than would a government composed of a single party. Moreover, it will be more difficult to assign credit and blame for what the government does in the case of a multiparty coalition than with a single party.

In a plurality system, coalition building occurs primarily within the major parties, not between them. Each of these parties tries to reach a broad cross-section of the electorate. In doing so, they have to balance diverse and often conflicting interests. Thus the major parties in a plurality system will be more heterogeneous and, conversely, more homogeneous in a proportional voting system.

As the plurality–proportional voting dichotomy suggests, election procedures and rules are not neutral. They benefit some at the expense of others. These clashes of interests create ongoing tensions within the democratic electoral system. They are what politics is all about.

TENSIONS WITHIN A DEMOCRATIC ELECTORAL SYSTEM

The problem of obtaining a fair election outcome underlies the natural tensions in a democratic political system—between political liberty and equality, between majority rule and minority rights, and between a free press and an informed electorate.

Liberty Versus Equality

If a democracy is based on the consent of the governed, then the ability to give that consent and, if need be, to take it away is essential. That's why political liberty is so important. Political liberty is the freedom to decide for oneself and act on the basis of that decision. Take that freedom away, and a democratic government cannot exist.

In the electoral process, liberty is the right to vote as one chooses, not to vote if one chooses, and in either case, to make the voting decision freely and without duress. It is the right to exercise personal choice within the framework of the political system. Accessible voting places, secret ballots, and privacy in casting votes help protect the exercise of this right.

Personal freedom to support the candidate of one's choice, however, can undermine the equity principle. A conflict is created because certain people have more resources at their disposal than others to use in campaigns. Should individuals and groups be free to spend as much money as they want to promote their ideas and beliefs, or should their spending be limited in order to allow every citizen equal opportunity to affect the outcome of the vote? Proponents of unlimited expenditures cite the constitutional protection of free speech. Opponents argue that elected officials are more likely to be responsive to large donors than to the average citizen who does not contribute or gives only a small amount. Moreover, they claim that the advantage of the wealthy extends past the election, to governing.[15]

A related issue is that of actual participation, of personally getting involved. For a variety of reasons, those with a higher income participate at a higher rate than do those at the lower end of the socioeconomic scale.[16] This higher rate of participation magnifies their influence.

There are many forms of participation, from the simple act of voting, to working for a candidate (ringing doorbells, handing out literature, sending e-mail, coordinating events, and the like), to contributing money to a candidate's campaign, to spending money to promote one's own views, which may or may not coincide with those of a particular candidate. Placing no restrictions on these activities allows those with the interest, time, resources, and will to do more and, as a result, to potentially exercise more influence. At what point should a line be drawn between voluntary citizens' actions in the electoral process, which should be encouraged, and actions that give an unfair advantage to those with superior resources at their disposal?

Majority Rule Versus Minority Rights

Plurality voting seems a pretty straightforward criterion for a democratic society. If every vote is equal, those with the most votes should win. The problem, as we've already mentioned, is that plurality voting systems overrepresent the majority; proportional systems give more representation to minorities than they would otherwise have. They also tend to inhibit the building and maintenance of a governing majority.

Many factors affect the majority-minority relationship: the ways the boundaries of electoral districts are drawn and the number of people to be elected within them; how the ballot is organized; whether candidates are listed by office or by party; and even where, when, and for how long voting occurs. If voting places are few and inaccessible, the hours for voting are too short, and the ballot is complicated and confusing, then turnout will be lower, those in power will more likely remain in power, and those who benefit under the current arrangement will continue to do so.

Representation of groups within the society can also be affected by ballot access. In 1992 and 1996, Ross Perot's Reform party spent millions of dollars and used hundreds of volunteers and paid workers to obtain the necessary signatures for its candidates to appear on all fifty state ballots. But for the Republican and Democratic candidates, ballot access is automatic. They have a built-in advantage. Is that fair?

The majority-minority issue extends to government as well. Should majority rule be restricted so that minorities will be better protected when public policy decisions are made? James Madison thought so. Fearing that the "tyranny of the majority" could deny the minority its basic rights, he argued successfully for a divided government, one that separates institutions representing differing constituencies so that no single group could easily dominate. But in the process, Madison and his colleagues at the Constitutional Convention created a system that has enabled powerful minorities to exercise a tyranny of their own, to prevent change and thereby thwart the desires of the majority or plurality—in violation of a basic precept of democratic theory.

A Free Press Versus an Informed Electorate

The framers of the Bill of Rights believed that a free press is essential. In a government based on the consent of the governed, those in office must be held accountable for their actions. Similarly, the qualifications, promises, and positions of candidates for elective office must be evaluated.

But the public cannot assess candidates running for office or the performance of those in office unless they have the necessary information to do so. The problem is that most providers of such information—the candidates, their parties, interest groups, policy-oriented think tanks, even government officials—have a stake in the outcome or an interest in the results. Although their information is still valuable, it must be evaluated with the interests of the source in mind.

Here's where a free press comes in. For some of the same reasons that we select others to represent us in government, we also depend on others to inform us about politics and government, to help us sort out what's going on and make an informed judgment about it. That's the role of the news media: to be a watchdog, to provide the information they believe we need to know or would be interested in knowing. Anticipating that the press will perform this role is itself an incentive for those running for and holding office to stay attuned to public opinion and not to behave in a manner that would draw unfavorable attention and admonishment.

A free press is unfettered but not necessarily neutral. News reporters describe the campaign as they see it. Naturally, their perceptions are influenced by their own political beliefs, their journalistic needs, and their personal feelings about the candidates and issues. To the extent that many in the news media share similar political and professional orientations, their reporting of the campaign reflects a pack mentality, a collective reading and interpretation of events.[17] This journalistic outlook colors the public's understanding and evaluation. The electorate gets a jaundiced view, one that highlights the dramatic and human elements of the campaign, usually at the expense of a debate over substantive issues.

What can be done about the media's orientation and their perceived bias? Restricting press coverage is not only impractical but also violates the First Amendment's protection of freedom of the press. Relying on the candidates to monitor the coverage they receive seems equally impractical, given their vested interest in favorable coverage. Nor can the government take on a supervisory role over political communication in a campaign, especially in light of the number of incumbents who seek reelection. How, then, can citizens obtain the information they need, particularly as it relates to policy issues and their impact on society—information that many consider essential for voters to make an informed vote?

Summary: Democratic Election Dilemmas in a Nutshell

In theory, a representative democracy is a government of the people, by some of the people, and for all of the people. It is connected to the people through elections. One democratic dilemma is to provide the citizenry with equal opportunities to affect the electoral and governmental processes without reducing their freedom to pursue their own interests and utilize their own resources. Another dilemma is to provide electoral mechanisms that are both efficient and representative, effective and accountable, dynamic and deliberative—a tall order, to be sure!

To meet these criteria, citizens must be accorded universal suffrage and equal voting power. They must have a meaningful choice in voting and timely information to make informed judgments. In practice, contemporary elections fall short of each of these criteria. There is universal suffrage in theory, but large-scale nonvoting in practice. There are many choices of candidates and some ballots of policy initiatives as well, but a lot of people still complain that their choices are unsatisfactory—because they are too narrow, too broad, or all distasteful.

All votes count equally, but all groups do not benefit equally from current electoral procedures and practices. Ethnic and racial minorities in particular seem to be disproportionately disadvantaged by plurality voting in single-member districts. Wealthy people have advantages. Finally, America has a free press but, in the view of much of the electorate, neither an objective nor a responsible one. Complaints that the media are too powerful, too judgmental, and too negative are regularly reported in survey and anecdotal research.[18] That much of the electorate is underinformed and underinvolved has been attributed in large part to the press's penchant for reporting entertaining news, as well as to weak party organizations and personal attacks by the candidates themselves.

These disjunctures between democratic theory and practice arise from many sources: the manner in which the electorate can and does participate in elections; the ways in which elections are structured and representatives chosen; the weakening of the party system and growth of candidate-oriented politics; the laws governing financial contributions and expenditures; press coverage, particularly its emphasis on the contest, its orientation toward personal character issues, and its general negativity; the parties' methods for selecting their nominees; the ways campaigns are conducted, appeals communicated, and images created; and incompatible outcomes, unclear meaning, and vacuous mandates.

Now It's Your Turn

Discussion Questions

1. How nearly universal must suffrage be for the popular will to be heard?
2. Can elections be structured to reflect majority sentiment as well as represent minority views and interests?
3. What current electoral issues pit individual liberty against political equality?
4. To what extent are the democratic goals of an informed electorate that makes a considered, hopefully rational political judgment on election day realistic and necessary?
5. How can the news media serve the informational needs of the electorate and the profit motives of media owners?
6. What are the most serious electoral problems today that threaten the democratic character of the political system?

Topics for Debate

Challenge or defend the following statements:

1. It is possible to have political freedom and equality simultaneously.
2. If the majority always rules, then the rights and interests of the minority cannot be adequately protected.
3. A press that is both free and fair is a contradiction in terms.
4. A democratic government cannot exist without a democratic electoral process.

Exercises

1. How democratic is the constitutionally prescribed electoral process?
   a. Answer this question by first examining what the Constitution requires and allows for national elections, noting its democratic and nondemocratic features.

b. To the best of your knowledge, have the nondemocratic features been changed by amendment, law, or practice? If so, how? If not, why not?

c. Is the electoral system becoming more or less democratic today and are the changes that have occurred in the electoral process good or bad for the country?

d. What aspects of the 2000 presidential election reflect negatively on the democratic character of the U.S. election system?

2. Advocates of democracy have urged that the electoral system be made as democratic as possible to achieve the ideal of a government of, by, and for the people. But others are reluctant to change a system that has worked so well for so long and has become part of America's political tradition. What do you think? Would more democracy be better, or would it actually impede the functioning of the electoral and governing systems? Might too much democracy be a bad thing? If you had to choose between liberty and equality or between majority rule and minority rights, how would you choose and why?

Internet Resources

The Internet is a rich and immediately available source of information on campaigns and elections. Here are some of the best generic sources for all kinds of information. Most of them contain links to the news media, public interest groups, ongoing political campaigns, polling organizations, and appropriate government agencies. In addition, you may access Houghton Mifflin's political science website, <http://www.hmco.com/college/polisci> for links to other sites of interest to students of American government.

Generic Sites on Campaigns

- C-SPAN <http://www.cspan.org>
  Contains up-to-date information on elections, including candidate speeches and critical commentary.

- Democracy Online <http://democracyonline.org>
  A site that examines the use of the Internet for political information. Includes reports on Internet usage and computerized voting.

- Web White & Blue <http://www.webwhiteblue.org/>
  Sponsored by the Markle Foundation, this site contains a lot of good information on nonprofit, nonpartisan resources relevant to the issues and candidates. Featured a rolling cyber debate among the presidential candidates in 2000.

- White House 2000 & '04 <http://www.niu.edu/newsplace/whitehouse.html>
  Frequently updated, this site, maintained by Professor Avi Bass, also has links to campaign humor, as well as the typical candidate and media links.

- Yahoo! <http://www.yahoo.com>
  Another comprehensive site; particularly useful for linkages to media outlets.

Government Sites on the Electoral System

- Federal Election Commission <http://www.fec.gov>
  Easily accessible data on electoral statistics, such as registration, turnout, and voting results, and extensive reports on campaign financial activities, filed by candidates and compiled in tabular form by analysts at the FEC. Bookmark this site!
- Library of Congress <http://thomas.loc.gov>
  You can use this site to access Congress, its committees, members, legislative process, rules, and schedules, as well as reports on campaigns and elections.
- National Archives and Records Administration: Office of the Federal Register <http://www.nara.gov/fedreg>
  Contains official statistics about past presidential elections, the Electoral College, election laws, and presidential documents.
- White House <http://www.whitehouse.gov>
  Contains not only information on presidential and vice presidential activities, speeches, press releases, and official business, but also links to all other parts of the government.

Selected Readings

Barber, Benjamin R. *A Passion for Democracy.* Princeton, NJ: Princeton University Press, 1998.

Dahl, Robert A. *Democracy and Its Critics.* New Haven, CT: Yale University Press, 1989.

————. *On Democracy.* New Haven, CT: Yale University Press, 1998.

————. *A Preface to Democratic Theory.* Chicago: University of Chicago Press, 1956.

Downs, Anthony. *An Economic Theory of Democracy.* New York: Harper & Row, 1957.

Dryzek, John. *Discursive Democracy.* Cambridge: Cambridge University Press, 1990.

Graham, Keith. *The Battle of Democracy: Conflict, Consensus, and the Individual.* Brighton, Sussex, United Kingdom: Wheatsheaf Books, 1986.

Held, David. *Models of Democracy.* Cambridge: Polity Press, 1996.

Hirst, Paul. *Representative Democracy and Its Limits.* Cambridge: Polity Press, 1990.

Warren, Mark, ed. *Democracy and Trust.* New York: Cambridge University Press, 1999.

Young, Iris Marion. *Inclusion and Democracy.* New York: Oxford University Press, 2000.

Notes

1. "Motor Voter Law Adds 7 Million Registrants," *Washington Post,* July 8, 1999, A7.

2. In the past the Court had stayed out of controversies over legislative districting by contending that they involved political and therefore nonjusticiable issues. In other words, they were not subject to judicial review.

3. U.S. Commission on Civil Rights, "Voting Irregularities in Florida During the 2000 Presidential Election," June 2001, <http://www.usccr.gov/vote2000>.

Florida state officials and Republican members of the commission criticized the conclusions of the report, asserting that there was no evidence that the disproportionate disfranchisement of African-American voters resulted from discriminatory behavior of state and county election officials.

4. Massachusetts Institute of Technology and California Institute of Technology, "Voting: What Is and What Could Be," report issued July 17, 2001.

5. Gallup Poll, "Seven out of 10 Americans Accept Bush as Legitimate President," July 17, 2001, <http://www.gallup.com/poll/releases/pr010717.asp>.

6. For example, see Stephen Ansolabehere and Shanto Iyengar, *Going Negative: How Political Advertisements Shrink and Polarize the Electorate* (New York: Free Press, 1995); and Thomas E. Patterson, *Out of Order* (New York: Knopf, 1993).

7. For a good basic discussion of democracy, see Robert A. Dahl, *On Democracy* (New Haven, CT: Yale University Press, 1998). Dahl has written extensively on this subject. Two of his other well-known works on democratic theory are *A Preface to Democratic Theory* (Chicago: University of Chicago Press, 1956) and *Democracy and Its Critics* (New Haven, CT: Yale University Press, 1989).

8. An excellent discussion of types of democratic systems appears in David Held, *Models of Democracy* (Cambridge: Polity Press, 1996).

9. In many of the southern states, judges are elected in partisan or nonpartisan elections. In other states, they are appointed by the governor, legislature, or special commission, in some cases later subject to an up or down vote by the electorate. At the federal level, judges are nominated by the president and appointed with the advice and consent of the Senate. Federal judges serve during good behavior for life.

10. James Madison, *The Federalist,* No. 10.

11. Gallup Poll, "Presidential Approval Trends, 1997–2000," <http ://www.gallup.com/poll/trends/pt.jobapp_BC.asp>.

12. For a classic discussion of the fundamental principles of democracy, see James W. Prothro and Charles M. Grigg, "Fundamental Principles of Democracy," *Journal of Politics* 22 (May 1960): 276–294.

13. Several southern states, such as Louisiana and Georgia, require runoffs if the winning candidate does not receive more than half the vote.

14. Dahl, *On Democracy,* 132–134.

15. Sidney Verba, Kay Lehman Schlozman, and Henry E. Brady, *Voice and Equality: Civic Voluntarism in American Politics* (Cambridge, MA: Harvard University Press, 1995), 512.

16. Ibid., 511–533.

17. S. Robert Lichter, Stanley Rothman, and Linda S. Lichter claim in their book *The Media Elite* (Bethesda, MD: Adler and Adler, 1986) that most national correspondents are liberal in ideology and Democratic in political allegiance.

18. *Striking the Balance: Audience Interests, Business Pressures, and Journalists' Values* (Washington, DC: Pew Research Center for The People & The Press, 1999); Pew Research Center For The People & The Press, "Big Doubts About News Media's Values: Public Votes for Continuity and Change in 2000," February 25, 1999.

The Popular Base of American Electoral Politics: Suffrage and Turnout

Did you know that . . .

- less than one-fifth of adults living in the United States were eligible to vote in the first election held under the Constitution?
- by 1800, about one-third of those eligible actually voted—practically all of them adult white males?
- Congress almost refused to allow Wyoming to enter the Union in 1890 because its state constitution allowed women the right to vote?
- 1.5 million African-American males are temporarily or permanently disfranchised because they have been convicted of a felony?
- at the beginning of the twentieth century, three out of four eligible voters cast ballots in the presidential election; at the end of the century, only two out of four did so?
- voter turnout has declined despite the enactment of laws to make it easier to vote?
- of all the countries with a long democratic tradition, the United States has one of the lowest rates of turnout among the voting-age population?
- the presidential election of 1996 was the first since 1924 in which less than 50 percent of those eligible failed to vote?
- the people who do vote are disproportionately better educated and have higher incomes than those who don't?
- election day is not and never has been a national holiday?
- nonvoters are less informed, less partisan, and less trustful of government than are voters?

Is this any way to run a democratic election?

T O BE democratic, an electoral system must allow all citizens to vote and to have their votes count equally.[1] Such a system should also encourage them to vote. To what extent do U.S. elections meet these democratic goals? To what extent do they achieve participatory democracy in theory and in practice?

This chapter will answer these two questions that underlie the popular foundation of American democracy. It begins with a historic overview of suffrage and turnout and then turns to the issues of who votes, why, and what difference it makes for a democratic electoral system. Proposals for increasing voter turnout are then assessed in light of contemporary trends in turnout and voting behavior.

THE EXPANSION OF SUFFRAGE

A participatory democracy was not what the framers had in mind when they drafted the Constitution. Most of the delegates who attended the Philadelphia convention neither desired nor encouraged large-scale public involvement in politics. The relatively low level of public education at the time, poor communications, and the distrust that pervaded relations among and within the states led those at the convention to design a government that would be responsive to various segments of the society but not necessarily to the popular mood of the moment.

Who should vote was a contentious issue in 1787. Not wanting to derail the Constitution's ratification by imposing conditions of suffrage to which the states might object, the framers decided not to decide who should be allowed to vote. They left the matter to the states, subject to any restrictions Congress might later establish.

Initially, most state constitutions limited suffrage to white male citizens over the age of twenty-one who owned property and were Christians. Gradually, these restrictions have been eliminated. By the 1830s, most states had removed religion and property ownership as conditions for voting, thereby enfranchising about 80 percent of adult white males.[2]

In some northern states, African-American males were also allowed to vote. The vast concentration of African Americans, however, was in the South, and not until after the Civil War were they granted suffrage. The Fifteenth Amendment, ratified in 1870, removed race and color as qualifications for voting. In theory, it enfranchised all African-American males who were citizens. In practice, only those who lived in the North and the border states could actually vote. A series of institutional devices, such as poll taxes, literacy tests, and restrictive primaries in which only Caucasians could participate (the so-called white primaries), effectively combined with social pressure to prevent African Americans in the South from voting for another hundred years.[3]

Women, too, were denied the right to vote. Wyoming was the first territory to grant women equal voting rights, in 1869, and the first state to do so after being admitted to the Union in 1890. Congress actually tried to compel Wyoming to rescind women's suffrage as a condition for statehood, but the Wyoming legislature refused, declaring, "We will remain out of the Union 100 years rather than come in without the women."[4] Congress relented. A few other states, primarily in the West, followed suit, but by 1904 only four states permitted women to vote.[5]

The almost exclusive authority that states exercised to determine eligibility began to break down after the Civil War. Over the next hundred years, Congress essentially nationalized the right to vote. A series of constitutional amendments and statutes limited the states' power to restrict suffrage. First, the Fifteenth Amendment (1871) prevented states from discriminating against otherwise eligible voters on the basis of race, color, or previous condition of servitude. The Seventeenth Amendment (1913) required all states to elect their senators by popular vote; the Nineteenth Amendment (1920) prohibited them from using gender as a qualification for voting; the Twenty-fourth Amendment (1964) precluded them from denying the vote for federal officials to residents who failed to pay a poll tax or any other taxes.[6] The last constitutional restriction on the states, the Twenty-sixth Amendment (1971), forbade them from setting an age of more than eighteen years as a condition for voting.

These constitutional strictures have been supplemented by legislation that has also limited state discretion on suffrage. The 1964 Civil Rights Act prevented a literacy test from being used for any citizen with a sixth-grade education in an accredited school in the United States or its territories. The 1965 Voting Rights Act authorized the federal government to send examiners to register voters in any legislative district in which 50 percent or more of the eligible adult population was not registered to vote. Amendments to this law further prohibited states from imposing a residence requirement of more than thirty days for voting in any presidential election. The 1993 motor voter law required states to make registration material available at their motor vehicle and social services offices, as well as at military recruitment centers, thereby enabling their residents to register at these offices or by mail.

Together, these constitutional amendments and statutes have established nearly universal suffrage. The only state restrictions that remain in place are those that prevent otherwise qualified citizens from voting because they are in jail or a mental institution. Thirteen states permanently disfranchise felons and those who have been dishonorably discharged from the military. The jail and felony restrictions would seem to be a minor and sensible limit on democratic participation, except for the fact that they disproportionately affect one demographic group: African-American males. Of the 10.5 million African-American men in the United States today, 1.5 million have been disfranchised temporarily or permanently by these restrictions.[7] To help rectify this problem, the National Commission on Federal Election Reform recommended that voting rights be restored to convicted felons.[8]

Since the 2000 election, there have also been allegations that minority voters, especially those in low-income areas, are much more likely than other voters to have their votes voided. A report by the U.S. Commission on Civil Rights criticized Florida election officials for their unequal treatment of African-American voters. The commission noted that 54 percent of the disqualified ballots were cast by African Americans, a group that constitutes only 11 percent of the state's electorate.[9] Another study, this one prepared for the Democratic minority on the House Governmental Reform Committee, found that 4 percent of all ballots cast in low-income districts were not counted, compared with 1.2 percent in higher-income districts.[10] Whether the differential in disqualified votes is a consequence of discriminatory behavior by state election officials, better voting machines in more affluent districts, or simply more errors made by less educated voters remains a subject of considerable controversy.

THE DECLINE IN TURNOUT

Although suffrage has been extended to most citizens, many do not exercise it much of the time. In the 1996 presidential election, a majority of the eligible population (51 percent) did *not* vote; in 2000, a bare majority did. In non-presidential elections, the proportion of nonvoters is even higher, usually in the range of 60 to 65 percent. In 1998, 64 percent of the population failed to vote—slightly less than two-thirds of the entire electorate. Turnout in primaries is even lower (see Figure 2.1). In 2000, turnout in the primaries averaged 15

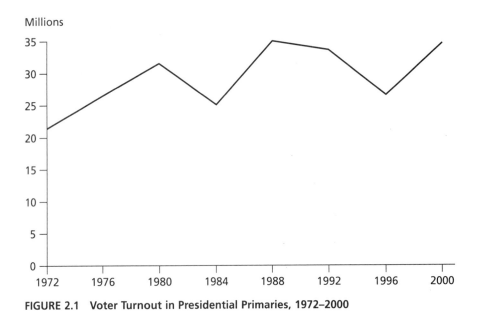

FIGURE 2.1 Voter Turnout in Presidential Primaries, 1972–2000

Source: William H. Flanigan and Nancy H. Zingale, *Political Behavior of the American Electorate*, 9th ed. (Washington, DC: Congressional Quarterly Books, 1998), 36; updated by author.

percent of the voting-age population. In states in which there were both Republican and Democratic contests, turnout was a little higher, in the range of 18 percent.[11]

It wasn't always this way. After 1800, the development of the party system provided the incentive and organizational mechanism to expand the proportion of the population that voted. Turnout rose, ranging from 25 to 50 percent of those eligible between 1800 and 1828, with the higher rates in elections in which the parties were most competitive. But the competition didn't last long. One of the parties, the Federalists, collapsed by 1816. With the advent of one-party dominance, turnout began to decline (see Table 2.1).

By the mid-1820s, however, factions within the dominant party led to a more competitive political environment and, ultimately, to the reemergence of a two-party system. As that system evolved, the parties tried to get more people involved and out to vote, and they were successful.[12] One of the tactics they used was to popularize election campaigns. Beginning in the 1840s, rallies, oratory, and parades were bringing out the faithful and the curious alike and were contributing to higher turnout.[13]

The new party activism continued in nonelectoral periods as well. Patronage jobs, political influence, and even a little monetary aid were given to loyal supporters, who in exchange were expected to return the favors on election day. This expectation was reinforced by the parties' oversight of the voting process. Precinct captains got out the voters; the parties printed their own color-coded ballots, which contained only the names of their candidates; poll watchers recorded who voted and how.[14]

As a consequence, turnout soared, involving more than 80 percent of the eligible electorate in the second half of the nineteenth century (see Table 2.1). But corruption and fraudulent voting practices also increased. Allegations of ballot stuffing, vote tampering, and irregularities in tallying the vote led states to print their own ballots and more closely monitor activities in and around the areas where people voted. Additionally, registration procedures were instituted to ensure that only the eligible voted.

Although these reforms were designed to protect the integrity of the electoral process, they also made the act of voting more difficult. People had to register first, sometimes well in advance of the election, and to do so at places and times designated by the states. Some states also enacted poll taxes to pay for the cost of the election. These taxes were particularly onerous for low-income voters.

But that wasn't the worst of it. The taxes and literacy tests were implemented in a discriminatory manner by election officials in the South. They became barriers to prevent African Americans, as well as many poor whites, from voting.

Decreasing competition between the political parties following the Civil War also contributed to lower turnout. The South became a one-party region, dominated by the Democrats. Because the winner of that party's nomination was a prohibitive favorite to win the general election, there was less incentive for southerners to vote. The Republicans also gained sufficient strength to dominate in the Northeast.

TABLE 2.1 Voter Turnout Rates, by Region and Total United States, 1789–2000 (Percentages)

Presidential Election Years			Off-Years			
Year	Outside the South	South	Total United States	Year[a]	Outside the South	South	Total United States
1789	11.0	13.5	11.4	1790	*	*	21.1
1792	*	*	2.6	1794	*	*	27.7
1796	*	*	20.4	1798	34.5	35.8	34.6
1800	39.2	28.0	31.4	1802	43.7	57.2	44.2
1804	28.7	11.9	25.3	1806	47.7	37.9	47.3
1808	43.0	17.8	36.9	1810	48.6	49.0	48.6
1812	47.1	17.8	41.6	1814	50.1	75.7	51.5
1816	26.8	8.3	20.5	1818	41.4	77.7	44.5
1820	12.0	3.8	9.8	1822	46.4	56.2	47.2
1824	26.5	27.4	26.7	1826	42.4	67.8	45.7
1828	62.8	42.6	57.3	1830	53.7	72.3	57.5
1832	64.2	30.1	56.7	1834	63.3	61.7	63.0
1836	58.5	49.2	56.5	1838	69.5	62.5	67.9
1840	81.6	75.4	80.3	1842	63.7	64.6	63.9
1844	80.3	74.2	79.0	1846	59.7	58.3	59.4
1848	74.0	68.2	72.8	1850	61.4	58.9	60.9
1852	72.1	59.5	69.5	1854	64.2	75.8	66.5
1856	82.3	67.9	79.4	1858	69.3	66.9	68.9
1860	83.1	76.5	81.8	1862	63.0	*	63.0
1864	76.3	*	76.3	1866	71.7	51.5	71.1
1868	82.8	71.6	80.9	1870	67.3	68.7	67.7
1872	73.7	67.0	72.1	1874	66.1	64.1	65.6
1876	85.0	75.1	82.6	1878	70.4	50.3	65.6
1880	85.5	65.1	80.6	1882	70.0	57.5	67.0
1884	83.1	63.3	78.3	1886	70.5	52.3	66.2
1888	85.5	64.2	80.5	1890	70.3	50.1	65.7
1892	80.7	59.4	75.9	1894	74.0	51.2	68.8
1896	86.2	57.6	79.7	1898	68.5	40.2	62.0
1900	82.6	43.5	73.7	1902	66.2	26.8	57.2
1904	76.5	29.0	65.5	1906	62.9	22.0	53.6
1908	76.1	30.7	65.7	1910	62.6	24.1	53.8
1912	67.7	27.8	59.0	1914	61.4	21.3	52.9
1916	69.1	31.7	61.8	1918	48.4	15.9	42.2
1920[b]	57.3	21.7	49.3	1922[b]	44.7	13.5	37.7
1924	57.5	19.0	48.9	1926	42.5	9.7	35.2
1928	66.7	22.5	56.9	1930	46.7	13.4	39.4
1932	66.2	24.5	57.0	1934	56.3	13.6	46.8

TABLE 2.1 (continued)

1936	71.4	25.0	61.0	1938	59.3	11.8	48.7
1940	72.9	26.5	62.5	1942	43.7	8.4	35.7
1944	65.1	24.5	55.9	1946	48.6	10.9	40.0
1948	61.8	25.0	53.4	1950	54.0	13.3	44.6
1952	71.4	38.4	63.8	1954	53.0	16.8	44.6
1956	69.2	36.6	61.6	1958	55.0	16.1	45.9
1960	72.8	41.4	65.4	1962	56.8	24.9	49.2
1964	68.6	46.4	63.3	1966	55.5	33.5	49.3
1968	65.7	51.8	62.3	1970	52.4	36.0	48.4
1972c	61.1	45.1	57.1	1974c	43.8	27.3	39.5
1976	57.9	47.5	55.2	1978	42.0	30.6	39.0
1980	56.6	48.1	54.3	1982	44.9	33.0	41.6
1984	57.8	48.7	55.2	1986	39.0	34.2	37.6
1988	54.5	46.6	52.2	1990	37.5	30.1	35.4
1992	58.9	51.7	56.8	1994	40.0	33.2	38.5
1996	52.4	47.1	50.8	1998	38.8	28.3	36.0
2000	55.0	44.1	51.2				

a. Before 1880, congressional elections were spread out almost an entire year rather than held on the same day. I calculated each state's potential electorate in a given year during the period from 1789 until 1880 and then aggregated it to a regional or national total.
b. General women's suffrage was introduced in 1920.
c. The vote was extended to eighteen-year-olds in 1971.
* Data not available.

Source: Walter Dean Burnham, "The Turnout Problem," in A. James Reichley, ed., *Elections American Style* (Washington, DC: Brookings, 1987), 113–114. Used by permission of Brookings Institution Press. Harold W. Stanley and Richard G. Niemi, *Vital Statistics on American Politics, 1999–2000* (Washington, DC: Congressional Quarterly Books, 2000), 13; updated for 2000 by author.

On top of all this, both parties seemed determined to establish as many safe seats as possible for their candidates. The adoption of the seniority rule in selecting the chairs of standing committees in Congress created added incentives for state parties to protect their congressional incumbents through "creative" districting that yielded as many safe seats as possible.

Although a reform movement at the end of the nineteenth century gave more power to rank-and-file voters through the introduction of presidential primaries in many of the states, it did not increase turnout. By the end of World War I, the reform movement had all but dissipated. States reverted to nomination procedures that facilitated control by party leaders. With the exception of the 1928 presidential election, turnout throughout the 1920s was less than 50 percent of those eligible to vote.

The realignment of political parties in the 1930s, and especially the appeal of Franklin Roosevelt's Democratic party to those on the lower rungs of the socioeconomic ladder (blue-collar workers, poor farmers, and racial and ethnic minorities), reenergized the electorate, contributing to a larger proportion of the population's voting, especially in presidential elections, for the next thirty years. Turnout, however, did not return to the levels of the second half of the nineteenth century.

And by the end of the 1960s, it was again on the decline. The civil rights movement and the Vietnam War created divisions within the majority party, the Democrats, marking the beginning of a trend of less intense partisan allegiance among supporters of both parties. Technological advances in communication, particularly the advent of television campaigning, increased the candidate-centeredness of elections and weakened party organizations and partisan loyalties even further. Because television proved to be a less effective way to mobilize voters than personal contact by party workers and volunteers, turnout continued to decline.

Who Doesn't Vote?

Identification with a political party is a motivation for voting. The stronger a person's partisan affiliation is, the more likely that person will vote. Thus the weakening of partisan identities and the increase in self-declared independents have resulted in lower turnout.

But other attitudinal factors have been contributing to the nonvoting trend. They relate to changing attitudes toward civic responsibilities and confidence in government. People have become more apathetic and less trusting. Many feel that the government is insensitive to their needs, that it is run by and for special interests, that politicians will say and do practically anything to get elected, that public officials are more interested in serving their own needs than those of their constituents, and that it just doesn't matter all that much who wins.[15]

There are other important distinctions between voters and nonvoters. Those who vote more regularly also tend to be more informed; have more well-defined issue positions, ideological perspectives, interest in the election, and concern about the outcome; and feel a greater sense of their own political efficacy—the belief that their vote can make a difference.[16] In contrast, nonvoters are more cynical and less "socially connected."[17] They belong to fewer politically oriented groups and associate with like-minded people who are also nonpolitical. Nonvoters are more likely to be single, younger, and less regular churchgoers.[18]

Educational levels also distinguish voters from nonvoters. The greater a person's education is, the more likely that person will vote.[19] Education provides the skills to maneuver through the intricacies of the electoral process: meeting the registration requirements, obtaining absentee ballots, and understanding the ballot and how to correctly indicate voting preferences on it. Education helps develop the cognitive skills necessary to process information and make an informed judgment.

Education also affects personal success. It increases a person's stake in the system, interest in the election, and concern over the outcome. Because the lesson that voting is a civic responsibility is usually learned in the classroom, schooling may also contribute to a more highly developed sense of civic responsibility about voting. And education and income levels tend to correlate with one another. Individuals with higher incomes also have higher rates of turnout.

Age is another variable that contributes to voting. Older citizens turn out at higher rates than do those who are younger. Older people have greater economic interests, which they perceive may be affected by the results of the election. They also have greater ties to the community, yet another reason for participating. For many of them, too, voting is habitual.

With education and income levels increasing, and with more of the population aging, one would expect turnout to be increasing—but it isn't. In fact, turnout has declined among almost all population groups, with the exception of African Americans living in the South.[20] Without the increase in education and income, turnout would have declined even further.[21]

The reduction in turnout has been greatest among "those less likely to vote in the first place."[22] The decreasing participation of those at the lower end of the socioeconomic scale has produced and extended a class bias in voting. Those who are most disadvantaged, who have the least education, and who need a change in conditions the most, actually participate the least. Those who are the most advantaged, who benefit from existing conditions and presumably from public policy as it stands, vote most often. These trends in voting behavior work to reflect, even to perpetuate, the status quo.

Generational and racial divisions accentuate the problem. Younger people and racial minorities are disproportionately found in the lower socioeconomic strata.

The demographic distinctions between voters and nonvoters have resulted in an electorate that is not representative of the general population. Overrepresented are the more educated, higher-income, older members of society; underrepresented are the younger, poorer, and less well educated. Moreover, the unrepresentative character of the electorate is even more pronounced in the nomination contests than in the general election.

Why Don't People Vote?

People think voting is important and regularly say that they vote. But many who claim to vote do not do so. Why do people lie about voting? The reason is that voting is seen as a civic responsibility. According to national surveys conducted by the Pew Research Center For The People & The Press, almost 90 percent of people agree with the statement "I feel it is my duty as a citizen to always vote."[23] More than 60 percent also add that they feel guilty when they do not do so.[24] Thus it is probably not surprising that survey researchers regularly find more people reporting to have voted than actually do vote. Table 2.2 indicates responses to the question "How often would you say you vote?"

The fact of the matter is that many people today lack the motivation to go out and vote. Even though they feel voting is important, even though they believe

TABLE 2.2 Percentage of People Who Claim They Vote, 1987–2000
Question: "How often would you say you vote?"

	Always	Nearly always	Part of the time	Seldom	Other	Never
June 2000	46	24	11	11	1	7
Late September 1999	28	41	15	9	1	5
Early September 1998	43	29	13	11	3	0
Late August 1998	38	30	16	14	*	6
June 1998	40	29	15	12	4	0
November 1997	33	38	15	9	*	5
September 1997	51	23	11	10	*	5
June 1996	41	30	12	12	1	4
February 1996	32	34	15	11	1	6
October 1995	41	32	12	11	*	3
April 1995	42	29	12	11	*	6
November 1994	43	24	11	13	1	8
October 1994	43	28	13	10	5	1
July 1994	40	30	14	11	*	5
June 1992	47	26	10	11	1	5
May 1992	41	32	13	11	*	3
November 1991	38	37	13	9	0	3
May 1990	33	35	12	10	1	8
February 1989	45	30	10	8	1	6
January 1989	39	33	12	8	1	6
May 1987	34	37	11	6	2	9

*Indicates less than 1 percent.

Source: Pew Research Center For The People & The Press, "Voter Turnout May Slip Again," July 13, 2000.

that voting gives them some say in "how government runs things," they also subscribe to the proposition that "most elected officials do not really care about what people like me think."[25] They are cynical. They don't see what difference it makes to them who wins, nor do they see their vote mattering all that much, although in Florida in the 2000 presidential election it would have made a difference. Because these citizens may lack the time and incentive to get involved, they also lack the incentive to get the information they need to sort out the candidates and issues and make a voting decision.

This lack of information and involvement prompted Congress in 1979 to amend the Federal Election Campaign Act to allow parties to raise and spend unlimited amounts of money in educational efforts and activities to get out the vote. But since the enactment of this legislation, turnout has not increased—hardly a testament to the success of the legislation.

Voter registration continues to be a problem for some. Despite enactment of the motor voter bill, potential voters are still plagued by registration mishaps of one type or another. A study conducted by researchers at the Massachusetts and California Institutes of Technology (MIT and Cal Tech) estimated that 3 million people were not able to cast valid ballots in 2000 because of registration mishaps.[26] To rectify this problem, the authors of the joint study recommended giving voters provisional ballots that would be counted when the registration difficulties were resolved. On-site voter registration on election day for the nation as a whole has also been proposed. Currently, only two states, Wisconsin and Wyoming, permit this practice, and only one, North Dakota, has no registration at all.

There are a myriad of other reasons or excuses why people do not vote. Some are too busy trying to earn a living, raise a family, and meet their day-to-day responsibilities. Single parents and elder caretakers fit into this category. Some are conflicted, unable to decide among competing candidates, parties, and policy alternatives. Their decision not to vote may be a considered one. The candidates may not seem appealing, qualified, or sufficiently different from one another. They make take positions with which people strongly disagree. The issues may not seem relevant. People may want to protest by not voting.

Another reason has to do with election rules and procedures. These rules and procedures increase the costs of voting. Finding the time, physically getting to the polls, understanding the intricacies of the ballot, and even knowing how to vote—which lever to push, hole to punch, or box to check—all are factors that discourage some people from voting—or disqualify votes that were cast improperly. The controversy over the "butterfly" ballot in Palm Beach County, Florida, in the 2000 election is a case in point.

Under Florida's election law at that time, individual counties were responsible for the design of the ballot, the monitoring of the election, and the tabulation of the vote. In Palm Beach County, Democratic election officials designed an easy-to-read ballot on which the names of all the candidates appeared on a single punch card. To fit everything on one side of the card, the ballot contained two columns of names but only one column of "chads," the perforated holes that voters were supposed to punch out (see Figure 2.2). Some voters were confused and punched the chads for the wrong candidates, and other voters punched two chads, thereby automatically voiding their ballots. Additionally some voters did not punch out the chads completely, leaving them dimpled or hanging. The voting machines undercounted chads that were not completely removed.

Florida was not the only state that had problems in 2000. Five states—Illinois, South Carolina, Idaho, Wyoming, and Georgia—had a greater percentage of voided and undercounted ballots according to the MIT-Cal Tech study. In fact, there were more invalidated votes in New York City and Chicago than there were in the entire state of Florida. Faulty voting equipment, errors in filling out ballots and casting them, lateness in submitting absentee ballots and invalid postmarks on them—all contributed to the 4 million to 6 million ballots that were not counted on election day 2000.[27]

A third factor, perhaps the most important, is the public's attitudes toward politicians and mistrust of their campaign positions and promises. Although

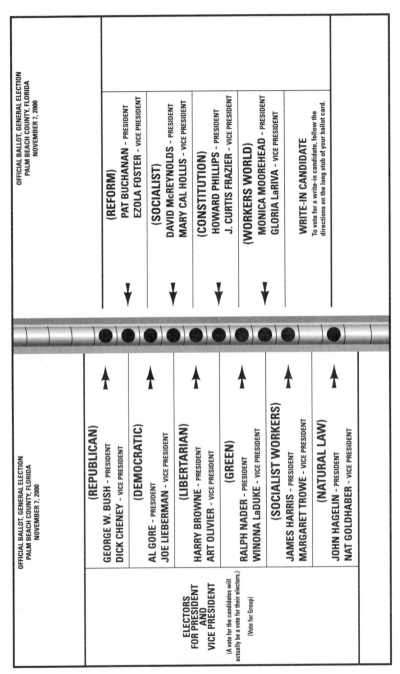

FIGURE 2.2   2000 Presidential Election Ballot Used in Palm Beach County, Florida

the public expressed more satisfaction with the 2000 campaign than with the three previous presidential campaigns—better candidates, more information, greater discussion of the issues, and less negative ads—turnout improved only marginally from its low in 1996.[28] When a national survey prior to the 1996 election asked voters what changes would improve the system the most, they most often cited candidate honesty and truthfulness, followed by more pertinent information and less negative campaigning.[29]

Some scholars allege that negative advertising also contributes to lower turnout. It turns off voters; it makes them more cynical about the candidates by emphasizing their negative personal characteristics or policy positions to which those who are the targets of the ads would strongly object. Experimental studies conducted by Stephen Ansolabehere and Shanto Iyengar found that negativism depresses turnout.[30] Empirical studies have also reported a correlation between the amount of negativity and voter turnout.[31] However, when this relationship is examined within the context of other variables that may be affecting attitudes, such as the level of mistrust people bring to the election, negative advertising seems to be a less important explanation of why people don't vote than the negative attitudes themselves.[32] Much depends on how the ads are viewed and by whom. If negative ads are deemed appropriate, as the Clinton ads about Dole were perceived by much of the electorate in 1996, they may actually increase turnout. But if they are seen as inappropriate—as mudslinging, harsh, or vindictive, as some of the ads critical of Dukakis were perceived in 1988—then they can adversely affect turnout and even boomerang against those who use them.[33]

Finally, the competitiveness of the election and the campaigns of the candidates also affect turnout—with more competitive elections contributing to a larger vote. The more competitive the election is, the more likely are the major party candidates to be well funded and hence conduct a more vigorous campaign, which in turn should turn out more voters. In the 2000 presidential election, the battleground states that both presidential campaigns targeted had higher turnout levels than did states that did not receive as much candidate attention (see Table 2.3).[34]

Are elections in the United States becoming less competitive? Some people believe so, citing increasing costs, incumbency advantages, and more sophisticated polling and targeting of voters as principal reasons.

THE CONSEQUENCES OF NOT VOTING

Does it *matter* that so many of those eligible don't vote? Most observers believe that it does, even though they concede that the outcome of most elections and the policies of newly elected officials would probably be the same even if nonvoters had participated. Postelection surveys of voters and nonvoters show little difference in their candidate and policy preferences.[35] The findings suggest that

TABLE 2.3   Citizen Voting Turnout in the Battleground States, 2000*

State	Percentage
Florida	57
Michigan	60
Ohio	55
Oregon	65
Pennsylvania	54
Washington	59
Wisconsin	68

*Figures based on eligible citizens rather than voting-age population. Citizen turnout estimated by Professor Martin P. Wattenberg to be 54 percent for the United States as a whole.

Source: Martin P. Wattenberg, "Getting Out the Vote," *Public Perspective* (January/February 2001), 17.

nonvoters support the candidates in roughly the same proportion as do voters. Moreover, the policy positions of voters and nonvoters are also similar.[36] Although nonvoters do tend to be slightly more liberal than voters, the ideological differences between them don't appear to be great enough to have a major impact on public policy.[37]

If the results of the election probably wouldn't change with more people voting, then what's the big fuss about nonvoting?[38] The answer lies in the link that voting forges between citizens and their elected representatives. Nonvoting weakens that link, creating a potential dichotomy between the general public and the voting electorate. Naturally, party and government officials are likely to seem and probably to be more responsive to those who elected them than to those who sit on the sidelines—hence the public perception that the interests and needs of nonvoters are less well represented by those in government.[39]

The representation problem is further aggravated by the demographic and attitudinal characteristics that distinguish voters and nonvoters. The fact that nonvoters are likely to be younger and less advantaged reinforces the participatory differences between those who are better off and those who are not. In an extensive study of political activity in America, Sidney Verba, Kay Lehman Schlozman, and Henry E. Brady found that

> participatory input is tilted in the direction of the more advantaged groups in society—especially in terms of economic and education position, but in terms of race and ethnicity as well. The voices of the well-educated and the well-heeled—and, therefore, of those with other politically relevant characteristics that are associated with economic and educational privilege sound more loudly.[40]

In short, nonvoting contributes to differential group influences on government, which can affect decisions on public policy, and does affect perceptions of influence on government.

Nonvoting can make the meaning of the election less clear, the claim of a public mandate more problematic, and the task of fulfilling campaign pledges and promises more difficult. It can also have a negative impact on building and maintaining a majority coalition, thereby adversely affecting governing.

Low turnout can be a policy issue as well. One of the cornerstones of U.S. policy since the end of World War II has been the promotion of and support for democratic institutions and processes abroad. The failure of a majority of American citizens to vote undercuts the credibility of the U.S. policy position that free and popular elections are critical to a democratic society. Compare voter turnout in the United States with that in other democratic countries, as shown in Table 2.4.

Some scholars actually see benefit in having a significant proportion of the electorate not voting on a regular basis. They claim that disinterest and inactivity mute political conflict, enhance social stability, and implicitly provide support for public policy decisions by not challenging those decisions or holding decision makers accountable.[41] In this sense, apathy can be viewed as satisfaction with existing conditions; otherwise, it is argued, people would be more likely to protest in the streets and at the ballot box. Those who support this position point to the fact that bad times and discontent normally bring out a larger vote than do good times and public contentment.[42] Compare turnout in 1968 (60.9 percent) to 1972 (55.5 percent), in 1992 (55.2 percent) to 1996 (49.0 percent). In the first of these elections, voters were responding to their unhappiness with the economic and social conditions, and in 1968 with the continuation of the Vietnam War; in the second of the elections they perceived conditions to be better and gave the incumbent a vote of confidence, but fewer turned out to do so.

Most democratic theorists, however, do not view apathy as a positive social trait. Rather, they see it as an illness, a symptom of discontent within the political system and its governing institutions. This discontent is amply documented by surveys taken over the last three decades.[43] If people feel the political system is no longer responsive to their needs and wishes, they may be less supportive of its decisions and less respectful of its authority.

POTENTIAL SOLUTIONS TO THE NONVOTING PROBLEM

Lower the Costs of Voting

What can be done about the problem of nonvoting? Describing the problem of nonvoting and the reasons people give for not voting is easier than solving the problem. Congress has dealt with the issue of nonvoting in two ways. First, it has enacted laws to remove or ease legal hurdles to voting. The motor voter law is an example. By making registration easier, more accessible, and less

TABLE 2.4   International Voter Turnout in Selected Countries

Country	Year	Type of election	Percentage of registered voters	Compulsory voting?	Work (W) or rest (R) day?
Argentina	1995	Presidential	80.9	Yes	R
Australia	1998	Parliamentary	95.2	Yes	R
Austria	1995	Parliamentary	82.7	Yes	R
	1998	Presidential	74.4	Yes	R
Belgium	1999	Parliamentary	90.5	Yes	R
Canada	1993	Prime Ministerial	73.0	No	W
	1997	General	67.0	No	W
Chile	1993	Presidential	90.0	Yes	R
Ecuador	1996	Presidential	73.0	Yes	R
Germany	1996	Parliamentary	67.5	No	R
Greece	1996	Parliamentary	76.3	Yes	R
	1996	Presidential	85.9	Yes	R
India	1998	Parliamentary	62.0	No	R
Israel	1999	Parliamentary	78.7	No	R
Italy	1995	Regional	77.4	No	W
Ireland	1997	Presidential	47.6	No	W
Japan	1995	Parliamentary	44.5	No	R
Mexico	2000	Presidential	60.0	Yes	R
Poland	1993	Parliamentary	52.1	No	R
	1995	Presidential	64.7/68.2*	No	R
Portugal	1995	Parliamentary	67.2	No	R
	1996	Presidential	66.3	No	R
Russia	1993	Parliamentary	54.8	No	R
	1995	Parliamentary	65.0	No	R
	2000	Presidential	67.8	No	R
Sweden	1994	Parliamentary	87.3	No	R
Turkey	1999	Parliamentary	87.1	Yes	R
United States	1992	Presidential	76.0	No	W
	1994	Legislative	68.5	No	W
	1996	Presidential	66.0	No	W
	1998	Legislative	63.8	No	W
	2000	Presidential	51.2	No	W
Zambia	1996	Presidential	58.2	No	W

* = Two rounds of elections.

Source: Table adapted from "International Voter Participation Figures," Federal Election Commission, <http://www.fec.gov/pages/Internet.htm> and updated by author.

time-consuming, Congress hoped that the proportion of the population that didn't vote because they weren't registered would decrease—perhaps by as much as 8 or 9 percent.[44] Although voter registration has steadily increased since the act went into effect in 1994, turnout has remained low.[45] However, it might be even lower had the motor voter bill not been enacted.

What else can Congress and the states do to reduce the personal costs of voting, costs measured in time, effort, and perhaps lost wages? One way to make it easier for people to find the time to vote is to hold elections on a nonworkday, a holiday, or Sunday. The United States is one of the few democracies that still conducts its elections on a workday. Although employers are required by law to give their employees time to vote and not penalize them financially for doing so, some people still find it difficult to take time off from work to vote.

Making election day a holiday might make it easier for more people to vote. However, there would be opposition to such a proposal. Some businesses would lose money by being closed or forced to pay employees extra for working on a holiday. Schools would be closed, thereby increasing the burden on single parents. And some people employed in essential or recreational services, such as police, fire, hospital, or even restaurant employees, would still have to work.

A second and somewhat less costly alternative would be to combine election day and Veterans Day, a proposal made by the Federal Election Commission in 2001. However, veterans groups might object to the diversion of focus from memorializing those who fought and died in defense of their country to the hurly-burly of contemporary electoral politics. Finally, even though Veterans Day is an official holiday, it is one that many in the private sector do not observe.

Instead of being held on a holiday, elections could be held on Sunday, as they are in many European countries. But Sunday elections would compete with religious services; recreational activities, such as professional football; and family events.[46] Besides, some people work on Sunday. Under the circumstances, it isn't clear whether turnout would increase all that much if elections were held on Sunday or whether the American people would support such a change. Turnout might even decrease.

Another possibility would be to extend the time people have for voting. Although most states keep their voting places open for at least twelve hours, some allow their citizens to vote up to twenty-one days before the election. Others permit "no-fault" absentee ballots so that people can vote by mail without having to certify that they will be out of the state at the time of the election. Oregon has gone even further. In 1998 voters in that state approved a ballot initiative that requires voting by mail ballot beginning in 2000. Voting over the Internet may also be a possibility in the not-so-distant future.

Another change that might facilitate voting would be redesigning the form and shape of the ballot. Some states still use a party-column ballot, in which all of a party's candidates are listed together below the party's label. Partisans have no difficulty discerning their candidates. The office-column ballot, on which candidates are listed by the position for which they are running, may confuse people who aren't familiar with the names of all the candidates. Besides, ballots may also contain complex policy initiatives, on which voters are asked to decide quickly so as not to delay those waiting to vote.

Extending the time for voting and making it simpler to vote might increase turnout, but how much? Despite the elimination of many of the institutional barriers to voting, turnout is still declining. It is unlikely that the elimination of the remaining barriers would substantially reverse this trend. More extreme measures may be necessary to achieve this objective.

Increase the Costs of Not Voting

The most far-reaching and controversial proposal for increasing voting is simply to require it as an obligation of citizenship and to fine those who fail to vote. Several countries, including Australia, Belgium, and Chile, have a mandatory voting system, and their turnout is 90 percent or over (see Table 2.4).

Requiring all citizens to vote would convert equality in theory to near-equality in practice. Moreover, it would reduce the distinction between the electorate and the population. Government officials would have to be more responsive to the entire adult population rather than to a portion of their electoral constituency. With mandatory voting, the poor, less educated, less informed, and less partisan would be better represented than they are today.

But mandatory suffrage could also result in a less informed and perhaps less intelligent vote. Besides, there would undoubtedly be strong opposition to such a proposal. Some argue that mandatory voting would prevent people from protesting the choices they have by boycotting the election. Others claim that mandatory voting is undemocratic, that a democracy that prides itself on freedom should allow its citizens the right to decide whether they wish to vote.

Enhance the Incentives for Voting

With individual choice a value and the tradition of voting a right, not a requirement, those interested in expanding voter participation have suggested other ways to encourage more people to participate in the electoral process. These include media campaigns in which prominent citizens urge others to vote; better civic education in schools and communities, in which the responsibilities of citizenship are stressed; and bipartisan informational campaigns by parties and nonpartisan groups, which would tell people why they should get out and vote. However, these so-called bipartisan efforts have themselves become controversial because they have been used by parties and groups to further their own political agendas and circumvent campaign finance regulations.

Stronger party ties might help motivate more people to vote, as would more effective grassroots party organizations. But these are not changes that can be legislated by Congress or the states. More competitive elections would also improve turnout, but the parties have little motivation for decreasing their number of safe seats. Holding fewer elections might boost turnout as well, but such a proposal would require longer terms of office, a proposition that a cynical and distrustful public is unlikely to support. Gaining better representation for those in the minority in electoral districts might encourage more people to vote, but to provide this representation would probably involve a fundamental change in the electoral system, moving from single-member districts and plurality voting to multimember districts with proportional voting.

Other proposals include shortening the election cycle, limiting negative campaigning, instituting voluntary candidate codes of conduct, and providing more and better information about the candidates and their positions. But instituting such changes might run up against the First Amendment protections of freedom of speech and of the press and are thus not likely to be legislated by Congress or upheld by the federal judiciary.

The bottom line is that citizens' attitudes about politics and government need to be changed if voter turnout is to be increased. And there's no easy way to do that. In fact, the events of recent years—the scandals in the Clinton administration, the campaign finance debacle in the 1996 election, and the increasing amount of money contributed and spent by powerful interest groups—have intensified, rather than alleviated, public cynicism and mistrust of politicians. On the other hand, the government's response to the terrorist attack on September 11, 2001, has increased confidence in government, but whether this new confidence will continue once the terrorist threat subsides is unclear.[47] In short, nonvoting remains an attitudinal problem, one that is not likely to go away soon.

Make It Easier to Vote

Getting people to the polls in only part of the problem; getting them to vote properly is another. Voting procedures need to be simplified; the tabulation of votes needs to be improved. Suggestions include eliminating confusing ballot designs, replacing aging voting machines and punch cards with optical scan equipment, allowing voters who accidentally spoil their ballots to get new ones, and having election officials explain how to vote to those who have difficulty doing so for whatever reason.

In the aftermath of the 2000 election controversy, the state of Florida revised its electoral procedures.[48] Bills were introduced in Congress to set a uniform national closing time for polls, provide federal assistance to the states to update their voting equipment, reduce discriminatory practices by having the Justice Department more vigorously enforce the 1965 Voting Rights Act, as well as reform campaign finance laws (see Chapter 5). Congress responded by enacting legislation that provided states with money to upgrade their voting equipment, better train election officials, improve the accuracy of registration lists, and prevent fraudulent voting.

Summary: Suffrage and Turnout Dilemmas in a Nutshell

The U.S. electoral system wasn't designed to be a participatory electoral democracy, but it has become one. In theory, today there is universal suffrage; in practice, more people don't vote than do. In theory, every adult citizen has an equal opportunity to participate; in practice, those with greater resources are in a better position to do so. In fact, their educational and economic advantages are both motivations for voting and consequences of voting. In theory, elected officials are supposed to be responsive to all the people; in practice, they tend to be more accessible and responsive to those who elect them, or so the public perceives.

Although low turnout is thought to be undesirable in and for a democratic political system, the remedies lawmakers have proposed and instituted to deal with the problem have not worked nearly as well as their sponsors had hoped. Removing barriers to voting should have increased the proportion of the electorate that votes, but with the exception of African Americans living in the South, it hasn't. Lifting federal campaign restrictions for the solicitation and expenditure of money used to get out the vote, engage in bipartisan educational efforts, and strengthen the parties' grassroots organizations was intended to increase turnout, but it hasn't. Instead, it has resulted in unexpected consequences that have broken down the campaign finance system and further alienated voters. Despite the pleas of public interest groups, the efforts of political parties, and the extended campaigns of those running for office, more and more people seem to be turned off by rather than turned on to campaigns and elections.

The problem of nonvoting has resisted easy solutions. It is as much an attitude problem as anything else. Changing these attitudes is difficult. Legislation alone cannot do so. It will require a major effort by those in and outside of government to reconstitute the civic culture, reenergize the political parties, and reestablish trust between the voters and their elected officials. There are no easy and quick fixes to the root causes of the nonvoting problem: alienation and cynicism.

Now It's Your Turn

Discussion Questions

1. Can the popular will be expressed if everyone does not vote?
2. Should voting be an obligation of citizenship? If so, should that obligation be enforced by penalties for those who do not vote?
3. Should people with little interest in the election and information about it be encouraged to vote?
4. Should registration be eliminated as a precondition for voting?
5. Should voting rules in presidential elections continue to be set by the states and counties, or should they be established by the federal government?
6. Should the Constitution be amended so that federal government conducts federal elections?
7. Should election day be a holiday or nonworkday such as Sunday?

Topics for Debate

Challenge or defend the following statements:

1. Universal suffrage is neither necessary nor desirable.
2. Nonvoting is not a problem for American democracy.

3. Literacy tests should be instituted in a nondiscriminatory manner to ensure that voters have sufficient information about the candidates and issues to make an informed judgment on election day.
4. States should abolish polling booths and permit voting from home via mail, Internet, or telephone over a designated period of time, not to be less than twenty-four hours.
5. Voting should be required as a condition of citizenship, with penalties imposed for nonvoters.

Exercises

1. Rock the Vote, a public interest organization dedicated to increasing turnout, particularly among younger voters, ran a public relations campaign during the last presidential election to increase electoral awareness, to provide potential voters with more information about the candidates and their campaigns, and, most important, to get more people registered to vote. It plans to run another educational campaign during the next election. If that organization asked you for advice on such a campaign, what would you say?
   a. To whom should it direct its campaign?
   b. What should its principal appeal be, and how should it be articulated to achieve maximum impact?
   c. Should the content of that appeal change over the course of the campaign?
   d. What should the principal means of communication be?
   e. In addition to a public appeal, what else could the group do to enhance its educational effort and achieve its principal objectives?
2. The National Commission on Federal Election Reform has proposed making election day a national holiday, allowing citizens whose registration is challenged to vote provisionally until the validity of their ballots is determined, establishing statewide systems of voter registration, replacing punch cards with ballots that can be optically scanned, and banning election-night predictions on the major networks until voting is completed within the continental United States. Assess each of these recommendations on the basis of
   a. its likelihood of increasing voter turnout,
   b. its costs to the governments that run the elections and to individuals who vote in them,
   c. its advantage or disadvantage to each of the major parties and to third parties and independent candidates.
   On the basis of your assessment, indicate which (if any) of the recommendations of the commission you support and which (if any) you oppose.

Internet Resources

- Democracy Network <http://www.dnet.org>
  Public affairs organization that provides a range of information on candidates and issues as well as other information in local areas.

- Federal Election Commission <http://www.fec.gov>
  Provides easy-to-use website for obtaining a national voter registration form and information on where to send it, as well as data on the numbers of those registered and voting.

- League of Women Voters <http://www.lwv.org>
  An established public interest group that publishes books and pamphlets on election activities, including information about the candidates and ballot initiatives. The league also lobbies Congress for campaign reform.

- Project Vote Smart <http://www.vote-smart.org>
  A public interest group dedicated to educating the electorate, particularly younger voters, on the issues, the candidates, and the records of public officials; distributes free citizen tool kits.

- Rock the Vote <http://www.rockthevote.org>
  Getting young people to register and vote is the primary goal of this public interest organization. The website provides a short form that can be used to begin the registration process. Rock the Vote will even remind those who registered through their site to vote on election day.

- Voter Information Services <http://www.vis.org>
  Another educational service to inform voters; provides information on the voting records of members of Congress.

Selected Readings

Bennett, Stephen Earl, and David Resnick. "The Implications of Nonvoting for Democracy in the United States." *American Journal of Political Science* 34 (1990): 771–803.

Burnham, Walter D. "The Turnout Problem." In *Elections American Style,* edited by A. James Reichley. Washington, DC: Brookings Institution, 1987.

Conway, M. Margaret. *Political Participation in the United States.* Washington, DC: Congressional Quarterly Books, 1991.

Crotty, William J. *Political Participation and American Democracy.* New York: Greenwood Press, 1991.

Gant, Michael M., and William Lyons. "Democratic Theory, Nonvoting, and Public Policy." *American Politics Quarterly* 21 (1993): 183–204.

Jackson, Robert A. "A Reassessment of Voter Mobilization." *Political Research Quarterly* (1996): 331–349.

Pew Research Center For The People & The Press. *Deconstructing Distrust.* Washington, DC: Pew, 1998.

Piven, Frances Fox, and Richard A. Cloward. *Why Americans Don't Vote.* New York: Pantheon, 1988.

Powell, G. Bingham, Jr. "American Voter Turnout in Comparative Perspective." *American Political Science Review* 80 (1986): 17–44.

Rosenstone, Steven J., and John Mark Hansen. *Mobilization, Participation, and Democracy in America.* New York: Macmillan, 1993.

Teixeira, Ruy A. *The Disappearing American Voter.* Washington, DC: Brookings Institution, 1992.

Verba, Sidney, Kay Lehman Schlozman, and Henry E. Brady. *Voice and Equality: Civic Voluntarism in American Politics.* Cambridge, MA: Harvard University Press, 1995.

Wolfinger, Raymond E., and Jonathan Hoffman. "Registering and Voting with Motor Voter," *PS* 34 (March 2001): 85–92.

Wolfinger, Raymond E., and Steven J. Rosenstone. *Who Votes?* New Haven, CT: Yale University Press, 1980.

Notes

1. Noncitizens, such as legal and illegal immigrants who are residents of the United States, also have a stake in the system. They have common interests, needs, and obligations including the payment of taxes on income earned in the United States. They are not afforded voting rights, however, until they become naturalized citizens. For illegal aliens, especially, it is often difficult to meet the legal requirements for citizenship.

2. For an excellent study of turnout since the beginning of the Republic, see Walter Dean Burnham, "The Turnout Problem," in *Elections American Style,* ed. A. James Reichley (Washington, DC: Brookings Institution, 1987), 97–133.

3. In every southern state, a majority of eligible African Americans were *not* eligible to vote until the mid-to-late 1960s. Earl Black and Merle Black, *The Vital South: How Presidents Are Elected* (Cambridge, MA: Harvard University Press, 1992), 217.

4. Susan Welch, John Gruhl, Michael Steinman, and John Comer, *American Government,* 3rd ed. (St. Paul, MN: West, 1990), 196.

5. Michael X. Delli Carpini and Ester R. Fuchs, "The Year of the Woman? Candidates, Voters, and the 1992 Elections," *Political Science Quarterly* 108 (Spring 1993): 30.

6. Two years later, the Supreme Court extended this prohibition to the election of state and local officials. It did so through its interpretation of the Fourteenth Amendment's equal protection clause, which holds that each person's vote be equal: one person–one vote.

7. Fox Butterfield, "Many Black Males Barred from Voting," *New York Times,* January 30, 1997, A12.

8. Janelle Carter, "Election Panel Submits Report to Bush," *Associated Press,* July 31, 2000.

9. U.S. Commission on Civil Rights as reported in Robert E. Pierre and Peter Slevin, "Florida Vote Rife with Disparities, Study Says," *The Washington Post,* June 5, 2001, A01.

10. "Votes of Poor More Likely Uncounted," *Associated Press,* July 9, 2001, <http://dailynews.yahoo.com/n/ap/20010709/ts/voter_study_1.html>.

11. There is considerable variation in turnout among states. In 2000, turnout ranged from a high of 71 percent in Minnesota and 68 percent in Wisconsin and Maine to a low of 43 percent in Arizona and 44 percent in Hawaii. Martin P. Wattenberg, "Getting Out the Vote," *Public Perspective* (January/February 2001): 17. See also Steven A. Holmes, "Many Stayed at Home," *New York Times,* September 1, 2000, A18.

12. In their provocative study, *Why Americans Don't Vote,* Frances Fox Piven and Richard A. Cloward argue that ethnic and religious identities reinforced partisan loyalties to mobilize the vote, particularly among the working class. Similarly, sectional issues and party competitiveness also contributed to the high turnout in the nineteenth century. France Fox Piven and Richard A. Cloward, *Why Americans Don't Vote* (New York: Pantheon, 1988), 26–29.

13. Keith Melder, *Hail to the Candidate* (Washington, DC: Smithsonian Institution Press, 1992), 69–100; Gil Troy, *See How They Ran* (New York: Free Press, 1991), 20–30.

14. The influx of immigrants, first predominantly from northern Europe during the period from 1840 to 1860, and later from southern Europe, from 1880 to 1910, provided fertile grounds for parties to recruit new partisans by providing them with social services and other benefits in exchange for their support.

15. Pew Research Center For The People & The Press conducted polls over the last decade that show declining trust and confidence in government. These results were collected in *Deconstructing Distrust,* which Pew published in 1998 and updated in Pew Research Center For The People & The Press, "Public Votes for Continuity and Change in 2000," February 25, 1999.
   Another contemporary survey, this one by the Center on Policy Attitudes, found strong support (74.5 percent) for the proposition that "the government is pretty much run by a few big interests looking out for themselves." "Expecting More Say: The American Public on Its Role in Government Decisionmaking," May 10, 1999.

16. Angus Campbell, Philip E. Converse, Warren E. Miller, and Donald E. Stokes, *The American Voter* (New York: Wiley, 1960), 102.

17. The term "social connectedness" was used by Ruy A. Teixeira in his book *The Disappearing American Voter* (Washington, DC: Brookings Institution, 1992), 36–37, to describe the degree to which a person has ties to the community. The stronger the ties, the greater is the motivation for voting.

18. Ibid.

19. Raymond E. Wolfinger and Steven J. Rosenstone, *Who Votes?* (New Haven, CT: Yale University Press, 1980), 13–26.

20. Teixeira, *The Disappearing American Voter,* 80.

21. Paul R. Abramson, John H. Aldrich, and David W. Rohde, *Change and Continuity in the 1996 Elections* (Washington, DC: Congressional Quarterly Books, 1998), 80.

22. Teixeira, *The Disappearing American Voter,* 72–74, 80.

23. Pew Research Center For The People & The Press, "Voter Turnout May Slip Again," July 13, 2000, 66.

24. Ibid., 67.

25. Pew Research Center For The People & The Press, *Retro-Politics* (Washington, DC: Pew, November 1999), 139.

26. Massachusetts Institute of Technology and California Institute of Technology, "Voting: What Is and What Could Be," report issued July 17, 2001.

27. Ibid.

28. Pew Research Center For The People & The Press, "Campaign 2000 Highly Rated," November 16, 2000.

29. Princeton Survey Research Associates, national survey conducted October 21 to November 2, 1996. The number of people surveyed was 1,881.

30. Stephen Ansolabehere and Shanto Iyengar, *Going Negative: How Political Advertisments Shrink and Polarize the Electorate* (New York: Free Press, 1995), 141–142.

31. Stephen D. Ansolabehere, Shanto Iyengar, and Adam Simon, "Replicating Experiments Using Aggregate and Survey Data: The Case of Negative Advertising and Turnout," *American Political Science Review* 93 (December 1999): 901–909; and Darrell M. West, *Air Wars*, 3rd ed. (Washington, DC: Congressional Quarterly Books, 2001), 71.

32. Martin P. Wattenberg and Craig Leonard Brians, "Negative Campaign Advertising: Demobilizer or Mobilizer," *American Political Science Review* 93 (December 1999): 891–899.

33. Steven Finkel and John Greer, "A Spot Check: Casting Doubt on the Demobilizing Effect of Attack Advertising," *American Journal of Political Science* 42 (April 1998): 573–595; and Kim Fridkin Kahn and Patrick J. Kenny, "Do Negative Campaigns Mobilize or Suppress Turnout?" *American Political Science Review* 93 (December 1999): 877–889.

Other factors, of course, can explain the differential in turnout. In both 1968 and 1992, there was a major third-party candidate running. In 1972 and 1996, there was not, and the incumbent presidents, Nixon and Clinton, were relatively popular in their reelection campaigns and seemed likely to win. As a result there was less interest in those campaigns, whereas in 1968 and 1992, the results were more in doubt, which in turn heightened interested and probably increased turnout.

34. Wattenberg, "Getting Out the Vote," 16–17.

35. Teixeira, *The Disappearing American Voter*, 95.

36. Stephen Earl Bennett and David Resnick, "The Implications of Nonvoting for Democracy in the United States," *American Journal of Political Science* 34 (1990): 771–802; and Michael M. Gant and William Lyons, "Democratic Theory, Nonvoting, and Public Policy," *American Politics Quarterly* 21 (1993): 183–204.

37. Teixeira, *The Disappearing American Voter*, 100.

38. Thomas E. Cavanaugh argues that elections have to be close and that the likely nonvoters who do cast ballots have to be disproportionately favorable to one candidate for the outcome to be changed. See Thomas E. Cavanaugh, "When Turnout Matters: Mobilization and Conversion as Determinants of Election Outcomes," in *Political Participation and American Democracy*, ed. William J. Crotty (New York: Greenwood Press, 1991), 89–112.

39. Sidney Verba, Kay Lehman Schlozman, and Henry E. Brady, *Voice and Equality: Civic Voluntarism in American Politics* (Cambridge, MA: Harvard University Press, 1995), 11.

40. Ibid., 512.

41. This argument was advanced by Bernard Berelson, Paul F. Lazerfeld, and William McPhee in their book, *Voting* (Chicago: University of Chicago Press, 1954). See also Lester Milbrath, *Political Participation* (Chicago: Rand McNally, 1965).

42. Blame tends to be greater than credit. Political scientists have found that people seem more motivated to turn out to vote during bad times than during good ones. See Howard Bloom and H. Douglas Price, "Voter Response to Short Run Economic Conditions: The Asymmetric Effects of Prosperity and Recession," *American Political Science Review* 69

(1975): 1240–1254; and Morris P. Fiorina, "Economic Retrospective Voting in National Elections: A Microanalysis," *American Journal of Political Science* 22 (1978): 426–433.

43. See *Why Don't Americans Trust the Government,* Washington Post, Kaiser Family Foundation, and Harvard University, 1996; and Pew Research Center For The People & The Press, *Deconstructing Distrust* (Washington, D.C.: Pew, 1998).

44. Teixeira, *The Disappearing American Voter,* 106–147; and Wolfinger and Rosenstone, *Who Votes?* 73.

45. In a report to Congress, "The Impact of the National Voter Registration Act on the Administration of Elections for Federal Officials, 1997–1998," the Federal Election Commission estimated that voter registration increased by 7.1 million in the first four years after the legislation was passed.

46. Moreover, churches are often the place where people vote in the United States.

47. Pew Research Center For The People & The Press reported a modest rebound in public trust in government after the Clinton impeachment. See its year-end report, "2000," p. 9, figure 14. For increase in public confidence since the terrorist attack, see Gallup Poll, "High Approval for Most People/Institutions Handling War on Terrorism," November 16, 2001, <http://www.gallup.com/poll/Releases/Pr011116.asp>.

48. The new Florida law provides $24 million to modernize voting machinery at the county and precinct level, $6 for voter education efforts, and $2 million to create a registration database for the state. In addition, the legislation standardizes recount procedures and provides for provisional ballots in the cases in which there are registration disputes.

3

How Representative
Are American Elections?

Did you know that . . .

- the constitutional system was designed to protect the rights of minorities, and the electoral system has evolved to reflect the influence of majorities (or at least pluralities)?
- drawing the shape of a legislative district to advance the party in power is an old American tradition? In fact, the term *gerrymander* was named after Massachusetts Governor Elbridge Gerry, whose party created a district in the shape of a salamander. The press termed it a "Gerry-mander."
- for most of U.S. history, the Supreme Court regarded the drafting of legislative districts as a political, not a judicial, issue and thus stayed away from this type of representational issue?
- the redrafting of congressional districts to gain more representation for African-American and Latino voters in the 1990s contributed to increasing the number of conservative Republican members of Congress?
- the Electoral College was originally designed to ensure that the most qualified, not necessarily the most popular, people were selected as president and vice president?
- twenty-two states have enacted laws to limit the terms of their legislative representatives?
- women make up 52 percent of the electorate but only 13.6 percent of members of Congress and 22.4 percent of state legislators?
- more than half of the members of Congress faced no opposition in their quest for renomination in 2000?
- nine members of the House ran unopposed in the 2000 general election while 97 others won with more than 75 percent of the vote?

- in the last three Senate elections, 25 percent of the incumbents received 65 percent or more of the vote while 60 percent won with more than 55 percent?
- groups that are less well represented in government support a stronger role for government than do those that are better represented?

Is this any way to run a democratic election?

I N A representative democracy, all citizens are entitled to have their interests represented. Is the U.S. electoral system, in which candidates are chosen by plurality vote in single-member districts, fair and equitable for all groups in the society? Many people say "no." They claim that the system overrepresents the majority and underrepresents the minority.

This chapter addresses the issue of representation. It examines how the electoral system affects the representative character of government. Beginning with a discussion of the concept of representation, the chapter turns to the relationship between the structure of elections and the type of representation that this structure produces. In the process, it focuses on those who have benefited from this representational struggle and those who haven't, and on the impact representation may have on attitudes toward government. The chapter also explores the necessity and desirability of imposing legal qualifications for office and their effect on a democratic electoral process.

THE CONCEPT OF REPRESENTATION

The concept of representation is central to American democracy and was so even before the colonists declared their independence from England.[1] "Taxation without representation is tyranny," the cry of those who wanted their representational rights as Englishmen restored, became part of the justification for revolution.

Although the issue for the colonists was nonrepresentation, for the framers it was devising a system that would permit diverse representation, but not majority rule. By overlapping constituencies between the federal government and the states, and within the federal government itself, the delegates at the Constitutional Convention hoped to achieve both state and popular representation without domination by a single interest, region, or group. The representational character of the American political system has been shaped by this artful constitutional design.

The Constitution gave the states the authority to determine how their representatives would be chosen. Most used their discretion to create institutions, paralleling those of the national government, in which representatives were to be chosen from clearly defined geographic areas. Within these areas, voters would select candidates directly, by popular vote, or indirectly, by voting for legislators who in turn would select the state's senators and presidential electors.

Who could be chosen was left to the states to decide. The Constitution specified only a few qualifications for federal office: a minimum age, a geographic residence requirement at the time of election, citizenship for a specified number of years, and, in the case of the president, being both native-born and a fourteen-year resident of the United States before the election. The Constitution also prohibited requiring a religious test as a condition for public office.

Types of Representation

In choosing their representatives, the states selected candidates from their pool of eligible voters: white, male Christians who owned property. Most elected officials were better educated than the average male citizen and usually prominent in the community. As the country became more diverse and as suffrage expanded, so did the acceptable qualifications for being elected to office. However, what were deemed acceptable criteria changed much more slowly than did the composition of the electorate. Even today, the initial dominant characteristics prevail: white, male, with above-average education and income.

Herein lies part of the representational dilemma. If one purpose of representation is to reflect the needs and interests of the society as a whole, then how can a government dominated by white males provide fair and equal representation?

Many say that it cannot. They argue that only a person who shares the characteristics of a particular constituency can effectively represent that constituency. Knowing how it feels to live in the constituency, having interests and needs similar to those of the people who reside there, and sharing their values and political beliefs are keys to effective representation. Taken to its obvious conclusion, this argument contends that the best representative for most people most of the time is a person who resembles them demographically and attitudinally. It follows that the composition of government should also reflect the composition of society, if the government is to be representative of that society. In other words, if a particular group, such as African Americans, constitutes a certain proportion of the voting-age population, 12 percent, then it should constitute a similar proportion of the government. When Bill Clinton promised in his 1992 campaign to appoint an administration as diverse as America itself, he was subscribing to this tenet of equal and fair representation.

Getting their fair share has become a goal of underrepresented groups and a hot-button political issue for them. Not only do the underrepresented want their needs addressed and their interests satisfied, but they also want to be represented in the institutions in which their own people, people who have their demographic and in some cases attitudinal characteristics, make public policy decisions. They see representation as a symbol of equality.

In addition to **descriptive representation,** how well the government reflects the composition of society, there is also the issue of **substantive representation,** how well public policy decisions affect various individuals and groups in the society. Whereas descriptive representation is reflected in the *who* of government (the people who make the decisions), substantive representation is reflected in the *what* of government (public policy and its impact). The distinction between descriptive and substantive representation arises in part because it is possible for a person who reflects the demographic characteristics of a particular group to hold beliefs that don't reflect the dominant sentiment of that group. To take an extreme example, do the beliefs and decisions of Justice Clarence Thomas or Representative J. C. Watts (Republican, Oklahoma) better reflect those of the African-American community than do those of Senator Ted Kennedy (Democrat, Massachusetts) and House minority leader, Richard Gephardt (Democrat, Missouri)?

Although substantive representation is more difficult to evaluate than descriptive representation, it is every bit as important. Not only do people want to see their own reflection in government, they also want that government to be responsive to their needs and interests.

Roles of Representatives

How to achieve equitable representation is an important issue; what role representatives should play in office is another. People want their representatives to serve their constituency and make intelligent decisions while doing so. But these two goals can be a problem for representatives who disagree with their constituents or who believe that, if constituents had more information, they would arrive at a different policy judgment.

There are basically two schools of thought about what the representative's proper role should be. The democratic school perceives the representative as a **delegate** of the people and, as such, duty bound to discern and reflect the majority opinion. If there is a consensus, the representative should follow it; if there isn't, then a representative may be able to exercise more personal discretion in deciding what to do about a public policy issue.

The other representational role is that of a **trustee,** a person charged with using the information and expertise at his or her disposal to make the best possible decision. Edmund Burke put it this way in a speech to the people of Bristol who elected him to Parliament:

> Parliament is not a congress of ambassadors from different and hostile interests, which interests each must maintain, as an agent and advocate, against other agents and advocates; but Parliament is a deliberative assembly of one nation, with one interest, that of the whole—where not local prejudices ought to guide, but the general good, resulting from the general reason of the whole. You choose a member, indeed; but when you have chosen him he is not a member of Bristol, but he is a member of Parliament.[2]

Those who favor a trustee role believe that the public has neither the desire, the ability, nor the knowledge to focus on policy matters. This is why they elect representatives to make policy decisions, people who have greater interest and desire (as indicated by their candidacy) and, one hopes, the knowledge and ability to do the job effectively. Moreover, this school of thought sees legislative institutions as deliberative bodies in which the deliberation may have an impact on a representative's decisions.

The American people are ambiguous about the role they want their representatives to play. They prefer leaders to followers, but they also believe that leaders should follow the views of the public closely.[3] They think that elected officials would make better decisions if they did what was right, but they also want their representatives to do what the majority desires.[4] They believe that members of Congress look out for their constituency's interests, but they also want them to do what's best for the country.[5] And they do not believe that elected and government officials do what the majority wants a great deal of time.

Naturally, they want their leaders to stay in touch with popular sentiment, but they are somewhat leery of public opinion polls as reflective of this sentiment.[6] Their skepticism about polling extends to why officials use them to gauge public opinion. More people believe that those in government use polls to stay popular and get reelected than because they want to give the public a say in what the government does.[7]

People believe that members of Congress should look out for their constituents' interests but think congressional representatives are more sensitive to special interests. However, they also believe that most members of Congress are too parochial and should do what is best for the country.

Contemporary political developments have been pushing elected representatives closer to their constituents than in the past. Candidates for office make representational promises that they are expected to fulfill. Failure to do so is frequently the subject of media attention and can become a campaign issue if the incumbent stands for reelection. Getting reelected is believed to be a primary motivation for legislators when they make policy judgments. Legislative offices are devoting more staff, more time, and more resources to servicing constituency demands. Members of Congress have received greater allowances for home travel, and even the legislative calendar has been adjusted to permit representatives to spend more time in their home districts.

Moreover, the use of public opinion polls and focus groups to dig more deeply into the opinions and attitudes of the populace; the development of rapid and easy communication by e-mail, fax, and telephone; and the growth and professionalization of interest groups have all kept legislators more closely in touch with their constituents than they were in the past. Similarly, the expansion of local news programming has allowed constituents to become better informed about the behavior of their representatives and created the perception among legislators that their words and actions are increasingly visible to the folks back home. Frequent elections keep these officials accountable.

Together, these factors have made legislators more cognizant of their delegate role, although the low level of public information and the absence of dominant constituency opinions on many issues have continued to allow them considerable discretion in making public policy decisions.

THE STRUCTURE OF ELECTIONS AND THE UNDERREPRESENTATION OF MINORITIES

How elections are structured shapes the representative character of the American political system—particularly its descriptive representation. The boundaries of legislative districts, the number of officials selected within them, and the procedure by which the winner is determined all affect the character of representation.

As we noted in Chapter 2, rules and procedures aren't neutral. The plurality voting system in single-member districts disproportionately benefits those in the majority. It also benefits the two major parties. Similarly, the way the Electoral College operates today favors the large states and groups within them.

Plurality Voting in Single-Member Districts

The Constitution does not prescribe single-member districts. What it does require is a reapportionment, every ten years, of the members of the House of Representatives on the basis of the national census. States gain or lose seats depending on how their proportion of the population compares to that of the country as a whole—with one proviso: every state must have at least one representative in the House.

Although the Constitution does not specify how the seats are to be allocated within the states, a single-member district system has generally prevailed since the Constitution was ratified. In such a system, the state drafts the boundaries of its legislative districts, and each district is represented by one legislator who is selected on the basis of the popular vote.

A voting system in which the candidate with the most votes wins favors those in the majority. It does so within each district as well as cumulatively among the districts within the state. It is difficult for a minority to gain representation unless it constitutes a majority within a district.

The best evidence supporting the proposition that plurality voting in single-member districts hurts minorities is the composition of bodies of elected officials. Take Congress, for example. Table 3.1 shows the percentages of African Americans, Latinos, and Asian Americans in Congress since 1981. Although African Americans constitute 12 percent of the voting-age population; Latinos, 10 percent (and growing); and Asian Americans, 4 percent, they have traditionally been underrepresented in Congress, more so in the past than at present.[8]

The underrepresentation of minority groups has become not only a political issue but also a legal one. Underrepresentation raises serious constitutional questions because the Fourteenth Amendment requires that states not deny their citizens equal protection of the laws, which in turn implies equal representation in the body that makes the laws.

Not until the 1960s, however, did the judiciary began to address constitutional issues associated with minority representation. In 1962 the Supreme Court decided in the case of *Baker* v. *Carr* (369 U.S. 186) that malapportioned state

TABLE 3.1 Minority Members of Congress, 1981–2001 (Percentages)

Congress/Year	African Americans	Hispanics	Asian Americans
	House of Representatives		
97th/1981	4	1	3
98th/1983	5	2	3
99th/1985	5	2	3
100th/1987	5	3	4
101st/1989	6	2	5
102nd/1991	6	3	3
103rd/1993	9	4	4
104th/1995	9	4	4
105th/1997	9	4	4
106th/1999	9	4	4
107th/2001	8	4	1
	Senate		
97th/1981	0	0	3
98th/1983	0	0	2
99th/1985	0	0	2
100th/1987	0	0	2
101st/1989	0	0	2
102nd/1991	0	0	2
103rd/1993	1	0	2
104th/1995	1	0	2
105th/1997	1	0	2
106th/1999	0	0	2
107th/2001	0	0	2

legislatures may violate the equal protection clause of the Fourteenth Amendment. The Court's judgment that legislative districting can be a judicial matter, not simply a political one, opened the floodgates to suits by those who believed that the size and shape of their districts discriminated against them and denied them equal representation.

In cases arising from these lawsuits, the Supreme Court ruled that all legislative districts, except for the U.S. Senate, had to be apportioned on the basis of population, according to the one person–one vote principle.[9] Additionally, the Court said that the size of congressional districts within a state cannot vary by more than 1.5 percent.[10]

The configuration of districts, however, wasn't subject to judicial scrutiny until 1986, when the Supreme Court decided, in the case of *Davis v. Bandemer* (478 U.S. 109), that partisan gerrymandering, the drafting of the boundaries of legislative districts to benefit the party in power, could also become a constitutional issue if it denied people equal representation.

By the 1980s, the battle over representation had spread to all institutions of the national government. Congress got involved when it amended the Voting Rights Act in 1982 to encourage states to create districts in which racial and ethnic minorities were in the majority. The Justice Department in the first Bush and in the Clinton administrations pressured the states to follow the dictates of the legislation after the 1990 census and legislative apportionment were completed.

The redrafting of state congressional districts resulted in an increase in minority representation in Congress (see Table 3.1), but it also contributed to a more Republican, more conservative Congress. Most of the newly crafted districts were in the South and Southwest. Because African Americans and Latinos are predominantly Democratic, their concentration in so-called majority-minority districts resulted in more conservative, "whiter" districts in other parts of the state—districts that benefited the Republicans at the expense of the Democrats. The gain in GOP seats helped the Republicans win control of Congress in 1994 and institute their more conservative policy agenda, which was opposed by the minority groups that the voting rights legislation was designed to help. Thus, in effect, the establishment of more districts in which a minority within the state became a majority within the district improved the descriptive representation for these minority groups but adversely affected their substantive representation.[11]

Legal challenges to these new minority districts were quickly initiated by Democrats and others who believed that they amounted to racial gerrymandering. A divided Supreme Court agreed. By a majority of only one, the Court held that race could not be a primary factory in drafting the boundaries of legislative districts.[12] The Court's decision was seen as a major setback for those desiring greater minority representation.

Not only do single-member districts with winner-take-all voting help the demographic majority, they also help the political majority, which is one or both of the major parties. In competitive districts, aspiring politicians have to run on the Democratic or Republican label if they are to have a reasonable chance of being elected to office. In noncompetitive ones, they have to vie for the nomination of the dominant party, whose primary is effectively equivalent to the general election.

Sometimes, to improve their chances, Democratic and Republican candidates in the general election will seek a third-party endorsement to get an extra line on the ballot and garner support from those who do not identify with either of the major parties. But rarely will a candidate who is endorsed only by a third party, or who runs as an independent, win.

There are only two members of the 107th Congress, Representative Bernard Sanders of Vermont and Virgil H. Goode Jr. of Virginia, who were elected as independents. During the first session of Congress, Senator James Jeffords of Vermont left the GOP and declared himself an independent. Jeffords voted with the Democrats to reorganize the Senate; thereby giving the Democrats a majority.

Improving Minority Representation

What can be done to improve demographic and partisan minority representation? There are several answers, but none of them affords much immediate hope of rectifying the representational issue. The principal structural change that would contribute to minority representation would be to create multi-member districts and use a proportional system of voting in which candidates are chosen roughly in proportion to the vote they or their party receive.[13]

Many countries, especially those with a parliamentary system of government, such as Brazil, Spain, and Israel, have proportional voting. Others, such as Italy, Japan, and Mexico, mix proportional and plurality voting systems for their legislative representatives. (Table 3.2 lists the electoral systems of other democratic countries.)

Some of the states in the United States use proportional voting in multi-member districts to choose their state legislators, city councils, and school boards. In the presidential nomination process, the Democratic party requires proportional voting for pledged delegates who attend its national nominating convention.

TABLE 3.2 Electoral Systems of Various Democratic Countries

Country	System of representation
Australia	Single-member districts (SMD) but uses proportional representation (PR) for senate elections
Austria	Proportional representation
Belgium	Proportional representation
Canada	Single-member districts
France	Single-member districts
Germany	Proportional representation
Greece	Proportional representation
Ireland	Proportional representation
Israel	Proportional representation
Italy	Combination of SMD and PR
Japan	Combination of SMD and PR
S. Korea	Combination of SMD and PR
Mexico	Combination of SMD and PR
Slovakia	Proportional representation
South Africa	Proportional representation
Spain	Proportional representation
Sweden	Proportional representation
United Kingdom	Single-member districts
United States	Single-member districts

Source: Data from "Voting in Major Democracies." Copyright © 1999 The Center for Voting and Democracy.

The principal advantage of proportional voting is that demographic and partisan minorities can gain representation roughly in proportion to their strength within the electorate. It also encourages turnout because representation is allocated according to the proportion of the vote that parties or candidates receive, thereby motivating all parties to try to maximize their vote. In noncompetitive, single-member districts, there is much less incentive to turn out.

A proportional election might require more complicated voting instructions and more complex ballots. It could also make it easier for candidates and parties with extreme political views to gain representation in government. In Israel, which has a proportional representation system, the small religious parties, some of which have strong fundamentalist beliefs, have exercised disproportional power because their support has been necessary to the formation of a governing majority.

The main disadvantage of a proportional system is that it is much less likely that one party will constitute a legislative majority. This forces the leader of the party with the most seats to try to form a governing coalition with other parties. A multiparty coalition is more fragile than a coalition composed of a single party. A vote against the government on a major issue frequently topples it and either forces new elections or requires a new person to try to form a viable governing coalition. It is also harder to pinpoint accountability in a multiparty government.

The other way to achieve fairer and more equal representation for minorities is to eliminate the allegiances and attitudes (some consider them biases and prejudices) that favor the majority. Although there is some evidence that a candidate's race, ethnicity, and religion aren't as important to today's voters as they were a decade or two ago, major attitudinal change takes time and, judging by the demographic composition of elected public officials, has a long way to go.

THE ELECTORAL COLLEGE SYSTEM AND THE OVERREPRESENTATION OF LARGE STATES

The Electoral College system also creates a representational bias. Initially designed as a dual compromise between the large and small states, and between proponents of a federal structure and of a more centralized national government, the Electoral College provided an alternative to legislative selection or a direct popular vote. The framers did not want Congress to select the president because they feared that would jeopardize the executive's independence. Nor did they want popular selection. They lacked faith in the people's judgment and the states' ability to conduct a fair and honest vote. Moreover, they wanted a leader, not a demagogue, a person selected on the basis of personal qualifications, not popular appeal.

According to the original plan, states would be allocated electors in proportion to their congressional representation. They could choose them any way they wanted, including popular vote. Initially, most had their legislatures do the selecting. The electors would meet and vote for two people. The person with the most votes would be president, provided the plurality winner had a majority[14]; the person with the second most votes would be vice president. In this way the framers hoped to ensure that the two most qualified people would be chosen president and vice president. The only restrictions they placed on the electors' choices were a few qualifications for eligibility: the candidate had to be at least thirty-five years of age and a native-born American who had been a U.S. resident for fourteen years prior to the election.

The system worked according to the original design in the first two elections, in 1788 and 1792. Washington was the unanimous choice of the electors, but there was no consensus on the other candidate. John Adams, the eventual second choice, benefited from some informal caucusing prior to the vote.

Partisanship and Winner-Take-All Voting

The development of the party system in the mid-1790s transformed electoral voting. Instead of making an independent judgment, electors exercised a partisan one. They were expected to vote the party line and did. Thus whichever party controlled the state also controlled the selection of electors, who in turn voted for their party's candidates.

The movement to the direct election of electors followed. In 1800 ten of the fifteen states had their legislatures choose the electors. By 1832, all but South Carolina elected them by popular vote. South Carolina began to do so in 1864.

The popular selection of electors made the Electoral College more democratic than it had been or was intended to be. However, the movement of states to a **winner-take-all system,** in which partisan slates of electors competed against one another, created a plurality-rule situation. It also created the possibility that the candidate who received the most popular votes might not receive the most electoral votes, a possibility that became a reality three times in American history, in 1876, 1888, and 2000.[15]

The most likely situation in which the candidate with the most popular votes would lose in the Electoral College is that of very close competition between the major parties, along with a strong third-party candidate who captures sufficient electoral votes to deny the leading candidate a majority. The elections of 1968 and 1992 could have produced such a scenario but did not. The election of 2000 probably did. Table 3.3 indicates the six states in which the winning candidate's margin of victory was less than the votes that third-party candidates Ralph Nader and Pat Buchanan received. According to the Voter News Survey exit poll, 47 percent of Nader voters said they would have voted for Gore, 21 percent for Bush, and 30 percent indicated that they would not have voted at all. Although Buchanan received a much smaller vote than Nader, most of his supporters indicated that they would have voted for Bush. Thus, had Nader not run, Gore would have won Florida (probably not New Hampshire) and, with

TABLE 3.3 The Potential Impact of Third-Party Candidates on the 2000 Presidential Election

States	Nader vote	Bush's margin	Number of electoral votes
Florida	97,488	537	25
New Hampshire	22,188	7,211	4
	Buchanan vote	**Gore's margin**	
Iowa	5,731	4,144	7
New Mexico	1,392	366	5
Oregon	7,063	6,765	7
Wisconsin	11,446	5,708	11

Florida's twenty-five electoral votes, the election. Had Buchanan not run but Nader remained in the race, Bush would have likely picked up three to four additional states. Had they both not run, Gore would have been advantaged because of the size of the Nader vote and probably would have won.

An undemocratic result is only one of the Electoral College's representational biases. The decision of most states—to create a general ticket system in which all of their electors are chosen by a single vote—gives an advantage to the very largest states, such as California, with the most electoral votes, and the very smallest states, whose three electoral votes overrepresent their proportion of the country's population. It also provides incentives for the candidates to concentrate their efforts in states that polls indicate are the most competitive. In 2000, the five major battleground states were Florida, Michigan, Pennsylvania, Ohio, and Wisconsin. Within the largest and most competitive states, groups that are geographically concentrated and unified in their voting behavior are also helped because they can exercise an influence disproportionate to their numbers.

Reforming the Electoral College System

Is the Electoral College a democratic problem, and if so, what should be done about it? Theoretically, any system that could upset a plurality choice is a problem for a democracy. The simple and what many consider the most equitable way to avoid this potential problem is to have a direct vote for president by the electorate. Such a change would simplify the election and prevent a discrepancy between the popular vote and the election results—provided that only a plurality was needed to win. If a majority were still required, however, another election, perhaps between the top two candidates, or a congressional resolution of the matter would be necessary.

In seven out of the twenty-five elections in the twentieth century, and one election in the twenty-first, the winner did not receive at least 50 percent of the vote. Clinton did not in 1992 or 1996, nor did Bush in 2000. One proposal for avoiding a two-tiered election is to elect the plurality winner, provided that candidate has at least 40 percent of the vote. The only winning candidate who got less than that percentage was Abraham Lincoln in 1860.

Rectifying the representative bias of the winner-take-all aspect of the system is another way to enhance the equity of the presidential vote. The general ticket system discourages turnout in those states that are least competitive, and, as a result, the major candidates put less effort into those states. Lower turnout can hurt the entire ticket of the party out of power, thereby perpetuating its minority status.

Allocating the electoral vote in proportion to the popular vote in each state (known as the **proportional plan**) would be another alternative. Such a system would more closely reflect the diversity of views and encourage turnout among the population, but it might also result in a proliferation of votes among different candidates and parties, thereby making it more difficult for any one to get a majority. Third-party and independent candidates would exercise more influence than they currently do.

Another option (known as the **district plan**), which the states of Maine and Nebraska use, is to give two at-large electoral votes to the candidate who wins the popular vote in the entire state and one vote to the winning candidate in each legislative district. It too would produce closer presidential elections than the current system, but it might also align the presidential election more closely to that of Congress, particularly the House of Representatives.

Table 3.4 lists the Electoral College vote since 1960 under the present system and the vote that would have resulted if these other systems had been employed. The results of only one of these elections would have changed. Under both the proportional and the district systems, Nixon probably would have defeated Kennedy in 1960.[16] In 1976 Carter and Ford would have tied under the district plan, but a Democratic Congress probably would have selected Carter anyway. In 2000 Bush wins in every voting system except direct election.

Despite the results in 2000, the present Electoral College system with its winner-take-all voting in forty-eight of the fifty states, has tended to enlarge the winning candidate's margin of victory, thereby giving the victor a larger mandate for governing than that candidate would otherwise have. However, acting on the basis of such a mandate can be hazardous. The current system has also compartmentalized voting problems although that compartmentalization in 2000 extended the indecisive outcome for five weeks.

AMERICAN POLITICS AND THE UNDERREPRESENTATION OF WOMEN

Women are a majority of the U.S. population today, almost 52 percent of the voting-age population. They are also a majority of the electorate, although their majority status in the electorate is of more recent origin. Women won the right to vote in 1919, but it took another sixty years for them to vote in equal

TABLE 3.4 Voting for President, 1956–2000: Four Methods for Aggregating the Votes

Year		Electoral College	Proportional plan	District plan	Direct election
1956	Eisenhower	457	296.7	411	57.4
	Stevenson	73	227.2	120	42.0
	Others	1	7.1	0	0.6
1960	Nixon	219	266.1	278	49.5
	Kennedy	303	265.6	245	49.8
	Byrd	15	5.3	14	0.7
1964	Goldwater	52	213.6	72	38.5
	Johnson	486	320.0	466	61.0
	Others	0	3.9	0	0.5
1968	Nixon	301	231.5	289	43.2
	Humphrey	191	225.4	192	42.7
	Wallace	46	78.8	57	13.5
	Others	0	2.3	0	0.6
1972	Nixon	520	330.3	474	60.7
	McGovern	17	197.5	64	37.5
	Others	1	10.0	0	1.8
1976	Ford	240	258.0	269	48.0
	Carter	297	269.7	269	50.1
	Others	1	10.2	0	1.9
1980	Reagan	489	272.9	396	50.7
	Carter	49	220.9	142	41.0
	Anderson	0	35.3	0	6.6
	Others	0	8.9	0	1.7
1984	Reagan	525	317.6	468	58.8
	Mondale	13	216.6	70	40.6
	Others	0	3.8	0	0
1988	Bush	426	287.8	379	53.4
	Dukakis	111	244.7	159	45.6
	Others	1	5.5	0	1.0
1992	Bush	168	203.3	214	37.5
	Clinton	370	231.6	324	43.0
	Perot	0	101.8	0	18.9
	Others	0	1.3	0	0.6
1996	Clinton	379	262.0	345	49.2
	Dole	159	219.9	193	40.7
	Perot	0	48.8	0	8.4
	Others	0	7.3	0	1.7
2000	Bush	271	260.2	271	47.9
	Gore	266*	258.4	267	48.4
	Others	0	19.4	0	3.7

*One Democratic elector in the District of Columbia cast a blank ballot.

Source: From *The Road to the White House, 2000, The Politics of Presidential Elections. The Post Election Edition,* 1st ed., by Stephen Wayne. © 2001. Reprinted with permission of Wadsworth, an imprint of the Wadsworth Group, a division of Thomson Learning. Fax (800) 730-2215.

proportion to men. Today, the proportion of women voting is actually slightly higher than that of men. Yet they represent a substantially lower proportion of members of Congress and of state legislative and top executive officials than do men. Why?

For most of the nation's existence, men dominated politics, and that domination to some extent still persists in election to office. It will take time for women to gain the electoral positions or professional status from which they can more successfully seek office. Moreover, women, who still take time off from their careers far more often than do men to raise a family, are disadvantaged politically for doing so.

Nonetheless, women have made gains in recent years, as indicated in Table 3.5, and are likely to continue to do so in part because they constitute a majority of the electorate and tend to be more supportive of women candidates than are men.

CONSEQUENCES OF REPRESENTATIONAL BIAS

Representational inequalities have contributed to public policy decisions that benefit those who are best represented. Not only does such policy work to benefit those who are already economically and educationally advantaged, but it could also lead to an attitudinal cleavage between the haves and have-nots.

We would expect those who perceive themselves to be less well represented in government to be more critical and less trusting of government, but they aren't. Surveys of public attitudes toward government find no major ethnic or gender differences in levels of trust, although there have been racial differences. For many years trust among African Americans has been less than among whites.[17]

Differences in perceptions of what government should do are also apparent. Generally speaking, those who are less well off and who consequently have less representation want a more powerful and active government, a government that will pay more attention to their interests and needs.

Table 3.6 reveals differences in public trust and confidence in government over a twenty-five-year period. Although it indicates that trust has declined among most population groups, it finds the largest declines among those who identify with the Republican party.

Table 3.7 indicates more variation in attitudes toward government power: individuals who are white, male, and Republican are more likely to believe that the government has too much power; conversely, women, minorities, and poorer, less educated people believe that the government should exercise more power. The former see the government as inhibitor of individual initiative; the latter see it as equalizer.

Demographic differences are also apparent in the public policy priorities that people think government should have. Although there is a general consensus that government should attend to the basic needs of the population, there is disagreement over the priority that government should and actually does place on those needs today. In general, men assign a lower priority to government's

TABLE 3.5 Women in Elective Office, 1975–2001 (Percentages)

Level of office	Year													
	1975	1977	1979	1981	1983	1985	1987	1989	1991	1993	1995	1997	1999	2001
U.S. Congress	4	4	3	4	4	5	5	5	6	10	10	11	12	13.6
Elected statewide Executive	10	10	11	11	11	14	14	14	18	22	26	26	28	27.0
State legislatures	8	9	10	12	13	15	16	17	18	21	21	22	22.5	22.4

Source: Used by permission of the Center for the American Woman and Politics, Eagleton Institute of Politics, Rutgers University, <http://www.cawp.rutgers.edu/Facts.html>.

TABLE 3.6 Trust and Confidence in the Federal Government to Handle Domestic Problems (Percentages)

	1972		1997	
	Great deal/ fair amount	Not much/ none	Great deal/ fair amount	Not much/ none
Total	69	29	60	40
Sex				
Male	65	34	58	42
Female	74	23	62	37
Race				
White	73	26	60	40
Black	60	39	63	36
Age				
18–29	65	33	60	40
30–49	69	30	59	40
50+	74	24	61	38
Education				
College graduate	70	30	64	36
Some college	67	32	58	41
High school	69	30	60	40
Less than high school	72	26	58	41
Party Identification				
Republican	80	18	56	44
Democrat	66	33	70	30
Independent	71	29	56	44

Source: 1972 data from Gallup polls; 1997 data from Princeton Survey Research Associates, "The National Trust Survey," September 25–October 31, 1997 as published in Pew Research Center For The People & The Press, *Deconstructing Distrust* (Washington, DC: Pew, 1998), 20.

involvement in health care, education, and concerns of the elderly than do women.[18] Racial differences aren't as great, but African Americans do believe more strongly than whites that government should put a higher priority on educational standards, affordable health care, and the reduction of poverty.[19]

What do these findings have to do with representational bias? The answer is, not much. Those at the lower end of the socioeconomic scale turn to government not because they are less represented in that government but because they have nowhere else to turn. Where representational bias may be a factor is in perceptions of how much attention those in office pay to certain groups. In its surveys of public opinion, the Pew Research Center For The People & The Press

TABLE 3.7 Attitudes Toward Government Power (Percentages)

	Gov't has too much	Gov't uses right amount	Gov't should use more	Don't know
Total	33	32	33	2
Sex				
Male	40	32	27	1
Female	27	31	40	2
Race				
White	35	33	31	1
Nonwhite	24	27	45	4
Hispanic	22	30	46	2
Black	25	25	47	3
Age				
Under 30	31	30	38	1
30–49	33	31	35	1
50–64	39	32	27	2
65+	28	38	29	5
Education				
College graduate	34	38	27	1
Some college	33	31	34	2
High school graduate	35	30	34	1
Less than high school	27	27	42	4
Family Income				
$75,000+	39	36	25	—
$20,000	29	25	41	5
Party Identification				
Republican	45	29	25	1
Democrat	18	39	42	1
Independent	38	28	32	2

Source: Pew Research Center For The People & The Press, *Deconstructing Distrust* (Washington, D.C.: Pew, 1998), 65.

found "striking differences among racial, gender, and income groups over the level of government attention afforded their own social groups and whether this amount was appropriate."[20] Table 3.8 indicates general perceptions of government responsiveness to various groups, and Table 3.9 indicates group perceptions of government responsiveness.

In short, those who are less well represented and more needful of government tend to trust the government as much as, if not more than, those who are

TABLE 3.8 Government Responsiveness to Group Needs: General Perceptions (Percentages)

	Less attention than deserved	Right amount	More attention than deserved	Don't know
Poor people	65	23	10	2
Elderly people	60	31	8	1
Middle-class people	54	36	9	1
Women	39	46	13	2
Religious people	27	46	22	5
Black people	26	46	24	4
White people	17	59	19	5
Business leaders	9	37	50	4

Source: Pew Research Center For The People & The Press, *Deconstructing Distrust* (Washington, DC: Pew, 1988), 48.

better represented in it, but they also perceive that government pays less attention to them and to their needs and interests.

The controversy that surrounded the Florida vote and the outcome of the 2000 presidential election generated considerable resentment within the African-American community and affected that community's attitudes toward government. A majority of African Americans believed that Bush stole the election, compared with only 17 percent of the white population.[21] African Americans became more critical of Congress and the Supreme Court than they were prior to the election and than the rest of the population. Moreover, African Americans are less satisfied than most Americans with the direction in which the country is heading, and they are much more disapproving of Bush's job performance than the country as a whole.[22] Whether these African-American evaluations would fade as the period from the election lengthened or would remain until the community's electoral and policy grievances were addressed was an issue that naturally engaged the Bush administration.

LEGAL QUALIFICATIONS AND DEMOCRATIC OUTCOMES

In a democratic political system, people should be able to select the candidate of their choice. In the United States, however, legal qualifications for office can and do inhibit that selection. The most controversial qualification for office is term limits, which prevent the electorate from reelecting a popular and experienced incumbent who has served the maximum number of years. Term limits currently apply to the president and to state legislators in twenty-two states. Many state constitutions limit governors' terms as well.

TABLE 3.9   Group Perceptions of Government Attention (Percentages)

	Get less than they deserve	Get more than they deserve	Right amount	Don't know
Black Respondents				
African Americans	61	7	28	4
Whites	21	26	49	4
White Respondents				
African Americans	7	56	31	6
Whites	19	12	64	5
Women				
Women	48	6	45	1
Men	29	20	48	3

Source: Pew Research Center For The People & The Press, *Deconstructing Distrust* (Washington, DC: Pew, 1998), 48.

The Twenty-second Amendment, ratified in 1951, limits a president to a maximum of two elected terms, or to only one if the president serves more than half his predecessor's term. Lyndon Johnson, who became president after John F. Kennedy's assassination in November 1963, would have been eligible for two elected terms; Gerald Ford, who succeeded Richard Nixon in August 1974, was eligible for only one.

Some states sought to impose restrictions on how long their members of Congress could serve, but the Supreme Court ruled that state-imposed limits on members of Congress were unconstitutional because they conflicted with Article I of the Constitution, which specifies only age and residence requirements for members of Congress.

The contemporary movement for term limits has been spurred by growing dissatisfaction with the performance of government and the behavior of public officials. There is a perception that these officials lose touch with those who elected them, that they become increasingly self-interested and self-promoting, and that they use the perquisites of their office to gain an unfair reelection advantage. Thus, the argument is that the only effective way to ensure turnover in office is to limit the terms of those elected.[23]

Those who support this argument contend that legislatures were initially designed to be popular assemblies in which concerned citizens represented their brethren to formulate and oversee public policy. The idea of an assembly composed of political professionals with job security gained through significant incumbency advantages is anathema to this original design and its intent to keep government close to the governed. Rotation in office keeps elected officials more in touch with the needs and interests of the electorate. It also creates more nonincumbency elections in which competition is stimulated and more voters turn out. It is argued as well that term limits prevent special-interest groups from becoming too cozy with those in power and thus less likely to use their resources to "buy, rent, or influence" elected officials.

The anti–term limits crowd contends that these limits are unnecessary, undesirable, and undemocratic.[24] They are *unnecessary* because there is sufficient turnover in most legislatures. Take the U.S. Congress, for example. More than half of the members of the 107th Congress were first elected in the decade from 1991 to 2001.

Term limits are *undesirable* because they result in less knowledgeable and less experienced public officials who lack the skills to be effective in office.[25] Inadequate information and understanding of the problem can result in unwise and ill-considered public policy decisions and on overdependence on staff—the so-called unelected representatives, who are not directly accountable to the electorate—and also may require longer learning periods during which government may not operate effectively.

Opponents of term limits argue that limits are *undemocratic* because they prevent the electorate from reelecting a particular representative who may have served well in office. Moreover, such limits remove the incentive for an incumbent to be responsive in his or her last term and contribute to the phenomenon of declining influence in that term.

The Twenty-second Amendment is a good example of the negative impact term limits can have. The amendment that prohibits presidents from running for a third term weakens them as the second term progresses, thereby inhibiting their leadership. The term *lame duck* is frequently used to describe their predicament in the last two years in office. Lame-duck presidents see power flow away from them, usually seek refuge in ceremony, travel, and speeches, tend toward concentrating on foreign policy, and make much more use of unilateral instruments of presidential power.

Supporters of the amendment believe that the loss-of-power argument is overblown, that presidents are reelected to continue their policies already in place, not to create a lot of new domestic programs. The greater danger, they contend, is that the cult of personality can upset the balance of power and effectively undercut the democratic electoral process.

Age, Residency, and Citizenship Requirements

In addition to term limits, there are several other constitutional qualifications that limit public choice. At the national level, these include minimum age and residency requirements for both Congress and the president, and a native-born requirement for president. Are such qualifications still necessary and desirable? Does it make sense to have a minimum age requirement but no requirement for maximum age? Ronald Reagan, the oldest president, suffered memory loss in his second term. Strom Thurmond, the oldest member of Congress, was reelected at the age of ninety-two and stood fourth in line for the presidency as president pro tempore of the Senate when the GOP controlled that body. About one-third of the electorate thought that the seventy-four-year age of Senator Robert Dole, the Republican presidential candidate in 1996, was a factor that could affect their voting decision.

The president has to be a native-born American. Being born in the United States might have been important in 1787, when the nation was young and patriotic ties to it were weak, but is it relevant today? Several prominent Americans have been precluded by this requirement. They held high positions in government, were in the line of succession, and would have been considered qualified in every other respect, but they were born in other countries. Included among them were Secretaries of State Henry Kissinger and Madeleine Albright.

Similarly, what is the purpose of a residency requirement, particularly in an age of international commerce in which business executives employed by multinational corporations often have to spend considerable time living abroad? Although the Constitution mandates residence in a state before a person can represent that state, it is still possible to achieve residency by moving into the state and declaring residence there at the time of the vote. Former Attorney General Robert Kennedy and First Lady Hillary Rodham Clinton both moved into New York in order to be candidates for the U.S. Senate. Both were elected although Kennedy hadn't lived in the state long enough to vote in the election in which he won.

Summary: Representational Dilemmas in a Nutshell

American democracy rests on the concept of representative government. In such a government, all citizens have the right to be equally and fairly represented. But theory and practice diverge. Structural biases affect the representative character of the political system.

Plurality voting in single-member districts overrepresents majorities at the expense of minorities, but it also contributes to stability and accountability in government by maximizing the number of seats that the majority party holds. A proportional voting system in multimember districts increases minority representation, but frequently at the cost of coalition government.

Winner-take-all voting in the Electoral College inflates the clout of the large states and cohesive groups within them; it also tends to enlarge the popular vote winner's margin of victory. Were states to apportion their electors on the basis of statewide and legislative district voting or on the proportion of the vote that candidates received in the state, the results of the Electoral College vote would be closer but also potentially more subject to dispute.

Women are underrepresented but not as a consequence of structural bias. Their failure to achieve representation equal to their proportion of the population is largely a residue of the restrictions placed on women's suffrage before 1920, traditional voting prejudices, and differing gender career patterns.

Although the underrepresentation of certain groups has been a source of discontent to them, it has had little direct impact on their attitudes toward government. These attitudes seemed to be conditioned more by economic and social need than by political representation.

Electoral and representational outcomes are also affected by restrictions placed on eligibility. Of the term, age, and residency requirements that shrink the pool of eligible candidates, limits on tenure are the most controversial and seem to have the greatest impact on the functioning of government.

To address representational bias and the policy problems that flow from it, the majority has to be more cognizant of the need for minority representation and willing to adjust the electoral system or their voting behavior to achieve it. A tall order, to be sure!

Now It's Your Turn

Discussion Questions

1. Is it possible to have a democratic electoral system in which the majority decides and the minority is fairly represented?
2. If women constitute a majority of the voting-age population, why are fewer women than men elected to positions in government?
3. Are age, residency, and place-of-birth requirements consistent with a democratic electoral process in which the people are supposed to be able to choose their elected leaders?
4. Is it important for a representative democracy to have demographic, issue, and ideological groups represented in proportion to their percentages in the population? If so, how can this representation be achieved? If not, why not?

Topics for Debate

Challenge or defend the following statements:

1. Descriptive representation is irrelevant and may be harmful to effective government.
2. The system of plurality voting in single-member districts is inconsistent with the Supreme Court's interpretation of the Fourteenth Amendment's equal protection clause.
3. The underrepresentation of women in elected positions does not adversely affect public policy.
4. Term limits are a good idea and should be permitted for all elected officials.
5. Age qualifications for office are unnecessary and undesirable and should be eliminated.

Exercise

A congressional committee is holding a hearing on how to improve representation in the national government. As an expert on representational issues, you've been invited to testify. Your assignment is to prepare and present your testimony. In your testimony, note the following:

1. How well the society is currently represented in federal government.
2. The principal groups that may suffer representational bias.
3. The source of their representational problems and what it would take to fix them.
4. The pros and cons of changing the system to remove these representational problems (including any unintended consequences that might occur).
5. Your recommendation to the committee on what (if anything) it should propose to Congress as a legislative solution to the problem.

Internet Resources

- Center for Voting and Democracy <http:///www.fairvote.org>
  Contains a wealth of information on various voting systems, especially proportional representation.
- Democracy Network <http://www.democracynet.org>
  A nonpartisan site sponsored by the League of Women Voters for up-to-date information on candidates and ballot initiatives.
- Democracy <http://www.democracy.org>
  An organization devoted to involving citizens in the democratic process; provides suggestions for improving representation and getting involved; has developed a classroom experiment on representation and electoral methods.
- Destination Democracy <http://www.destinationdemocracy.org>
  This public interest group, sponsored by the Benton Foundation, examines changes to the electoral system that will make it more democratic and less influenced by special interests.
- The Pew Research Center For The People & The Press <http://www.people-press.org>
  Conducts surveys on public knowledge, attitudes, and opinions toward candidates, government, and the media.
- Voter Information Services <http://www.vis.org>
  Provides a database on congressional voting that can be downloaded for analysis.

Selected Readings

Abbot, David W., and James P. Levine. *Wrong Winner: The Coming Debacle in the Electoral College.* New York: Praeger, 1991.

Best, Judith. *The Choice of the People? Debating the Electoral College.* Lanham, MD: Rowman and Littlefield, 1996.

Glennon, Michael J. *When No Majority Rules: The Electoral College and Presidential Selection.* Washington, DC: Congressional Quarterly Books, 1993.

Guinier, Lani. *The Tyranny of the Majority.* New York: Free Press, 1994.

Hardaway, Robert M. *The Electoral College and the Constitution: The Case for Preserving Federalism.* Westport, CT: Praeger, 1993.

Jackson, John S., III, J. C. Brown, and David Bositis. "Herbert McClosky and Friends Revisited: 1980 Democratic and Republican Elites Compared to the Mass Public." *American Politics Quarterly* 10 (1982): 158–180.

Jackson, John S., III, J. C. Brown, and Barbara Leavitt Brown. "Recruitment, Representation and Political Values: The 1976 Democratic Convention Delegates." *American Politics Quarterly* 6 (1978): 187–212.

Lublin, David. *The Paradox of Representation.* Princeton, NJ: Princeton University Press, 1997.

Malbin, Michael J., and Gerald Benjamin, eds. *Limiting Legislative Terms.* Washington, DC: Congressional Quarterly Books, 1992.

Nye, Joseph S., Jr., Philip D. Zelikow, and David King. *Why People Don't Trust Government.* Cambridge, MA: Harvard University Press, 1997.

Pitkin, Hanna F. *The Concept of Representation.* Berkeley: University of California Press, 1967.

Swain, Carol M. *Black Faces, Black Interests: The Representation of African Americans in Congress.* Cambridge, MA: Harvard University Press, 1993.

Warren, Mark E. *Democracy and Trust.* Cambridge: Cambridge University Press, 1999.

Will, George. *Restoration: Congress, Term Limits, and the Recovery of Deliberative Democracy.* New York: Free Press, 1992.

Notes

1. For a theoretical discussion of the concept of representation, see Hanna F. Pitkin, *The Concept of Representation* (Berkeley: University of California Press, 1967).

2. Edmund Burke, "Speech to the Electors,"*Burke's Politics,* quoted in ibid., 171.

3. In a national survey conducted for the Center on Policy Attitudes, respondents were asked the following:

> I'm going to read you a set of arguments that some people have used when discussing the role of the public in government. For each one, I'd like you to tell me whether you find it convincing or unconvincing.
>
> • Nobody knows what's best for the people better than the people. Paying attention to the views of the majority would probably lead to policies that are best for the country as a whole. Do you find this argument convincing or unconvincing?

Convincing	73.6%
Unconvincing	22.4
Don't Know/Refused	4.0

- The public is emotional, volatile and uninformed. Therefore it is better for policymakers not to be very influenced by the public's wishes when making decisions. Do you find this argument convincing or unconvincing?

Convincing   19.9%
Unconvincing   77.0
Don't Know/Refused   3.1

Steven Kull, "Expecting More Say: The American Public on Its Role in Government Decisionmaking," Center on Policy Attitudes, May 10, 1999, 37.

4. • Elected officials would make better decisions if they thought more deeply about what they think is right.

Agree   79.2%
Neither Agree nor Disagree   5.9
Disagree   12.2
Don't Know/Refused   2.8

- When your Representative in Congress votes on an issue, which should be more important: the way voters in your district feel about that issue, or the Representative's own principles and judgment about what is best for the country?

Way voters feel   68.5%
Principles and judgment   25.3
Both equal (volunteered)   4.0

Ibid., 35, 40.

A survey conducted by the Henry Kaiser Family Foundation, in collaboration with *Public Perspective*, asked the following question: "Please tell me which [statement] comes closer to your views. . . . Elected and government officials should use their knowledge and judgment to make decisions about what is the best policy to pursue even if this goes against what the majority of the public wants. . . . Elected and government officials should follow what the majority wants, even if it goes against the officials' knowledge and judgment." The responses were as follows:

Officials should follow the majority   54%
Officials should use judgment   42
Don't know/Refused   4

"Polling and Democracy," *Public Perspective* (July/August 2001): 18.

5. • Generally, do you think most members of Congress are more interested in doing what's best for the country, or what's best for their own congressional district?

What's best for the country   19.1%
What's best for their congressional district   71.4
Neither/Both/It Depends/Don't Know (volunteered)   9.5

- Do you think your own representative in Congress should be more interested in doing what's best for the country, or what's best for your congressional district?

What's best for the country   52.2%
What's best for your congressional district   37.7
Neither/Both/It Depends/Don't Know (volunteered)   10.1

Kull, "Expecting More Say," 41.

6. "Polling and Democracy," 24. They also believe that public officials place too much attention on polls. Gallup Poll, "Public Opinion Polls, April 15, 1999, <http://www.gallup.com/poll/indicators/indpolls.asp>.

7. "Polling and Democracy," 23.

8. U.S. Census Bureau, "California, Texas, and Florida Will Show Biggest Increases in Voting-Age Population in November," July 31, 2000.

9. *Reynolds* v. *Sims,* 377 U.S. 533 (1964).

10. *Wesberry* v. *Sanders,* 376 U.S. 1 (1964).

11. For an excellent discussion of this quandary for minorities, see David Lublin, *The Paradox of Representation* (Princeton, NJ: Princeton University Press, 1997).

12. *Shaw* v. *Reno,* 509 U.S. 630 (1993); *Miller* v. *Johnson,* 115 S.Ct. 2475 (1995); *Bush* v. *Vera,* 116 S.Ct. 1941 (1996); *Meadows* v. *Moon,* 117 S.Ct. 2501 (1997).

13. Lani Guinier, a law professor and unsuccessful nominee for assistant attorney general for civil rights in the Clinton administration, argues in her book *The Tyranny of the Majority* (New York: Free Press, 1994) that only with cumulative voting in multi-member districts can the minority hope to achieve fair and equal representation. Guinier's proposal is to give citizens as many votes as there are candidates and allow them to distribute their votes any way they choose. They could, for example, give all the votes to one of the candidates, perhaps a person who shares their demographic characteristics or attitudinal views, or they could divide them among several of the candidates. Guinier contends that such a system would accord with the one person–one vote principle but not involve the state in racial districting. Without such a system, she contends that the prejudices of the majority will dominate. This proposal, which conservatives found so alarming, forced Guinier to withdraw her nomination when she failed to obtain sufficient support in the Senate.

14. If no candidate received a majority, the House of Representatives would choose from among the top five candidates. The Twelfth Amendment later reduced this number to three when it provided for separate ballots for the president and vice president. In the event of a House election, voting would be by state, with each state delegation possessing one vote.

15. In 1876 a dispute over twenty electoral votes and a resolution of it by a congressionally established commission resulted in the election of Republican Rutherford B. Hayes, who had fewer popular votes than his opponent, Samuel J. Tilden. In 1888 Republican Benjamin Harrison received a majority of the electoral votes, while his opponent, President Grover Cleveland, received a majority of the popular votes. In 2000 Republican George W. Bush won a majority of the electoral vote, while Democrat Al Gore had a plurality of the popular vote.

16. In Alabama and Mississippi, fourteen unpledged electors voted for Democratic Senator Harry Byrd of Virginia.

17. Orlando Patterson, "Liberty Against the Democratic State," in *Democracy and Trust,* ed. Mark E. Warren (Cambridge: Cambridge University Press, 1999), 190–191.

18. Pew Research Center For The People & The Press, *Deconstructing Distrust* (Washington, DC: Pew, 1998), 46.

19. Ibid.

20. Ibid., 48.

21. Gallup Poll, "Seven Out of 10 Americans Accept Bush as Legitimate President," July 17, 2001, <http://www.gallup.com/poll/releases/pr010717.asp>.

22. Gallup Poll, "With the Advent of Bush Administration, Blacks Have Become More Negative About All Three Branches of Government," July 10, 2001.

23. For arguments in favor of term limits, see Mark Petracca, "Rotation in Office: The History of an Idea," in *Limiting Legislative Terms,* ed. Michael J. Malbin and Gerald Benjamin (Washington, DC: Congressional Quarterly Books, 1992), 19–52; George Will, *Restoration: Congress, Term Limits, and the Recovery of Deliberative Democracy* (New York: Free Press, 1992).

24. Malbin and Benjamin, *Limiting Legislative Terms,* 198–221.

25. John R. Hibbing, *Congressional Careers: Contours of Life in the U.S. House of Representatives* (Chapel Hill: University of North Carolina Press, 1991), 180; and John M. Carey, *Term Limits and Legislative Representation* (Cambridge: Cambridge University Press, 1996), 193–194.

4

Are Political Parties Still Relevant?

Did you know that . . .

- the Democratic party of the United States is the oldest political party anywhere?
- the strength of the electorate's partisan loyalties has declined, but partisan voting in Congress has increased?
- more people claim to be independents today than claim to be either Republicans or Democrats?
- the largest group of Democratic voters consists of those sixty-five years or older?
- although changes in the nomination process were designed to improve the representative character of the parties, more people think the parties are less representative today than they were in the past?
- the key factor that has led to a resurgence of party influence during electoral campaigns is money—lots of it?
- no third-party or independent candidate ever won the presidency?
- only two independent or third-party members of the House of Representatives have been elected since the end of World War II?
- the group that is most desirous of a strong third party today is the youngest group of eligible voters: those between eighteen and twenty-nine?
- the keys to the longevity of the major parties are their moderation in policy and their pragmatic outlook, whereas the keys to the longevity of minor parties are their consistent policy positions and ideological orientations?
- the United States is one of the few democratic countries with a two-party system?

Is this any way to run a democratic election?

PARTIES AND AMERICAN DEMOCRACY

Why Political Parties Are Important

Political parties are considered an important part of a democratic electoral system. In fact, some scholars consider them absolutely essential.[1] They provide critical links among the electorate, the candidates, and the government. Parties help orient and organize voters. They tie candidates to one another and allow them to make both generic and specific appeals, replete with partisan imagery. And they provide the people with a basis for evaluating the performance of elected officials and holding them collectively responsible for their actions or inaction in office. These links have a direct impact on the responsiveness and accountability of elected officials, two critical components of a representative democracy.

In a heterogeneous society like that of the United States, interests are many, varied, and often conflicting. Political parties provide a structure for aggregating these interests, for packaging them and presenting them to voters. Parties articulate the interests in their platform, their campaign communications, and the collective campaigns of their candidates. Finally, parties provide a mechanism for governing, for bringing together elected officials on the basis of their shared values, interests, and policy goals and holding them accountable for their performance in office.

In elections, as in government, parties are likely to be the most effective coalition builders. They can unite diverse elements of the electorate, as well as overcome the institutional separation of powers to facilitate the operation of government. But parties can also have the opposite effect. Divided partisan control of government reinforces the separation of powers and impedes consensus building across institutional bodies.

Each of these functions—interest aggregation, articulation, and electoral accountability—is critical to a viable democratic political system.[2] That's why parties are important.

What Parties Do in Elections

Within the electorate, parties organize and orient voters. They create alliances among groups and allegiances among individuals. They inform people about the issues, get them involved in the campaign, and encourage them to vote.

Parties also structure electoral choices. They enable voters to transcend the many individual decisions they must make and allow them to superimpose a collective judgment that both guides and justifies their micro-level decisions. For the vast majority of voters, a major party label conveys legitimacy, whereas a minor party label does not. The candidates' partisan association gives the electorate some sense of whether the candidates will be able to affect other elected officials' actions in achieving the public policy goals and positions they articulated during the campaign.

Parties anchor policy preferences. Parties have an organizational history and a policy record that enable the electorate to learn what they've stood for and evaluate how successful they've been.

For the candidates, parties provide a collective presence and perspective, an organizational base, and the potential for enhancing their individual influence if elected. The collective presence is the party organization and its perspective, shared values, beliefs, and opinions. The organization has the resources, money, media expertise, and grassroots mobilization to aid candidates in their campaigns and extend their influence in government. Partisanship provides candidates with a core of faithful supporters; it also gives them the opportunity to reinforce some of the ideas, beliefs, and interests they have in common with fellow partisans. These benefits that parties give to candidates have led one astute observer, John H. Aldrich, to theorize that parties exist because office-seekers and officeholders find them useful. They contribute to the outcomes that these ambitious politicians desire.[3]

Parties also provide a framework for evaluating election results, organizing for the government, and subsequently for assessing its performance. In doing so, they convert individual victories into a collective effort, help define priorities for newly elected officials, and provide a continuing incentive—reelection—for keeping public officials sensitive to the interests and opinions of those who elected them.

This chapter examines each of the ways parties help electoral democracy. It looks at parties and the electorate, parties and electoral choice, and parties and electoral accountability. First, however, we present a brief overview of the evolution of American political parties, to provide a historical context for evaluating how well parties are serving the needs of electoral democracy today.

THE EVOLUTION OF U.S. POLITICAL PARTIES

Parties aren't mentioned in the Constitution, nor did the framers anticipate them when they created the electoral system. They did anticipate that groups would be active within the political arena, however. Fearing domination by any one of these groups, they divided institutional spheres of authority and created separate but overlapping constituencies as a hedge against any one group, including a majority, disproportionately influencing the formulation of national policy.

Implicit in this constitutional design, however, was the assumption that a lot of public policy wouldn't be necessary at the national level. With an ocean for protection, a huge frontier, seemingly unlimited natural resources, this nation composed largely of self-sufficient farmers wasn't thought to need or desire a very active national government. Although economic and social needs have changed, and government has grown and become more active, its constitutional structure has essentially remained the same—hence the dilemma of how to bridge the institutional divide and facilitate the operation of government. By providing common perspectives, policy goals, and political structures, parties can unify what the Constitution separates if they control the institutions of government. However, if institutional control is divided between parties, then partisanship can reinforce the constitutional division, thereby impeding the functioning of government. Over the course of American history, parties have done both.

Birth and Infancy

The creation of parties at the end of the eighteenth and beginning of the nineteenth centuries presented the political system with both a challenge and an opportunity. The challenge was to prevent a major party from dominating the system in such a way as to deny the minority its rights and disregard its interests. The opportunity was to utilize common beliefs, goals, and interests as a consensus-building mechanism within and among the institutions of government.

Thomas Jefferson's Democratic-Republican party, which emerged as the first broad-based political party in the United States, controlled national politics and government for more than twenty-five years, from 1800 to 1828. It was the majority faction that the framers feared, but it also bridged the gap that was developing between an expanding and more diverse electorate and the national elites that had controlled the government since its founding. By the 1820s, the Federalist party, which supported the policies of the Washington and Adams administrations, had faded from the scene, and the Democratic-Republicans, the only viable party remaining, divided into factions along regional lines. Two of these factions eventually evolved into broad-based parties: the Democrats, who backed Jackson, and the Whigs, who opposed him.

Adolescence: A Growth Spurt

Between 1828 and 1844, state party organizations, loosely affiliated with the two major parties, developed and subsequently changed the character of the two-party system by federalizing it.[4] The parties began increasingly to reflect the federal structure of the government. The national parties became little more than collectivities of state parties, and the state parties began to aggressively build a mass base. Beginning in the 1840s, both parties used their presidential campaigns to mobilize voters. During nonelectoral periods, they used their resources and political influence to provide their supporters with tangible economic and social benefits (see Chapter 2, page 24.) Thus, by energizing the electorate, the parties not only extended their political influence but also began to address the economic and social needs of the society.

In the 1850s, sectional rivalries, inflamed by the passions of slavery and westward expansion, splintered the parties and eventually led to the demise of the Whigs and the division of the Democrats into northern and southern factions. The Republican party emerged out of this political chaos. Organized in 1854, the Republicans appealed to Whigs and northern Democrats who opposed slavery (abolitionists), to those who objected to its expansion (white laborers and small farmers), and to others (industrial workers) who feared that the influx of new immigrants would lower their wages or cost them their jobs.

Out of the turmoil created by the Civil War and Reconstruction, new partisan coalitions emerged. Big-business tycoons who had profited from the industrial revolution gained control of the Republican party and dominated it for over fifty years. The Democrats remained divided into a rural southern faction, controlled by the socially conservative white elite, and a more industrialized northern one, influenced by banking and commercial interests.

The popular bases of both parties shrank in the second half of the nineteenth century; voter turnout declined; and the partisan political environment became less competitive. Increasingly, poorer farmers, blue-collar workers, and newly arrived immigrants found themselves alienated from both major parties.[5]

Adulthood: The Eras of Partisan Majorities

The Republican Era, 1896–1928

A recession in 1893 during the administration of Democrat Grover Cleveland, combined with the Populist movement in the West, which further splintered the Democratic party into "free silver" and non–free silver factions, resulted in the emergence of a new Republican majority. Strong in the North, popular among Protestants and older immigrant groups, buoyed by the support of business and also increasingly by labor, benefiting from the country's economic prosperity, the Grand Old Party (GOP), as it had come to be called, dominated American politics for the next three decades. Although the Democrats were still a major party, ruling the South and even managing to gain control of both the White House and Congress from 1912 to 1918, the Republicans held onto their numerical advantage with voters until the Great Depression.[6]

The Democratic Era, 1932–1968

A major realignment of parties occurred in the 1930s. The Democrats, riding on the coattails of Franklin Roosevelt and his New Deal policies, broadened their base by appealing to those at the lower end of the socioeconomic scale, while the Republicans held onto the allegiances of the business community and the well-to-do members of society. The principal exception to this economically based division of the electorate was in the South, where, regardless of socioeconomic status, voters retained their Democratic loyalties.

The economic division between the parties became evident in their policy perspectives as well. The Democrats looked to government to take the lead in solving the nation's economic and social policies, whereas the Republicans viewed government involvement in the economy as a threat to the free enterprise system. Whereas the Democrats supported Roosevelt's efforts to redistribute resources on the basis of individual need, the Republicans did not. They continued to believe that a capitalistic system, free from government control, would provide the greatest benefit to the society as a whole.

The Democrats maintained the allegiances of a majority of voters until the end of the 1960s. However, changes in the economic environment following World War II, growing prosperity, an expanding middle class, and gains for organized labor all weakened the economic foundation on which the Democrats had built their electoral and governing coalitions. New social and international issues—the civil rights movement; the Korean and Vietnam wars and the public's reaction to them; violent demonstrations on college and university campuses; deteriorating conditions in the cities, with associated increases in crime, drug trafficking, and racial unrest—all divided the Democrats and helped unify the more socially conservative Republicans. By the 1970s, the Democrats had lost their status as the majority party; by the 1980s, they had lost their electoral plurality; by the 1990s, the parties were operating at rough parity with each other and continue to do so today.[7]

Although the Republicans benefited from the fraying of the Democrats' electoral coalition, they didn't become the new majority, except in the South. Rather, the electorate entered into a period of partisan dealignment, with neither party able to gain a permanent partisan advantage.

Modern Maturity: Dealignment or Realignment?

Scholars have disputed whether the dealignment of partisan allegiances augurs a new antiparty era. Will the electorate now be less tied to parties and more independent in their voting behavior? Or is this really the beginning of a new party realignment, albeit a slower and more gradual one than occurred in the 1930s, with the Republicans becoming the more dominant of the two parties?

The proponents of the dealignment theory point to the weakening of partisan attachments and the absence of corresponding reattachments. With the exception of southern whites, who have shifted their political allegiances from the Democrats to the Republicans, Democratic losses have resulted not in large-scale Republican gains but rather in a growing number of voters, now a plurality, who consider themselves independent.

Some see the changes as the precursor of a new Republican era in which the GOP will become the plurality party and eventually perhaps the majority party. They point to the steady rise in the Republican vote at all levels of government, to the election of a Republican Congress in 1994, to control of a majority of state legislatures and governorships in the mid-1990s, and to the registration preferences of new voters, which favored the Republicans throughout the Reagan era. They believe that such idiosyncratic events as the Watergate scandal during the Nixon administration, the economic recession during the first Bush administration, and the unpopular, failed attempt to remove President Clinton from office through the impeachment process slowed but did not reverse Americans' growing Republicanism.

Although the dealignment-realignment debate hasn't been resolved, the weakening of partisan attitudes has had a major impact on the electorate, the campaign, and the government.

- Voters have become more independent, more candidate-centered, and more volatile in their voting behavior.
- Party leaders have lost control of the nomination process, and their organizations no longer run their candidates' campaigns.
- The advent of television as a principal means of electioneering, the computer-based technology of modern campaigns, the professionalization of the campaign industry, and the rise of outside groups active in the electoral process have all weakened the party's role as the major intermediary between candidates and voters. However, political parties have begun to reassert themselves in the campaign process by virtue of their fund-raising skills and issue advocacy advertising.
- Governing at the national level has been made more difficult. Divided control of Congress and the presidency has become the rule, rather than the exception, since 1968.
- Ideology has reinforced partisanship. And the increasingly public arena in which government must operate has intensified the partisan and ideological divisions.

All of this has contributed to less legislation, more oversight, and greater partisan and institutional conflict. People have become less trustful of politicians. They also believe that elected officials lose touch with the average people and really don't care what that person thinks.[8] Increasingly, people have become turned off to national politics.

Each of these consequences has affected the major parties' influence on the electorate, on electoral choice, and on government. We examine these changes in the next three sections.

PARTIES AND THE ELECTORATE: THE WANING OF PARTISANSHIP

Partisan attitudes influence voting behavior in two fundamental ways: they are a motivation for voting, and they are a shorthand way of deciding for whom to vote. Thus any change in the direction and strength of these attitudes is bound to have an impact on the electorate's voting behavior.

Partisan attitudes aren't as strong as they used to be. A smaller proportion of the population identifies with the major parties today than did several decades ago, and the partisan loyalties of those who do identify are less intense. Table 4.1 documents some of these changes. It indicates that today only about two-thirds of the electorate currently identify with a major party, compared with almost three-fourths in 1960. It also shows some weakening in the intensity of people's allegiances to parties. Despite the decline in partisan indentities, people still seem to have a favorable view of both major parties (see Table 4.2). They support the idea of a third party but do not have a favorable view of most third parties operating today.

One reason for the weakening of party loyalties is the increasing candidate orientation of elections. Not only do more people, especially those between the ages of eighteen and twenty-nine, identify themselves as independents, but more claim to vote for the person, not the party.[9] How many times have you heard people say proudly, "I vote for the best person regardless of the party?"

Nonetheless, the proportion of the electorate that identifies with the major parties has been relatively constant since the 1970s. Moreover, voting analyses reveal strong correlations between partisanship and voting behavior especially in recent elections. And partisan attitudes seem to have a greater influence than any other factor on the way people vote. So how do shifts in partisanship and perceptions of parties affect the electorate?

TABLE 4.1   Partisan Identification of the American Electorate, 1960–2000 (Percentages)

Year	Democrats		Republicans		Independents	Other
	Strong	Weak	Strong	Weak		
1960	20	24	15	14	22	5
1964	27	25	11	13	22	2
1968	20	25	10	14	29	2
1972	15	25	10	13	35	2
1976	15	25	9	14	36	2
1980	18	23	8	14	34	2
1984	17	20	13	15	34	2
1988	17	18	14	14	36	2
1992	18	17	11	14	38	2
1996	19	20	13	15	32	1
1998	19	18	10	16	35	2
2000	19	15	14	13	30	9

Source: "National Election Studies," Center for Political Studies, University of Michigan. Data provided by the Interuniversity Consortium for Political and Social Research; 2000 data from Pew Research Center For The People & The Press, "2000 Typology Questionnaire," conducted August 24–September 10, 2000.

TABLE 4.2 View of Political Parties, 1999–2001 (Percentages)

	Partisan Identification*			Overall		
	Republican	Democrat	Independent	1999[†]	2000[‡]	2001[§]
View of Republican Party						
Favorable	91	29	58	53	53	56
Unfavorable	8	68	34	41	40	35
View of Democratic Party						
Favorable	43	94	70	61	60	60
Unfavorable	56	5	23	33	35	30

Sources: *Gallup Organization, Gallup News Service, April 9, 1999, <http://www.gallup.com/poll/release/pr990409c.asp>.
[†]Gallup News Service, January 14, 2000, <http://www.gallup.com/poll/release/pr000114.asp>.
[‡]Pew Research Center For The People & The Press, "2000 Typology Questionnaire."
[§]Pew Research Center For The People & The Press, "Clinton Nostalgia Sets In, Bush Reaction Mixed," January 11, 2001.

Partisanship as a Political Attitude

Partisanship is important because it acts as a lens through which political activity is viewed, a conceptual framework that helps people sort out the candidates and the issues, tell the "good guys" of one party from the "bad guys" of the other. Partisan attitudes reduce the burdens of voting for those who identify with a political party by providing an easy guide to follow when casting ballots. These attitudes also provide an incentive to become more involved, to get more information, to be more active, and to vote.[10]

In contrast, weaker partisan allegiances have contributed to the decline in turnout, to the lower level of information that much of the electorate possess, and to the unpredictability of voting decisions.[11] In theory, voters without a partisan mindset and the emotional ties that go with it should be in a better position to make an informed voting decision. In practice, such people often lack the interest and information to do so. Isn't it ironic for a democracy that the most informed and involved voters are also the most partisan and thus the least able to make an independent, nonpartisan judgment?

The Personification of Electoral Politics

With weaker party ties, people look to other factors when deciding how to vote. They look to the images of the candidates and to their positions on salient issues. Candidates, in turn, have contributed to the personification of electoral politics by deciding whether to run for office, how to organize their own campaigns, and what policy positions to take. In fact, their independence is often a selling point in their campaign. They argue that they are beholden to no one but their constituents.

Is the personification of politics a good or a bad development for an electoral democracy? Most observers think that it's bad because it directs attention toward personal traits and behavior, which may have little to do with governing, and away from policy issues and their impact, which can have a far greater effect on society.

Moreover, the emphasis on personality has turned into an emphasis on negative character traits. More and more campaign messages are geared toward explaining why people should *not* vote for a particular candidate rather than why they *should*.[12] News media coverage of campaigns has become more negative as well[13] (see Chapter 6). This negativity leaves a bad taste in the mouths of many voters. It makes a difference in the attitudes toward parties and the candidates who run on their label if people feel they're voting for the least bad candidate or for the best one. Excessive negativism dampens public enthusiasm, contributes to lower turnout, and undermines confidence in elections, candidates, and elected officials.

In an effort to overcome their own negative portrayal, candidates turn to professional image makers and pollsters to find images and appeals that will resonate with the voters. Sometimes, in their desire to win, they create images and make promises that become impossible to fulfill, with the result that public expectations are not met.

Finally, the emphasis on individuals rather than on parties also undermines accountability in government. It's one thing to hold a party responsible if that party controls the White House or is a majority in one or both houses of Congress. But how can an individual within a system based on separation of powers be held accountable for anything other than his or her own personal behavior?

The Division of Government

Another major argument against the personalization of politics is that it increases the probability of a divided government. By voting for the person and not the party, the electorate ends up with a mixed government composed of individuals who may not have common unifying priorities, positions, or even personal relationships that would facilitate the compromise that is essential to governing in a large and diverse society. Under such circumstances, consensus building becomes harder to achieve, policy coalitions shift from issue to issue, and legislative output decreases. Table 4.3 indicates that the number of laws between 1987 and 1996 declined significantly although in recent years that number has begun to increase. As a consequence, the public becomes disillusioned, disengaged, and, if conditions merit it, discontented. Periods of disillusionment and disengagement have plagued the United States since the personification of

TABLE 4.3   Legislation, 1987–2000

Congress	Public laws	Private laws
100th (1987–1988)	713	48
101st (1989–1990)	650	16
102nd (1991–1992)	590	20
103rd (1993–1994)	465	8
104th (1995–1996)	333	4
105th (1997–1998)	394	10
106th (1999–2000)	580	24

Source: National Archives and Records Administration, "Catalogue of Public Laws," <http://www.access.gpo/nara>.

politics began in the 1960s and 1970s. Periods of outright public anger have been rarer but still evident according to some observers.[14]

PARTIES AND ELECTORAL CHOICE: AN ECHO OR A SCHISM?

Another function of political parties in a democratic electoral process is to structure choice in elections. They do so through the philosophy they profess, the positions they take, the record on which they stand, and of course, by virtue of the candidates who run on their ticket. As we noted in Chapter 1, meaningful choice is an essential criterion for democratic elections. But how meaningful is the choice that parties provide?

To make such a choice, voters need to be presented with discernible options. Obviously, if the major parties support essentially the same issue agendas and similar policy proposals, then from the perspective of the voters and the public policy that results, it doesn't matter all that much who wins. From the perspective of the party, however, it matters a great deal.

One of the most persistent criticisms of parties over the years is that they aren't sufficiently different from one another. Their social and economic goals, their orientation toward government, their positions on major policy issues have more in common than not. The explanation for this lack of distinctiveness is the parties' broad-based composition, their inclusive character, and their desire to build and maintain as large an electoral coalition as possible. In order to accommodate the diverse and shifting interests of their partisans, the major parties have been forced to emphasize pragmatism over principle. They've tended to pursue mainstream policies at the expense of ideological politics. And they've chosen to emphasize reelection by making politically expedient policy decisions when they govern.

For those who adhere to well-defined belief systems, those who value policy over politics, those who claim that they'd rather be right than victorious, the choices that the major parties have presented over the years may not have been satisfactory. Third-party candidates such as George Wallace and Ross Perot voiced this criticism, as did Ralph Nader and Pat Buchanan more recently. Ideological and issue group leaders also complain that the parties are unresponsive to their views and interests.

Political scientists who have examined party platforms, campaign oratory, and policy achievements in government, however, have found consistent differences between the major parties over the years. Gerald Pomper's analysis of Republican and Democratic platforms from 1944 to 1976 revealed that they were more distinctive than duplicative, more policy oriented than simply rhetorical. Pomper found that many of the differences centered on issues that one party addressed and the other did not.[15] He argued that differences were important because the parties tried to keep their promises.[16] Jeff Fishel also found that presidential candidates tried to fulfill their campaign promises and were reasonably successful in doing so.[17]

The public also had perceived differences between the parties on policy issues (see Table 4.4). These perceptual differences first appeared in the National Election Surveys of 1964, have continued, and are even more pronounced today.[18] The public sees Democrats in general and their presidential candidates in particular as more liberal, and Republicans and their presidential candidates as more conservative.[19] These perceptions accord with scholarly studies that have also found ideological orientations that distinguish the major parties and their electoral coalitions from one another.[20]

In fact, the parties' ideological orientations have been criticized by those who believe that the Democrats in the 1970s and 1980s and the Republicans in the 1990s espoused views that were too extreme and thus unrepresentative of their own rank and file, much less of the public as a whole. The cleavages appear to be most extreme at the leadership level. Party leaders and activists tend to have more consistent belief systems than do their rank-and-file partisans.[21] Not only do these more distinctive ideological perspectives divide the Republican and Democratic parties, they create divisions within them.

Do the parties provide a meaningful choice in elections? The answer depends on how satisfied people are with the candidates who are running and with the views they express. To the extent that the candidates are more extreme in their beliefs than the electorate as a whole, the choices they provide will be less satisfactory. So why would parties nominate candidates like these? We answer this question in Chapter 7, where we discuss reforms in the nomination process that have shifted power from party leaders and to rank-and-file

TABLE 4.4 Degree of Perceived Differences Between the Democratic and Republican Parties, 1987–1999 (Percentages)

Question: Thinking about the Democratic and Republican parties, would you say there is a great deal of difference in what they stand for, a fair amount of difference, or hardly any difference at all?

Date	Great deal	Fair amount	Hardly any	Don't know
1999	33	46	18	3
1998	28	45	23	4
1997	25	48	25	2
1995	34	46	18	2
1994	23	51	24	2
1990	24	45	27	4
1987	25	45	25	5

Source: Pew Research Center For The People & The Press, "Public Votes for Continuity and Change in 2000," February 1999.

partisans—particularly to those activists who feel more strongly about issues and exercise disproportionate influence in the selection of party nominees.

PARTIES AND GOVERNMENT: IS COLLECTIVE ACCOUNTABILITY POSSIBLE?

Throughout this book we've argued that elected officials must be held accountable for their decisions and actions. Since the 1970s it has become easier to hold individual government officials accountable because of the increasingly public arena in which policy decisions are made, the multitude of information sources on government that are available, the investigative bent of the news media, and the continuous scrutiny of policymaking by interested outside groups. Personal accountability is also enhanced during elections by the amount of research that parties and candidates conduct about their opponents, as well as by their campaigns themselves, which highlight the candidates, their achievements, and their responsiveness to constituents.

But what about *collective* responsibility? Do contemporary parties contribute to that as well? Most observers are less sanguine about how responsible parties are or can be today.

The doctrine of having more responsible parties was first proposed by Professor Woodrow Wilson in his book *Congressional Government*.[22] Wilson lamented the fact that American parties were not as cohesive as those in the British parliamentary system; he urged the adoption of practices designed to make them more responsible, such as proposing a national program, campaigning for it, and carrying it out if elected.

The idea of responsible parties appealed to political scientists as the discipline of political science developed after the Second World War. E. E. Schattschneider, a proponent of this view, headed a committee of the American Political Science Association that called for the Democrats and Republicans to offer clear-cut alternatives to the voters, pursue them if elected, and be held accountable for their success or failure.

But no matter how good the idea sounded in theory, it would have been difficult to implement in practice. U.S. parties are more diverse than their British counterparts, in large part because the United States is a larger, more diverse country than the United Kingdom. Moreover, power is more dispersed within the American governmental system. In Britain, control of the House of Commons amounts to control of the government; in the United States, control of the House of Representatives, the people's house, is a far cry from control of the government. So is control of Congress, for that matter, if the president is of the opposite party from Congress. Besides, even when parties constitute a legislative majority, they aren't usually able to dictate their public policy outcomes. The committee and subcommittee systems in both houses, the unlimited debate rule in the Senate, and the strong constituency orientation of most members have made it difficult for the parties' legislative leaders to impose discipline on their members, much less take collective responsibility for the policies and practices of government.[23]

Ironically, in light of these obstacles, the parties demonstrated more unity during the voting stages of the congressional process in the 1990s than they did in the two preceding decades. The more ideological orientation of members of Congress, the visible public arena in which decisions are made and votes are cast—all covered by C-SPAN and the twenty-four-hour television news networks—as well as the decline of the civility and informality that facilitated compromise in the past, have all contributed to the warring camps atmosphere prevalent in Congress during the last decade.

Partisan bickering has been highlighted by national press coverage, with the consequence that the public is less likely to perceive Congress as an effective governing body.[24] Individual members tend to get more positive assessments from their constituents. The evaluative gap between the representatives individually and their representative body undercuts the consequences of a collective judgment. The lack of competition in most legislative elections, either because an incumbent is so advantaged or because the district is dominated by the partisans of one of the major parties, also makes it difficult to read a general judgment by the electorate in their vote for Congress. Voters are critical of the party in power but still reelect a representative of that party. For a collective judgment to be made, a partisan victory would have to occur as in the congressional elections of 1946 and 1994, which switched legislative control from one party to the other.

PARTIES AND THE POLITICAL SYSTEM

The weakening of partisanship and the growth of independents suggest that Americans see contemporary parties as less responsive than parties were in the past. Similarly, the dissatisfaction with electoral choices, as indicated by low turnout, low candidate evaluation, and the periodic support, at least in theory, for a new third party, may be evidence that many do not think they have a meaningful choice today. Finally, the public's inability to assign and the parties' inability to assume accountability for their performance in office also contribute to lower public confidence in the parties and the government.

Given these problems, is the current two-party system serving the needs of the American electorate, or would a multiparty system be better?

Multiparty Politics: Pros and Cons

There are those who believe that two parties can never satisfactorily represent a country as large and diverse as the United States. Instead of having two broad-based parties reaching out to accommodate those with very different, even conflicting philosophies and issue positions, they would rather have a multiparty system that could more effectively represent a diverse set of policy interests and political needs.[25]

Smaller and less diverse countries than the United States, such as Germany, France, and Spain, have such a system and have been able to maintain stable and effective government for relatively long periods of time. Others, however, such as Italy and, to a lesser extent, Israel, have not been as successful. Italy has had more than forty governments since the end of World War II. And the major governing party in Israel has to depend on the support of minor parties to gain and maintain a parliamentary majority. Table 4.5 lists the various types of party systems in major democratic countries.

In a multiparty system, the parties themselves combine to form governing coalitions, and compromise occurs among them. In the United States, if there is a majority party, as there was between 1932 and the late 1960s, compromise occurs within it, among the various groups competing for influence. If the major parties share power as they have for most of the time since 1968, then they must compromise within and between themselves.

Whether a two-party or a multiparty system is best may depend on the priorities placed on representation, accountability, and effective governance. But the question may also be academic, given the long and dominant two-party tradition in America, to which both major parties are committed and from which both derive benefit.

The Two-Party Tradition and American Diversity

Why does a heterogeneous society like that of the United States have a two-party tradition? There are two types of answers to this question. The first focuses on the incredible ability of the major parties to adjust and survive in the light of the changes that have affected American society. The major parties have successfully weathered these changes because they have been more pragmatic than ideological, more inclusive than exclusive, and more decentralized than centralized. They also haven't attempted to impose their beliefs and issue positions on their supporters, their candidates for office, or even their elected officials as a condition of party affiliation or electoral acceptability—although obviously they try to persuade them to follow the party line.[26]

The second type of answer focuses on the built-in advantages that the two major parties possess and jealously guard. The major parties are well recognized and have standing. They have organizations in all the states, a leadership structure, and, despite weaker allegiances, a core of supporters and financial benefactors. Independent candidates and especially third parties generally lack these resources.

The major parties have systemic advantages as well. They are automatically on the ballot in all fifty states as long as they win a certain percentage of the vote. Third parties are much less likely to have won that percentage. Their candidates and those running independently usually have to collect a certain number of signatures of registered voters just to get on the state ballots. Besides, as we noted

TABLE 4.5 Types of Party Systems

Taking account of relative size of parties	Strictly by Number of Parties			
	Predominant party systems	Two-party systems	Party systems with three to five parties	Party systems with more than five parties
Predominant party systems	Japan			
Two-party systems		Great Britain New Zealand U.S.A.		
Two-and-a-half-party systems			Australia Austria Canada Germany Ireland	
Systems with more than two-and-a-half parties				
One large party			Norway Sweden	
Two large parties				Israel Italy
Even-party systems			France Iceland Luxemburg Netherlands	Belgium Denmark Finland Switzerland

in Chapter 3, the single-member district system in which the person with the most votes wins also benefits the major parties at the expense of minor parties.

The presidential election system confers the same advantage on the major parties. The winner-take-all method of Electoral College voting used by forty-eight of the fifty states disadvantages third-party candidates whose support is widely distributed across the country, as was Ross Perot's in 1992 and 1996. If the election moves into the House, the major parties are also advantaged. Campaign finance laws that benefit the major parties reinforce these structural features, as does the more extensive media coverage they receive.

Despite public opinion, which periodically looks to third parties and independent candidates when the people are dissatisfied with the major parties, third parties have had difficulty gaining acceptance and maintaining public support. The argument that they can't win contributes to their difficulty in winning.

If third parties and independent candidacies were the only ways minority viewpoints could be heard and minority groups represented, then the bias of the system would be a serious failing in a democratic political process. But, as we've seen, there are many other ways minorities can and do get representation and exercise influence on elections and government. In fact, many believe that demographic and ideological minorities are overrepresented within the major parties and exercise disproportionate influence on them, much to the dismay of moderate, mainstream, rank-and-file voters. And outside of the parties, interest groups have proliferated: political action committees (PACs) within the electoral arena and lobbying groups within the governing arena.

Summary: Partisan Dilemmas in a Nutshell

Parties are important to a democratic selection process. They provide a critical link between candidates and voters, and between elected officials and the people who elected them. Without such a link, it would be more difficult to hold elected officials collectively responsible for their actions and thereby to hold government accountable to those who elected them.

Parties organize ideas, people, and institutions. The allegiances they engender, the attitudes they shape, and the electoral behavior they influence provide the electorate with a framework for the campaign, a motivation for participating in it, and an orientation that can be used to arrive at a voting decision.

The partisan dilemma stems from the weakening of political attitudes, the structuring of electoral choices, and the absence of responsible parties in government, all of which have contributed to the apathy, instability, and mixed judgments of the electorate.

The major parties have lost adherents; their electoral coalitions have frayed; their candidates have become increasingly independent and, conversely, less willing to follow the party line when running for office. And, to make matters worse, these candidates are held in lower esteem by the public. *Politician* has become a dirty word, which people associate with the ambitious pursuit of self-interest, with candidates who will say and do anything to win and keep public office.

Activists have been able to gain control of the nomination process and choose candidates whose beliefs and policy positions are more extreme than those of rank-and-file partisans and much more extreme than those of the general electorate. The combination of ideology and divided government has made policy-making more difficult and collective responsibility harder to establish. Prior to the terrorist attack, the last three decades have seen the growth of political alienation, apathy, and cynicism.

Despite the weakening of the major parties, new parties have failed to capture the heart and soul of the American people. The Reform party tried to take advantage of disenchantment with the Democrats and Republicans but has not been successful on a national scale. One of the reasons that third parties have had such a difficult time is the broad-based composition of the major parties, their pragmatic approach over the years, and their decentralized character. Another has been the stranglehold the major parties have on the current electoral system and their unwillingness to let go. One can see the marks of that stranglehold in the structuring of elections, the laws that regulate campaign finance, and the manner in which the news media cover electoral politics.

What can be done to resurrect or replace the major parties without government intervention that either reinforces the current system or forcibly imposes change on it? Can a two-party system be relevant and responsive to a country as large and diverse as the United States? Can parties be held accountable in a candidate-driven electoral process? These are the critical party-related issues that America's electoral democracy must address.

Now It's Your Turn

Discussion Questions

1. Why have partisan loyalties declined in intensity while the partisan influence on voting behavior has remained so strong?
2. Have interest groups weakened parties or substituted for them in the electoral and governing processes?
3. How has the increasing personification of elections affected the composition and disposition of the major political parties?
4. Are political parties the key to collective responsibility in government? If not, how can government be held accountable for its public policy decisions?
5. Does having only two major parties facilitate or impede the conduct of elections and the operation of government?
6. Can America's political diversity be adequately represented in a two-party system?
7. Does having two major parties make it more or less likely that public policy will reflect the views and interests of the majority of people in the United States?
8. Are the views and interests of those who do not identify with a major party represented in elections and government? If so, by whom?

Topics for Debate

Challenge or defend the following statements:

1. All candidates who run on a party label should be required to promise that they will support the principal tenets of their party as stated in the last party platform or be removed from the party line on the ballot.
2. Every person should register with the party of her or his choice as a condition of voting or participating in that party's nomination process.

3. State and national party chairs should be elected every four years by the party's rank and file, not by some "invisible" party committee.
4. Partisanship is undesirable; thus all candidates for office should run in non-partisan elections.
5. Political parties are unnecessary to the functioning of democratic government and should be abolished.
6. Interest groups should be required to affiliate with a political party in order to contribute money to it or its candidates or to spend money on its behalf in elections.
7. A new third party should be created that speaks for the average American voter.

Exercises

1. Design a strategic memorandum for a new political party that addresses the needs and desires of your generation. In your memorandum, indicate the following:
   a. the key issues and the new party's position on them,
   b. the campaign appeals that your party would make, not only to your generation but also to others,
   c. likely sources of income for the party and its nominees and methods you would use to raise the money,
   d. other nonparty or even party groups to which you might appeal for funds and votes in an election,
   e. what your first order of business would be if your party were to win control of a legislative or executive branch.
2. The major parties in the United States have been criticized for being too inclusive, for trying to satisfy too many divergent and even conflicting interests, for being everything for everyone. Do you think that this criticism is valid? Answer this question by comparing the major parties today on the basis of the following:
   a. their demographic and regional composition,
   b. their positions on the major issues before Congress and the president,
   c. their ideological orientations,
   d. the distinctiveness (if any) of their candidates for elective office.

Internet Resources

- Democratic National Committee <http://www.democrats.org>
  This is the main website of the national Democratic party, with links to other Democratic organizations, as well as to state Democratic parties.
- Republican National Committee <http://www.rnc.org>
  This is the main website of the national Republican party, with links to other Republican organizations, as well as to Republican state parties.

- Other political parties:
  Communist Party of the United States <http://www.cpusa.org>
  Democratic Socialists of America <http://www.dsausa.org>
  The Green Party <http://www.greenparties.org>
  Libertarian Party <http://www.lp.org>
  Reform Party <http://www.reformparty.org>
  Socialist Party <http:www.sp-usa.org>
  Socialist Labor Party <http://www.slp.org>

Selected Readings

Aldrich, John H. *Why Parties? The Origin and Transformation of Political Parties in America.* Chicago: University of Chicago Press, 1995.

Bibby, John F., and L. Sandy Maisel. *Two Parties—or More?* Boulder, CO: Westview, 1998.

Black, Earl, and Merle Black. *The Vital South: How Presidents Are Elected.* Cambridge, MA: Harvard University Press, 1992.

Clubb, Jerome M., William Flanigan, and Nancy H. Zingale. *Partisan Realignment: Voters, Parties, and Government in American History.* Boulder, CO: Westview, 1990.

Fiorina, Morris P. "The Decline of Collective Responsibility in American Politics." *Daedalus* 109 (Summer 1980): 25–45.

Gerring, John. *Party Ideologies in America, 1828–1996.* New York: Cambridge University Press, 1998.

Green, John C., and Daniel M. Shea, eds. *The State of the Parties.* Lanham, MD: Rowman and Littlefield, 1999.

Margolis, Michael. "From Confusion to Confusion: Issues and the American Voter." *American Political Science Review* 71 (1977): 31–43.

Miller, Warren E. "Party Identification, Realignment, and Party Voting: Back to the Basics." *American Political Science Review* 85 (1991): 557–570.

Nie, Norman H., Sidney Verba, and John R. Petrocik. *The Changing American Voter.* Cambridge, MA: Harvard University Press, 1976.

Niemi, Richard G., and Herbert F. Weisberg. *Controversies in Voting Behavior.* Washington, D.C.: Congressional Quarterly Books, 1993.

Pomper, Gerald M. "From Confusion to Clarity: Issues and American Voters, 1956–1968." *American Political Science Review* 66 (June 1972): 415–428.

Pomper, Gerald M., with Susan S. Lederman. *Elections in America.* New York: Longman, 1980.

Rapoport, Ronald B. "Partisanship Change in a Candidate-Centered Era." *Journal of Politics* (1997): 185–199.

Schattschneider, E. E. *Party Government.* New York: Rinehart, 1942.

Shafer, Byron E., and William J. M. Claggett. *The Two Majorities.* Baltimore, MD: Johns Hopkins University Press, 1995.

Wattenberg, Martin P. *The Decline of American Political Parties: 1952–1988.* Cambridge, MA: Harvard University Press, 1990.

Notes

1. E. E. Schattschneider, *Party Government* (New York: Rinehart, 1942), 1.

2. These party functions are presented and discussed in Samuel J. Eldersfeld, *Political Parties: A Behavioral Analysis* (Chicago: Rand McNally, 1964).

3. John H. Aldrich, *Why Parties? The Origin and Transformation of Political Parties in America* (Chicago: University of Chicago Press, 1995), 18–27, 277–296.

4. Ibid., 118–135.

5. Frances Fox Piven and Richard A. Cloward, *Why Americans Don't Vote* (New York: Pantheon, 1988), 64–95.

6. The Democrats' success in the second decade of the twentieth century came as a result of a split within the Republican party at the national level, between those supporting William Howard Taft and those backing Theodore Roosevelt's candidacy for the presidency in 1912.

7. Gallup Poll, "Major Political Parties in Competitive Situation," December 3, 1999, <http:www.gallup.com/poll/releases/pr991203.asp>.

8. Data collected by the Pew Research Center For The People & The Press since 1987 indicated that three out of four people subscribe to the proposition "Generally speaking, elected officials in Washington lose touch with people pretty quickly." "Issues and Continuity Now Working for Gore," September 14, 2000, 43. Almost 40 percent believe "Most elected officials don't care what people like me think." *Retro-Politics,* November 1999, 139.

9. In a poll taken by Gallup in April 1999, 24 percent of those under thirty years of age identified themselves as Republican; 35 percent, as Democratic; and 41 percent, as independent. Gallup Organization, Gallup News Service, April 9, 1999, <http://www.gallup.com/poll/release/pr990409c.asp>.

10. Angus Campbell, Philip E. Converse, Warren E. Miller, and Donald E. Stokes, *The American Voter* (New York: Wiley, 1960), 133–136.

11. Ibid.

12. See Lynda Lee Kaid and Anne Johnston, "Negative Versus Positive Television Advertising in U.S. Presidential Campaigns, 1960–1988," *Journal of Communication* 41 (Summer 1991): 53–64; L. Patrick Devlin, "Contrasts in Presidential Campaign Commercials of 1992,"*American Behavioral Scientist* 37 (November 1993): 272–290; and Patrick Devlin, "Contrasts in Presidential Campaign Commercials of 1996," *American Behavioral Scientist* 41 (August 1997): 1058–1084.

13. Thomas E. Patterson, *Out of Order* (New York: Knopf, 1993).

14. See Susan J. Tolchin, *The Angry American* (Boulder, CO: Westview, 1996).

15. Gerald M. Pomper, "Control and Influence in American Politics," *American Behavioral Scientist* 13 (November–December 1969): 223–228; and Gerald M. Pomper, with Susan S. Lederman, *Elections in America* (New York: Longman, 1980), 161.

16. Naturally, the party controlling the White House has an advantage in accomplishing its policy goals. According to Pomper and Lederman, the party that controlled the presidency achieved almost four-fifths of its program, but even the losers gained some of their objectives. Pomper, with Lederman, *Elections in America*, 161.

17. Fishel found that, from 1960 to 1984, presidents initiated legislation or signed executive orders that were broadly consistent with about two-thirds of their campaign pledges. Of the legislation, the percentage that became law ranged from a high of 89 percent during the Johnson administration to a low of 61 percent during Nixon's. Jeff Fishel, *Presidents and Promises* (Washington, DC: Congressional Quarterly Books, 1994), 38, 42–43.

How much of the platform becomes public policy depends largely on the partisan composition of the new government. Obviously, the more control one party exercises, the more likely is that party to be able to implement more of its platform planks, which will be deemed to have public support because the party was victorious.

18. See Gerald M. Pomper, "From Confusion to Clarity: Issues and American Voters, 1956–1968," *American Political Science Review* 66 (June 1972): 415–428; and Michael Margolis, "From Confusion to Confusion: Issues and the American Voter," *American Political Science Review* 71 (March 1977): 31–43.

19. Paul R. Abramson, John H. Aldrich, and David W. Rohde, *Change and Continuity in the 1996 and 1998 Elections* (Washington, DC: Congressional Quarterly Books, 1999), 132.

20. John Gerring, *Party Ideologies in America, 1828–1996* (New York: Cambridge University Press, 1998).

21. Herbert McClosky, Paul J. Hoffman, and Rosemary O'Hara, "Issue Conflict and Consensus Among Party Leaders and Followers," *American Political Science Review* 54 (June 1960): 425–426.

22. Woodrow Wilson, *Congressional Government* (1885; reprint, New York: Meridan Books, 1960).

23. Morris P. Fiorina, "The Decline of Collective Responsibility in American Politics," *Daedalus* 109 (Summer 1980): 25–45.

24. General Social Surveys conducted by National Opinion Research Center.

25. Theodore J. Lowi, *The Personal President* (Ithaca, NY: Cornell University Press, 1985), 195–208.

26. When David Duke, a former Nazi sympathizer and member of the Ku Klux Klan, announced that he would run for governor of Louisiana as a Republican, the party denounced his candidacy, although it could not prevent him from running or claiming he was a Republican. The Democrats have had similar problems with Lyndon LaRouche, who has run for the Democratic nomination for president—the last time, from his jail cell.

Has Money Corrupted
Our Electoral Process?

Did you know that . . .

- Nixon spent six times as much money in his last race for the presidency in 1972 as he spent for his first in 1960?
- ever since Congress amended the law to allow parties to raise and spend an unlimited amount of money to get people out to vote, the percentage of people turning out to vote has declined in most national elections?
- about $3 billion was spent on the 2000 elections for president and Congress?
- the more money incumbents spend in the general election, the more it is a sign that they fear they may lose?
- despite the use of the White House to raise funds for Clinton and the Democrats in 1996, the Republicans raised more money for that election?
- there may be no causal relationship between campaign spending and electoral success?
- the party that controls Congress tends to receive a larger proportion of its funds from PACs than does the congressional minority?
- most people don't contribute to political campaigns, and less than 14 percent of taxpayers check off the box that allows three dollars of their taxes to go to a federal election campaign fund?
- foreign governments and multinational corporations spend much more money lobbying elected officials than they do trying to influence their election?
- political advertisers spent five times more on broadcast television ads across the country in 2000 than they did in 1980, even after adjusting for inflation?
- the Federal Election Commission is permanently immobilized by its statutory composition of three Democrats and three Republicans?

Is this any way to run a democratic election?

MONEY AND DEMOCRATIC ELECTIONS

What does money have to do with democracy? The answer is a lot, especially if

- it gives wealthy people and groups an unfair advantage in influencing the election outcome;
- it affects who votes and how they vote;
- it becomes a condition for who runs for office and who doesn't;
- it affects information that the electorate receives about the candidates and their issue positions;
- it affects public perceptions of how the system is working and whether it's fair.

Money can and does affect the democratic character of American elections. If a basic tenet of an electoral democracy is every adult citizen's right to an equal opportunity to influence an election outcome, then the unequal distribution of resources within society threatens that right. Does the average citizen have the same opportunity to affect an election campaign as does billionaire Bill Gates, CEO of Microsoft, or to run for office as did Ross Perot and Steve Forbes? Do two equally qualified candidates have the same chance to win if one is wealthy and willing to use a personal fortune to advance his or her political ambitions, while the other doesn't have the wealth to do so? Is everyone equally protected by the law if some people are able to gain more access to policymakers by virtue of their campaign contributions and expenditures than are those who cannot or do not contribute?

The difficulty in providing equal opportunities for all citizens stems in large part from the value that Americans place on personal freedom and private property. The Constitution protects people's freedom to use their own resources as they see fit, provided they do so legally. Moreover, the Supreme Court has equated campaign spending with freedom of speech. In 1976, in the case of *Buckley* v. *Valeo* (424 U.S. 1), the Court held that the independent expenditure of funds by individuals and groups in a political campaign was protected by the First Amendment. Subsequently, the advocacy of issue positions in campaigns by party and nonparty groups was also deemed to fall under this protection. So how can campaign spending be restricted if that restriction violates fundamental First Amendment rights?

Not only does the Constitution protect the rights of people and groups to express their feelings and to "petition the government for grievances," but the electoral and governing systems are designed to allow them to do so, to enable those who feel most intensely about a candidate or issue to try to convince others. Should a democratic electoral system allow those with greater resources and more intense feelings to exercise more influence over the selection of candidates, the issue agenda, the campaign debate, organizing activities, the vote, and even the interpretation of the results? Should the giant companies of the communications industry be able to condition the scope, content, and "spin" of the information the electorate receives and needs to make an informed voting decision? Should they profit from the election campaign as they did in 2000?[1]

Most people believe that special interests and the press exercise too much influence on elections and government. These perceptions, documented in recent public opinion polls, have undoubtedly contributed to (and perhaps followed from) the dissatisfaction that is regularly expressed today about politics and politicians, elections and candidates, and government and public policy makers.[2] For many, money is the root of all evil, but it is also the "mother's milk of politics." Herein lies the problem.

This chapter explores the impact of money on electoral politics. It begins with a description of the rising costs of elections, the problems associated with those costs, and how Congress has attempted to deal with the problems through legislation. It then describes the unintended consequences of some of this legislation, which has led to the breakdown of the campaign finance system. Subsequent sections of the chapter deal with the relationship between money and electoral success, public perceptions of the money problem, and proposals for campaign finance reform.

MONEY AND POLITICS: AN OVERVIEW OF CONGRESS'S ATTEMPTS TO REGULATE CAMPAIGN FINANCE

The costs of elections have skyrocketed in the last thirty years. In 1960 Richard Nixon spent about $10 million in his race for the presidency. Eight years later, he spent $25 million. Running for reelection against weak opposition in 1972, he spent over $61 million. The Center for Responsive Politics estimates that $1.8 billion was spent on federal elections during the 1991–1992 election cycle, $2.2 billion during 1995–1996, and $3 billion during 1999–2000.[3]

Various factors have contributed to the rapid rise in expenditures. The nomination process became more competitive. Successful candidates often have to run in two elections: one for the nomination and one for the general election. The techniques of the modern campaign—television advertising, survey research, direct-mail fundraising, and grassroots organizing—have added to the costs.

Fearing that the election process had become too expensive; that candidates had to spend too much time raising money; that they were becoming too dependent on large donors, who in turn were exercising too much influence over the electoral and governing processes; that money was being given secretly and perhaps illegally to candidates and parties, Congress went into action.

Setting Limits: The Federal Election Campaign Act

Legislation was enacted in the 1970s to reduce the costs of elections, decrease dependence on large donors, and open the process to public view. The Democratic Congress had an additional objective in passing this legislation: to reduce the Republican party's financial advantage.

The laws were directed primarily at the presidential election, but some restrictions were placed on congressional elections as well. The amount of money that individuals and groups could give to candidates for federal office, as well as to the political parties, was strictly limited. In addition, a restriction was placed on how much money candidates could contribute to their own campaign; federal subsidies and grants for major party presidential candidates and grants for the major parties were provided; spending limits in the presidential campaign were established; corporations and unions, prevented from contributing money, could allow their employees, members, and stockholders to form political action committees and contribute up to $5,000 per candidate per election.[4] A Federal Election Commission, composed of six members, two appointed by the president and four by Congress, was set up to monitor and police election activities.

The Federal Election Campaign Act (FECA) was the first comprehensive law that Congress enacted to regulate campaign finance activity and the first to provide partial public funding. Previous legislation had prohibited direct business and labor contributions but had done little else to regulate the overall source and amount of campaign contributions and expenditures. Prior to the 1970s, the only public funding was at the state level, and it paid for the conduct of the election. In providing public subsidies, the United States followed the practices of several European countries that also subsidized candidates or their parties' elections. Table 5.1 summarizes the grants and subsidies of other democratic governments.

The FECA, scheduled to go into effect after the 1972 elections, was immediately challenged as unconstitutional. Critics charged that the limits on contributions and spending violated the constitutionally guaranteed right to freedom of speech, that the funding provisions unfairly discriminated against third-party and independent candidates, and that appointment of four of the commissioners by Congress violated the principle of separation of powers.

In 1976 the Supreme Court declared two parts of the law unconstitutional. Although the Court upheld Congress's right to regulate campaign contributions to candidates seeking federal office, it held that independent spending by individuals and groups was protected by the First Amendment and thus could not be regulated.[5] It also voided Congress's selection of four of the six election commissioners.

The Court's decision forced Congress to redraft the legislation. A new law, enacted in 1976 at the start of the presidential nomination campaign, retained the contribution and spending limits and public funding of the presidential campaign. But the funding was to be voluntary. Candidates didn't have to accept government funds; and if they did, they were limited in how much they could contribute to their own campaign and how much that campaign could spend. The Federal Election Commission was reconstituted with all six members, three Republicans and three Democrats, to be nominated by the president and appointed with the advice and consent of the Senate.

With limited money available, the candidates decided to spend the bulk of their resources on television advertising. Absent was much of the political paraphernalia that usually accompanied presidential campaigns—buttons, bumper stickers,

TABLE 5.1 Public Subsidies to Political Parties and Candidates

Country	Recipient	Direct Subsidies			Specific grant/services	Indirect subsidies
		Interval	Basis	Eligibility		
Australia	Candidates, parties		Per vote	At least 4% of vote, must be registered with EC	Transportation, get out the vote, broadcasting	
Belgium	No direct subsidies	n/a	n/a	n/a	Broadcasting, encouragement of voting	
Canada	Candidates, parliamentary groups	Election	Per vote	Candidate: 15% of votes in district, parties must spend 10% of limit	Broadcasting, encouragement of voting	Tax credits
Denmark	Parliamentary groups	Annual	Per seat		Broadcasting, press and publications, women/youth groups	
France	Presidential candidates	Election			Bill posting, broadcasting, printing ballots, press/publications	Kickbacks of deputy salaries
Germany	Parties	Election	Per vote	5% for national party lists*	Broadcasting, subsidies to party foundations	Tax deductions
India	No direct subsidies	n/a	n/a	n/a	Broadcasting	
Ireland	No direct subsidies	n/a	n/a	n/a	Broadcasting	
Israel	Party groups	Annual, every election	Per seat	†	Broadcasting, get out the vote	
Italy	Parties, parliamentary groups	Annual, every election	Per vote		Broadcasting, education, women's and youth groups	Kickbacks of deputy salaries
Japan	Candidates	Every election			Transportation, publications, broadcasting, advertising, use of public halls	Tax benefits

Country	Direct Subsidies					Indirect subsidies
	Recipient	Interval	Basis	Eligibility	Specific grant/services	
Mexico	Parties	Annual, every election	Per vote	Party should obtain more than 1.5% of total ballot	Broadcasting	Tax exemptions
Netherlands	No direct subsidies	n/a	n/a	n/a	Broadcasting, get out the vote, party foundations, women/youth	Tax deductions
Poland	No direct subsidies	n/a	n/a	n/a	Broadcasting, use of public halls, printing/mailing, get out the vote	Limited tax exemptions for parties
Spain	Parties	Annual, every election	Per vote		Party must have won one electoral seat (at 3% threshold)	
Sweden	Parties, parliamentary groups	Annual	Per seat, per vote		Publications, encouragement of voting, broadcasting	
United Kingdom	Parliamentary groups	Annual			Publications, mailing, broadcasting, use of public halls	Gifts to parties exempt from inheritance tax
United States	Candidates in presidential primaries and elections	Election	Matching grant in primary, fixed sum in election from earmarked funds		Nomination costs, mailing, most states pay for voter registration/ballots	Tax credits and deductions

*0.5% of votes for national party lists of candidates, or 105 of first votes cast in a constituency if no regional list has been accepted.
†Had at least 1 MP in last parliament or has been recognized as a group by the legislature.

Source: Lawrence LeDuc, Richard G. Niemi, and Pippa Norris, eds., *Comparing Democracies: Elections and Voting in Global Perspective* (Thousand Oaks, CA: Sage, 1996), Table 5.1, 38–41.

campaign literature, and the like. To see the campaign, people had to turn on their televisions. When voter turnout continued to decline, Congress assumed, with some justification, that it was because the candidates had spent too much on television and not enough on grassroots organizing and get-out-the-vote activities.

Encouraging Turnout: The Soft Money Loophole

So in 1979 an amendment to the law was enacted that enabled the parties to raise and spend unlimited amounts of money for their voluntary efforts to promote voting through educational campaigns, get-out-the-vote drives, and other party-building efforts. To stimulate state and local parties, the law allowed them as well as the national party to raise "soft money." The national party could distribute the money to its state and local affiliates and their candidates. The

Raising the Stakes: The Selling of the Government

I N JUNE 1995, the president's political advisers, notably Dick Morris, recommended to Bill Clinton that a preemptive advertising campaign be launched to reinforce the president's image as a moderate, mainstream Democrat and to help pave the way for his reelection. The campaign was directed at the early caucus and primary states, to discourage anyone from challenging the president. Approximately $2.5 million was devoted to this early advertising effort, which had the additional goal of undercutting public support for the Republicans' balanced-budget proposals in Congress.[6]

The expenditure of so much money so early provoked considerable division within the Clinton White House. Some of the president's advisers believed that the spending put the president in a potentially vulnerable position should a Democratic challenger emerge or should the Republicans unite behind a single candidate and then turn their attention to the president. But the president supported Morris's advertising initiative, remembering all too well how the administration's health care proposals in 1993–1994 had been defeated by a multi-million-dollar public relations campaign supported by the Health Insurance Association of America.

Where to get the money became the critical issue for the White House. In September 1995, Harold Ickes, deputy chief of staff, came up with an idea: Let the Democratic party pay for the ads with soft money (which the president could help raise), because the commercials aired were policy oriented and didn't directly urge the president's reelection. The White House quickly approved Ickes's plan, which Democratic lawyers believed to be perfectly legal.

What followed was a frantic, no-holds-barred fund-raising effort in which the Democrats raised $124 million in soft money, much of it in sizable donations from wealthy patrons. Working closely with the White House, using the perquisites of the office to great advantage, the Democrats brought in more money than they ever had before. So fast did only prohibition was that soft money couldn't be spent directly on candidates running for federal office.

The "soft money" amendment created a gigantic loophole in the law. It permitted, even encouraged, parties to solicit large contributions and distribute the money as they saw fit. Unlike "hard money," which is strictly regulated and reported, so-called soft money isn't. By 1996, the loophole had effectively scuttled the contribution and spending limits of the Federal Election Campaign Act.

In the first two presidential elections after the soft money amendment was enacted, the Republicans enjoyed a large financial advantage. Helped by negative reaction to the Carter presidency, by Reagan's popularity among wealthy conservative donors and conservative business interests, and subsequently by Reagan's own general popularity in 1984, the GOP raised $31 million in soft money, compared with only $10 million for the Democrats. Since 1988, the soft money race has become closer and reaped a much larger bounty for both major

the dollars flow that the party didn't take the time to ensure that the contributions were legal, were voluntarily given, and came from respectable donors. In the end, the Democrats were forced to return millions of dollars to contributors whose legal status to make them could not be established.

The active involvement of the president and vice president also raised questions about whether the effort was really the party's or the Clinton-Gore campaign's. The specter of taxpayer facilities' being used for political purposes captured the attention of the press, public interest groups, and Republicans. All of them suggested that laws were being violated by donors' being invited to dinners and coffee hours with the president, vice president, and other top administration officials; by sleepovers at the White House and trips on Air Force One; and through U.S. trade missions abroad.[7] The president arranged his travel schedule to participate in as many of these fundraising activities as possible.[8] The vice president personally solicited contributions from his own White House office.[9] There were even allegations that campaign donors—even donors who represented foreign governments and companies—were directly influencing policy decisions.

To make matters worse, the Democratic National Committee was distributing the money to certain key states designated by the Clinton-Gore campaign. The state parties, in turn, were directed to spend it on advertisements produced by the president's media consultant, Robert Squire. In other words, the national party was circumventing the limit imposed on its spending for presidential campaigns by creating the fiction that these were advertisements bought and aired by state parties.

Meanwhile, the Republicans were also raising soft money—even more than the Democrats. They, too, offered inducements, such as meetings with congressional leaders and access to committee chairs' unlisted telephone numbers. They, too, directed the money to their state and local parties, to spend on behalf of their candidates in both the congressional and the presidential campaigns. In other words, they had followed the Democrats' lead.

This pattern of fundraising continued and even accelerated in 2000.

parties, although the Republicans have continued to maintain their financial advantage even when a Democrat was in the White House (see Table 5.2).

Soft money revenues and expenditures of both parties have been increasing, in part because the Federal Election Commission broadened the scope of "legitimate" soft money activities and political parties and political action committees rushed to take advantage of that broadened scope. Table 5.2 lists the hard and soft money raised and spent in 1996 and 2000. Table 5.3 lists the expenditure breakdown between candidates and their parties.

COSTS, CONTRIBUTIONS, AND CONSEQUENCES

Are the Costs Excessive?

House Majority Whip Tom Delay didn't think so. In claiming that the campaign finance issue was overblown, Delay stated, "Americans spend twice as much per year on yogurt than they spend on political campaigns."[10] Does it take hundreds of millions of dollars to educate the public about the candidates and the issues? A subsidiary issue—how well campaigns are educating the public— is discussed in the next chapter, on the media.

Elections have become much more expensive, but the public is participating in them less. Clearly, all that soft money presumably being spent on get-out-the-vote activities isn't working. But if less effort were made and less money were spent, even fewer people might turn out.

Nor is there any evidence that the public today is any better informed or more attentive to election issues than the public was a decade or two ago, when campaign expenditures were less. In fact, the contemporary electorate may actually

TABLE 5.2 Major Party Revenues and Expenditures in 1996 and 2000 (in Millions)

		1996		2000	
		Revenues	**Expenditures**	**Revenues**	**Expenditures**
Democrats	Hard	$221.6	$241.3	$ 275.2	$ 265.8
	Soft	123.9	121.8	245.2	244.9
	Total	$345.5	$363.1	$ 520.4	$ 510.7
Republicans	Hard	$416.5	$408.5	$ 465.8	$ 427.0
	Soft	138.2	149.7	249.9	252.8
	Total	$554.7	$558.2	$ 715.7	$ 679.8
Grand Totals		$900.2	$921.3	$1,236.1	$1,190.5

Source: Federal Election Commission, "FEC Reports Increase in Party Fundraising for 2000," May 15, 2001.

be less knowledgeable about the issues than voters were when newspapers were the prime source of campaign information. The cost of elections doesn't seem to be paying off in terms of a more educated electorate, but fewer expenditures might result in an even less educated one.

Does money win elections? Clearly, many candidates and their managers believe that it does. A large war chest is an important deterrent to competition. Candidates who begin with a lot of money often discourage a credible challenger from running against them. In his quest for reelection, President Clinton raised the maximum amount permitted by law in order to preclude a Democratic challenger. Four years later, Al Gore wasn't as successful in drying up Democratic money as Clinton had been and had to compete against former Senator Bill Bradley (Democrat, New Jersey) for the Democratic nomination.

Having money up front gives a candidate greater flexibility in deciding when and where to campaign and what to spend it on. It also helps in getting press coverage. The news media view those who are well financed as more likely to wage a credible campaign and thus take them more seriously. In fact, the size of the candidates' treasury is often seen as an indication of how popular they are and how well they're likely to do. News coverage, in short, takes on the aura of a self-fulfilling prophecy. The media anointed George W. Bush as an almost prohibitive favorite to win the 2000 Republican presidential nomination because he had raised so much money the year before the primaries—almost as much as all of his opponents combined.

In addition to the psychological and public relations advantages that early money gives a candidate, it also provides more options. Bush, for example, decided that he could afford to forgo federal matching funds and thus not be bound by their expenditure limits. Only Steve Forbes, who was willing to pay for his campaign with his own inherited fortune, could compete on an even financial footing with Bush.

For most candidates, money is most important early in the campaign because it buys them what they need most: visibility. As a candidate becomes known, the expenditure of money is less critical for identification and credibility. But, although money buys recognition and other needs, such as fundraising,

TABLE 5.3 The Costs of the 1996 and 2000 Federal Elections (in Millions)

	1996	2000
Congressional candidates	$ 765.3	$1,018.5
Presidential candidates	453.8	343.1
Parties (hard money)	622.8	692.7
Parties (soft money)	271.5	497.7
Total	$2,113.4	$2,552.0

Source: 1996, Federal Election Commission; 2000, The Center For Responsive Politics.

staff support, and grassroots organizing, it may not buy much more than that. It certainly doesn't guarantee electoral success, as Ross Perot and Steve Forbes can attest.

Nonetheless, the public perceives that money contributes to electoral success.[11] And it is true that candidates with war chests larger than their opponents' have won more often than they've lost. What isn't clear, however, is whether the money was key to their victory or whether the likelihood of their victory encouraged donors to contribute.

Political science research suggests that challengers need more money than incumbents in order to defeat incumbents. When incumbents spend a lot of money, it's usually a sign that they're in trouble, that they fear they may lose, not that they're confident of victory. In fact, money seems to be more of a factor in the election outcome when less is known about the candidates.[12]

Who Pays and What Do They Get for Their Money?

For many, more troubling than the high cost of elections is who pays and what they get for their money. Contributors are unequally distributed among the population. Only about 5 percent of the people give any money at all to candidates or parties. Less than 1 percent make a contribution of $200 or more, the minimum amount that needs to be reported to the Federal Election Commission. Most of the big bucks come from wealthy donors or well-financed groups.[13] Table 5.4 lists the groups that gave and spent the most in 1999–2000.

The concentration of contributors among wealthy individuals and of expenditures among corporations, trade associations, and labor PACs raises important issues for a democracy. To whom are the winning candidates likely to be more responsive? From the public's viewpoint, the answer is clear: big-money contributors. In a survey conducted by Princeton Survey Research Associates for the Center for Responsive Politics and paid for by the Pew Charitable Trusts, more than half of the respondents expressed the belief that money buys political influence, that members of Congress are more likely to respond to campaign donors outside of their districts than to nondonors within their districts, and that legislative representatives support policies primarily because these policies are desired by their donors, and *not* because they believe them to be in the best interests of the country.[14] The public is particularly troubled by foreign money in American elections, because of implications that it could jeopardize national interests and security.[15]

Whether or not these public perceptions jibe with reality, the fact that most people believe them is significant. A democratic political system is not enhanced if its citizenry believes that government is conducted by and for special interests rather than in the public interest. Such a belief undoubtedly continues to contribute to (and may also be a product of) declining trust in government.

TABLE 5.4   The Big Contributors, 1999–2000*

PAC Name	Total amount contributed (in dollars)	Contributions to Democratic candidates (%)†	Contributions to Republican candidates (%)†
National Association of Realtors	3,423,441	41	59
Association of Trial Lawyers of America	2,661,000	86	13
American Federation of State, County, and Municipal Employees	2,590,074	95	5
Teamsters Union	2,565,495	93	7
National Auto Dealers Association	2,498,700	32	68
International Brotherhood of Electrical Workers	2,470,125	96	4
Laborers Union	2,255,900	90	9
Machinists/Aerospace Workers Union	2,188,138	99	1
United Auto Workers	2,155,050	99	1
American Medical Association	2,028,354	48	52
Service Employees International Union	1,871,774	89	11
National Beer Wholesalers Association	1,871,500	21	79
Carpenters & Joiners Union	1,869,920	84	15
National Association of Home Builders	1,824,599	36	64
United Parcel Service	1,755,065	35	65
United Food & Commercial Workers Union	1,743,652	97	2
National Education Association	1,717,125	95	5
Verizon Communications	1,677,617	33	67
American Bankers Association	1,657,615	35	64
American Federation of Teachers	1,599,555	98	2

For ease of identification, the names used in this section are those of the organization connected with the PAC, rather than the official PAC name.

*Based on data released by the FEC on Friday, June 1, 2001.

†Percentages were rounded and therefore percentages do not necessarily total a hundred.

Source: Center for Responsive Politics, <http://www.opensecrets.org/pacs/topacs.asp>.

Who Gains and Who Loses?

The issue is also one of equity. If the groups that contributed and spent the most money were representative of the population as a whole, the situation wouldn't be as bad as if they represented a particular economic stratum. But, alas, they do, as Table 5.4 suggests. Business, labor, trade, and professional groups give the most; the contributions of consumer groups and nonprofessionals, including non-unionized labor, pale by comparison. And when was the last time you heard that a group representing people out of work, single parents, prisoners, or the mentally disabled elected or influenced a public official through campaign contributions or expenditures?

Multimember issue groups, some masquerading as "concerned citizens" but really created and funded by an industry or labor union, spend the most. They do so to educate the public and mobilize their sympathizers. They use issue advocacy and grassroots campaigning to do so. Much of their financial support comes from dues and contributions from their members and from wealthy donors.

The Annenberg Public Policy Center at the University of Pennsylvania has tracked issue advocacy advertising from these nonparty and party groups. Expenditures for these types of political ads have more than tripled since the 1995–1996 election cycle, when between $135 million and $150 million was spent. The Center estimated $509 million was expended on issue ads in 2000 in the seventy-five major media markets. One-third of these expenditures was funded by the political parties through their soft money accounts, the rest by single-issue groups. Two groups, both supported by the health care industry, spent $85.4 million alone.[16] As noted previously, (see note 1), the Alliance for Better Campaigns calculated that $234 million was received by major television networks for all types of political ads.[17]

Who benefits from these election expenditures? Candidates, parties, advertisers, and the media stand to gain the most. Candidates who support or have supported the policies advocated by the groups are prominently featured in many of the advertisements, which thus indirectly but not subtly help their campaigns by promoting their candidacies. They also benefit from group efforts to get out their vote. Similarly the national parties extend their influence over their state and local affiliates by soliciting money for them and distributing it to them. In the process, the national parties circumvent the spending limits on federal elections. Nonparty groups help their cause by using the election process to educate the public about the merits of their positions as well as identifying candidates who support or oppose those positions.

As the public sees it, the politicians, parties, and special interests are inextricably bound together in this money game.[18] Politicians get elected, their parties gain influence; and special interests obtain the public policy they desire. The only losers are the general public and its interests; or at least that is what people believe.

This perception explains why the public strongly favors campaign finance reform but is pessimistic about whether it would improve the situation very much.

When Gallup, Pew, and other polling organizations asked the public about the merits of campaign finance reform, two out of three respondents said that major changes or complete reform is needed and should be enacted. But when asked whether such a reform "would make our democratic form of government work much better than it does now," only 22 percent said that it would; 37 percent thought it might make it "a little better," 32 percent thought the result would be "about the same," and 5 percent believed that it would be "a little or much worse."[19] As the people see it, "special interests will still find a way to maintain their power in Washington."[20]

THE POLITICAL DEBATE OVER CAMPAIGN FINANCE REFORM

Why have members of Congress been so slow to reform campaign finance? Some are philosophically opposed to government regulation in general and to campaign finance regulation in particular. Others object to using taxpayers' money to fund national elections, in part or entirely. Partisanship also plays a role. Republicans have been able to raise more money than Democrats and thus stand to lose more if the playing field were leveled by expenditure limits or public funding.

Until recently there hasn't been much pressure on Congress to act. Although the public wants campaign finance reform, for most people it hasn't been a priority issue, one that they cite when they list the major problems facing the country today.[21] Moreover, most people have very limited knowledge of the current law, much less how to change it.[22]

But even if there were public pressure to fix the campaign finance problem, how to do so is a complicated question. There are serious constitutional concerns, for one thing. As we noted at the beginning of this chapter, the First Amendment, as interpreted by the Supreme Court, protects independent spending and campaign advocacy, including the cost of financing it. Congress has to be careful not to intrude on constitutionally protected rights.

There's also the history of reform to consider when legislating. Despite good intentions, the law has produced unintended and undesirable consequences, particularly the soft money and issue advocacy provisions. Changes could make things worse. Besides, politicians are known to be particularly creative when it comes to finding ways to circumvent legal obstacles.

Certain practices—especially the solicitation of soft money, unrestricted issue advocacy, contributions from foreigners and foreign-owned companies, PAC activities, and limits on individual and group donations—have been subject to the most criticism and seem ripe for change. The next section explores some of the proposals for reform and their potential impact on the democratic character of the American political system.

PROPOSALS FOR REFORM

Eliminate Soft Money

Soft money has become the focus of much discontent because it has increased so much in recent elections. Opposition to soft money is based on the belief that it has become a corrupting influence. The perception is that donors want something in return for their "gift"—a favorable policy decision, access to those in power, consultation when the issue affects them directly, even such personal benefits as invitations to social events with the political establishment. Whatever the desire, the effect is the same: people and groups with money have more influence and seem to get more of what they want. That's undemocratic!

Take the case of the gambling industry. In 1998 that industry feared that Congress might try to raise revenues by eliminating tax write-offs for gambling losses. The industry, headed by a former chair of the Republican National Committee, Frank Fahrenkopf, met with two Republican senators whose states receive considerable revenues from gambling: Mitch McConnell of Kentucky, home of the Kentucky Derby, and Trent Lott of Mississippi, a state that profits from riverboat casinos. The purpose of the meeting was to persuade both senators to stop the proposal before it got out of committee and into the public arena. Because the additional revenues were intended to fund scholarships for poor children, the industry feared a debate over the interests of high-rolling gamblers versus the needs of poor kids. To demonstrate good faith, gambling PACs donated $250,000 in soft money to the Senate Republican Campaign Committee. In the previous year, Senate Republicans had received over $500,000 from organized gambling.

Lott (then Senate majority leader) and McConnell prevailed on their colleagues on the Senate Finance committee to drop the provision. The industry escaped the tax. Did the soft money contribution and the likelihood that the gambling industry would continue to fund Republican candidates "buy" the elimination of this taxing provision for the industry?[23] Although it can't be proved that it did (and the concerned parties—Lott, McConnell, and other Republicans—would certainly deny that the contribution in any way affected their judgment), the public perception is that this kind of contribution does affect policymaking, that "Money talks."[24]

Preventing soft money contributions and expenditures for federal elections, or limiting their size, would help close a loophole that has encouraged parties and politicians to circumvent the reporting, fund-raising, and expenditure limits of the current law. It would also reduce the amount of money that wealthy individuals and groups could funnel to their political friends, thereby reducing their influence or at least the perception of their influence.

But the elimination of soft money would force candidates and parties to search for new sources of revenue, if elections continue to be as expensive as they have been in recent years. Candidates would probably have to devote *more* time and money to fundraising, not less—an undesirable consequence from the perspective of most election observers, especially the candidates them-selves. Besides the distaste that many candidates have for fundraising, the time they spend doing it takes away from the time available for campaigning or, if in office, for attending to official duties. Eliminating or limiting soft money might also weaken the national parties, whose centralized fund-raising efforts have strengthened their influence after two decades of decline.

From the perspective of contributors, the absence of soft money might save them money, but it would also require them to find other ways to exert their influence. Independent spending might increase, as might lobbying activities. The demise of soft money might even advantage wealthier candidates, who would still have their own resources on which to rely. Finally, less soft money might result in less advertising, less party building, and less grassroots mobi-lization, all factors that work to educate, inform, and turn out voters. Some minority groups, African Americans in particular, fear that without large, soft money benefactors they will be unable to mount aggressive campaigns to turn out their vote, as they were able to do in 2000.

Restrict Issue Advocacy Advertisements

Banning or restricting issue advocacy ads is another proposal that has received considerable attention and support. The problem with issue advocacy during a campaign is that it can take over an electoral debate, refocusing attention on the interests of the group at the expense of those of the candidates and the elec-torate. Besides, many of the ads are thinly veiled partisan or candidate appeals. There's usually very little subtlety about which party and which candidate the group thinks is "right" on its issue. These issue ads have much the same impact as candidate-sponsored ads. In fact, most of the public cannot tell them apart.[25]

Banning the ads or restricting when they can be aired, however, strikes per-ilously close to limiting freedom of speech and might be declared unconstitu-tional by the courts. Restricting ads and limiting references to the candidates and parties in ads face a similar legal hurdle. At the present time, the parties and candidates can't tell groups what to say in their ads or when and how to run them, although attempts by the auditors of the Federal Election Commission to enforce this restriction haven't been successful.

However, if issue advocacy ads aren't restricted but soft money is, then the ads become the perfect vehicle for business, labor, and other interest groups to pursue their agendas within the electoral arena. And the legislators contemplat-ing such restriction know this.

Prohibit All Foreign Money

Another source of public concern is foreign contributions. Under the existing law, contributions are restricted to U.S. citizens or noncitizens who are perma-nent residents. American subsidiaries of foreign-owned companies may also create PACs or make contributions, provided they do so with money that has been earned in the United States. A foreign company cannot give its American subsidiary money to spend in U.S. elections.

Congress could prohibit any individual contribution from a person who isn't a U.S. citizen. It could also prevent foreign-owned companies from making contributions. It probably couldn't prevent American employees of these companies from forming PACs and making contributions, however. Nor would Congress want to do so and thereby potentially discriminate against American workers.

In today's interdependent, international economic environment, Congress must be very careful how it treats foreign companies, for fear of hurting American interests abroad. Although the problem is perceived as foreign influence, as often as not the beneficiaries are American companies that do business abroad. Take the case of Loral Space and Communications, whose chief executive officer, Bernard Schwartz, gave $100,000 to the Democratic National Committee during the 1995–1996 election cycle. Loral wished to sell satellite technology to the Chinese government to help it launch commercial satellites. Fearing that this technology could be used for military purposes, the State and Defense Departments opposed the sale, but the Commerce Department and the White House supported it. The president ultimately approved the sale. Did Schwartz's $100,000 have anything to do with the president's decision?

Eliminate or Reduce PAC Contributions

Another reform would be to eliminate or reduce PAC contributions. The law currently restricts the amount donated to $5,000 per candidate per election. But it sets no overall limit on how much PACs can contribute and spend. One proposal would be to reduce the amount that could be donated to $1,000, the same as the limit for individuals. Alternatively, Congress, which created PACs in the legislation that established the campaign finance system, could prohibit them from making contributions to individuals at all. It could also set an overall cap on the total amount of their contributions in any election cycle, specify a maximum percentage of funds that candidates could receive from PACs, or, in the most extreme case, eliminate PACs altogether.

Reducing or eliminating PAC contributions would certainly appeal to the general public, which perceives these nonparty groups as a large part of special-interest politics in the United States. In reality, however, PAC contributions amount to less money than the soft money contributions of wealthy individuals and corporate America. Moreover, if PACs were eliminated, it's doubtful that their interests would be eliminated as well. Rather, they would find other ways to affect the political process. PACs are required to report their contributions and expenditures to the Federal Election Commission. Whether and to what extent other entities that replaced them would be required to do so is unclear. Finally, the elimination of PACs could result in less information and control of election activities than currently exist.[26]

Increase Individual Contribution Limits

If Congress were to further restrict or eliminate soft money, PAC contributions, or foreign money, a substantial portion of the revenues now used to fund national campaigns would be eliminated. How could these funds be replaced?

One proposal is to increase the amount that individual and nonparty groups can contribute to candidates during the election cycle. Since the law was enacted in 1974, the contribution limit per candidate per election has been set at $1,000 for individuals and $5,000 for nonparty groups. These are much lower limits than those in other countries, such as Germany, Japan, and Mexico. Nor has this amount been adjusted for inflation, as have candidate spending limits and federal grants in the presidential election.

Increasing the individual and group limits would reduce the financial burden on the candidates. The greater the increase, the less dependent they would be on outside groups for money and campaign-related activities. Even an increase limited to the rate of inflation since 1974 could more than triple revenues in the next election.

But the greater the increase in allowable donations, the more influence those in the upper-income strata would have on the election and could have on the government. The lower the increase, the longer and harder candidates would have to work raising money. Any limit on contributions advantages those candidates who are personally wealthy.

For increasing limits to have an effect and make up the gap left by the elimination of soft money, PAC contributions, and foreign money, more people would have to be encouraged to contribute, and to contribute more. One incentive might be to give tax credits or deductions to contributors of up to a certain amount. Currently such provisions are written into the tax codes of three states and the District of Columbia. The federal government had one as well but abandoned it at the time when many other deductions were also eliminated. The problem with such incentives is twofold: they benefit the wealthy, and they lower government revenue.

Limit Voluntary Spending

Limiting campaign spending would obviously cut down the costs of elections and make candidates less dependent on outside sources of revenue. The limits would have to be voluntary, because the Supreme Court has stated that involuntary restrictions on campaign spending violate freedom of speech. But, if candidates agree to such limits as a condition of receiving other benefits such as matching funds and subsidies, then spending limits would be a viable option. Several countries, including the United Kingdom and Canada, impose spending limits on candidates for national office, although they do not limit party spending.

A voluntary ceiling for House and Senate elections, such as $600,000 for House races (about a dollar per person in the district) and $950,000 to

$5,500,000 for the Senate, depending on state population, is another option. Candidates who abide by these ceilings could receive in return free or reduced-cost television time and lower mailing rates.

Voluntary limits with inducements for complying would equalize spending and keep costs from getting out of hand. Incumbents who could raise more money might seem disadvantaged by this arrangement, but most wouldn't be. Challengers usually need more money to balance the incumbent's advantages of recognition, constituency service, and record of accomplishments in office. But voluntary spending limits could also give greater advantage to wealthy candidates who don't have to abide by them.

Providing free or low-cost communications might also be a problem. The television industry strongly opposes it because of the lost revenue. Lower mail rates would have to be subsidized either directly, by the taxpayers, or by raising other postal rates. Countries such as Germany, Mexico, and the United Kingdom do require their television broadcasters to provide free time to political parties, but not to individual candidates. The United States could do the same as a condition for renewal of television licenses. But what about minor parties and independent candidates? What about stations that don't use the airwaves but operate via cable or satellite?[27]

Provide Public Funding

Another way to deal with the campaign finance issue would be to prohibit all contributions from individuals and groups and use public funds to pay for federal elections. Since the current voluntary checkoff of three dollars per taxpayer would not be sufficient, the amount could be increased, or more likely, funds could be appropriated directly from the federal treasury.

The benefits of public funding are many. It would level the playing field for the major parties. It would reduce the advantage incumbents have in fundraising, although it would not eliminate their other electoral advantages (see Chapter 7, pages 166–168). Public funding would curtail the amount of time government officials have to spend raising money for their next election. It might also weaken the public's perception that special interests exercise disproportionate influence on public officials by virtue of their campaign contributions. However, other electoral activities of individuals and groups would be more difficult to restrict without violating the protections of the First Amendment.

The argument against public funding is that it would be expensive, a drain on the budget, which might have to be balanced by reducing or eliminating other government programs. Moreover, it would force the all taxpayers to contribute—even those not entitled to vote, such as resident aliens and citizens under eighteen who have taxable incomes. The wealthy would no longer bear the financial burden of paying most of the costs of elections. Moreover, public funding would most likely benefit the major parties at the expense of the minor ones. Then there is the issue of choice. If citizens have the right not to vote, should they also have the right not to have their taxes spent on federal elections?

Despite public dissatisfaction with the current system of campaign finance, despite the public perception that it needs a major overhaul, despite public support for banning soft money and reducing the power of special-interest groups and wealthy individuals, there is not and has not been widespread support for publicly funded national elections. Because of the absence of public support, pollsters who have examined opinions on campaign finance reform have rarely even asked respondents for their position on the matter. When a 1999 CBS News Poll did ask, the findings revealed broad-based opposition to the idea among Democrats, Republicans, and independents.[28]

The Shays-Meehan and McCain-Feingold Bills

Since 1999, Congress has considered legislation aimed at curbing soft money and issue advocacy. The legislation prohibits the major parties at the national level from accepting soft money contributions; it also bans state parties from using soft money in federal elections. To compensate for the elimination of soft money, individual and group donations to the candidates and parties are increased. Issue advocacy, which the parties and outside groups have used to circumvent the restrictions on hard money, is also restricted in the final weeks of the campaign.

The Senate enacted the McCain-Feingold bill in 2001. The House, which had passed the Shays-Meehan bill in 1999, got caught up in a procedural debate on the issue in June 2001, forcing postponement of the issue until the Republican leadership, which opposed the bill, could be persuaded to bring it to the floor. The terrorist attack on the World Trade Center and the Pentagon further delayed House consideration of campaign finance issues.

Basic Provisions of the McCain-Feingold Bill, Enacted by the Senate on April 2, 2001

1. Prohibits national political party committees from soliciting or receiving soft money.
2. Prohibits parties at all levels from soliciting money for or donating money to a tax-exempt organization.
3. Prevents labor unions, corporations, and many non-profit groups from sponsoring political advertisements that refer to a candidate by name or contain a candidate's likeness in the final thirty days before a primary, caucus, or convention and the final sixty days before a general election.
4. Raises the limits on individual contributions to $2,000 per candidate per election and to $25,000 to non-candidate, political committees. The act also provides for the indexing of these contribution limits to inflation.

Summary: Campaign Finance Dilemmas in a Nutshell

American elections are getting more and more expensive. For some candidates, it seems almost as if the sky's the limit when it comes to campaign spending. And there's no end in sight. Each election has become more costly than the previous one.

The need for money has become an obsession for candidates, encouraging them to spend more and more time, energy, and money raising money. Their drive to fill their own war chest has created, at least in the public's mind, a political system in which the wealthy wield the most influence, thereby undermining the equity principle of a democratic political system.

For the last thirty years, Congress and the presidency have had to contend with the campaign finance issue and the scandals, allegations, and demoralization arising from it. Initially, the solution was thought to lie in requirements that limited contributions to candidates for federal office, established voluntary spending limits for presidential candidates who accepted government subsidies and grants, and established comprehensive reporting requirements monitored by an election commission.

The legislation that was enacted in the 1970s achieved some of these objectives. It broadened the base of public participation; for a time, it decreased the influence of the wealthy on the election process; and it did bring campaign finance into full public view. But many of these achievements have subsequently been dissipated by the soft money loophole, created in 1979 but exploited most fully in 1996 by the Supreme Court's interpretation of independent spending as free speech, and by the creative efforts of candidates of all political persuasions to find ways around the law.

As a result, the campaign finance system has effectively broken down. The public has lost faith in politicians and confidence in the political system. The general perception today is that government is for sale to the highest bidder. Money, once seen as the mother's milk of politics, is now perceived as the root of all evil, a poison pill.

There have been investigations of abuses and campaign and congressional debates on proposed solutions, but achieving a consensus on what to do has proved to be difficult. The issue is extremely complex. The consequences of changes are unknown. Skepticism about politicians remains high. The dilemmas that policymakers face are multiple. How can campaign spending be equalized without impinging on constitutionally protected freedoms? How can candidates be assured of having sufficient money to get their messages across without increasing the burden on taxpayers, forcing the media to provide free time, or maintaining a situation in which those who have access to money are advantaged? And, finally, how can incumbents who have profited from the current system be induced to change it in a manner that may reduce their electoral advantage?

The most likely candidates for financial reform are soft money, foreign money, and PAC money, because, in the public mind, they create the most inequities and present the greatest potential for abuse. But elections as they are currently structured need money. If certain kinds of contributions are eliminated, new sources of revenue will have to be found. And if the past is prologue to the future, politicians will find them.

Now It's Your Turn

Discussion Questions

1. Is money really as corrupting an influence on politics and government as people believe?
2. Do the wealthy exercise disproportionate influence on the conduct of elections and, through that influence, on the operation of government?
3. Are American elections really too expensive? What would be a helpful criterion by which to evaluate whether the costs of elections are excessive?
4. Can money in elections be regulated without violating First Amendment protections of freedom of speech? If so, how? If not, why not?

Topics for Debate

Challenge or defend the following statements:

1. All laws regulating campaign finance, except for reporting requirements, should be abolished.
2. All federal elections should be publicly funded.
3. Congress should raise individual and group contributions and eliminate soft money.
4. The required political composition of the Federal Election Commission— three Democrats and three Republicans—should be abolished and replaced by the appointment of independent commissioners.
5. The McCain-Feingold and Shays-Meehan bills are fatally flawed and should not be enacted into law.
6. The Federal Election Campaign Act should be terminated.
7. The Constitution should be amended to specifically exclude campaign spending from the free speech protection of the First Amendment.

Exercise

This exercise has two parts. In the first you are to design, for a public interest group such as Common Cause or the Center for Responsive Politics, a public relations campaign about the need for campaign finance reform in the United States today. In your campaign, indicate

- why the system should be reformed,
- what are its principal problems, and
- how these problems threaten America's electoral democracy.

Make sure that you try to anticipate the objections that different groups may raise. Remember, you're involved in a nonpartisan public relations campaign, with the objective of rousing the general public to force Congress to act.

For the second part of your exercise, assume that your campaign has worked, that you've generated enough of a public outcry to move Congress to action. Assume the role of a Democratic or Republican member of a committee (your choice, depending on your own political persuasion) charged with investigating the issue and proposing a legislative solution.

1. Outline the major points of a bill that addresses the problems you've cited in your public relations campaign. Remember, you're now a partisan, so your bill should *not* adversely affect the interests of your party. However, if it is to be enacted into law, it must not adversely affect the interests of the other party either. In your statement, anticipate likely criticisms from committee members of the other party, and respond to them.
2. At the end, with your class as the full committee, hold a vote to see whether your proposals should be sent forward to the floor of Congress.

Internet Resources

- Brookings Institution <http://www.brookings.org>
  Contains information from scholars at a well-known think tank who have been exploring finance issues and possible reforms.

- Campaign Finance Information Center <http://www.campaignfinance.org>
  Collects and disseminates campaign finance information from investigative reporters and editors.

- Campaign Finance Institute <http://www.cfinst.org>
  An institute that focuses on campaign finance issues and how to fix inequities within the system.

- Center for Responsive Politics <http://www.opensecrets.org>
  A public interest group that focuses on money and elections. The center publishes alerts, news releases, and major studies on campaign finance issues.

- Common Cause <http://www.commoncause.org>
  An organization that considers itself a citizens' lobbying group and Washington watchdog; for years, it has been at the forefront of campaign finance reform.

- Destination Democracy <http://www.destinationdemocracy.org>
  Another public interest group sponsored by the Benton Foundation, with a concern about money and politics. Take their road test to see where you come out on campaign finance reform.

- Federal Election Commission <http://www.fec.gov>
  The official source of campaign revenues and expenditures for federal elections; puts candidates' financial reports on its website, analyzes data from these reports, and makes them available to the public.

Selected Readings

Alexander, Herbert B., et al. "New Realities, New Thinking: Report of the Task Force on Campaign Finance Reform." Citizens Research Foundation, University of Southern California, March 1997.

Corrado, Anthony. *Paying for Presidents: Public Financing in National Elections.* New York: Twentieth Century Fund Press, 1993.

Gierzynski, Anthony. *Money Rules.* Boulder, CO: Westview, 2000.

Magleby, David B., and Candice J. Nelson. *The Money Chase: Congressional Campaign Finance Reform.* Washington, DC: Brookings Institution, 1990.

Mann, Thomas E. "The U.S. Campaign Finance System Under Strain: Problems and Prospects." In *Setting National Priorities: 1999,* edited by Robert D. Reischauer and Henry J. Aaron. Washington, DC: Brookings Institution, 1999.

Ornstein, Norman J., et al. "Reforming Campaign Finance." In *Campaign Finance Reform: A Sourcebook,* edited by Anthony Corrado, Thomas E. Mann, Daniel R. Ortiz, Trevor Potter, and Frank J. Sorauf. Washington, DC: Brookings Institution, 1977.

Politics and Money. Washington, DC: Center for Responsive Politics, 1997.

Princeton Survey Research Associates. "Money and Politics: A National Survey of the Public's Views on How Money Impacts on the Political System." Washington, DC: Center for Responsive Politics, 1998.

Sabato, Larry J. *PAC Power.* New York: Norton, 1985.

Sorauf, Frank J. *Money in American Elections.* Glenview, IL: Scott Foresman, 1988.

West, Darrell M. *Checkbook Democracy: How Money Corrupts Political Campaigns.* Boston: Northeastern University Press, 2000.

Notes

1. According to the Alliance for Better Campaigns, the major networks received $234 million from political advertising in 2000. "Gouging Democracy: How the Television Industry Profiteered on Campaign 2000," Appendix I.

2. See the 1998 Pew Research Center For The People & The Press survey on public trust in government, *Deconstructing Distrust.* A more recent report on a national survey conducted for the Center on Policy Attitudes in January 1999, "Expecting More Say: The American Public on Its Role in Government Decisionmaking," also found a majority of the populace believing that government is run by special interests, not for the benefit of all the people (question 12, p. 36).

3. Center for Responsive Politics, "Campaign Finance Reform," <http:www.opensecrets.org/campaignfinancereform>.

4. In an effort to control spiraling media expenses, the law limited the amount that could be spent on advertising. This provision was later eliminated when new legislation was drafted in 1976 following the Supreme Court's *Buckley* v. *Valeo* decision, which voided several provisions of the initial law.

5. Subsequent court decisions have reaffirmed contribution limits on candidates and coordinated expenditures of parties.

6. The ads were designed not only to paint Clinton as a moderate but also to suggest that the Republicans' proposed budgetary cuts were extreme and would devastate such popular programs as health care for the elderly, environmental cleanup, and education.

7. Such inducements had been used in the past to raise money, but not to the extent that they were used during the Clinton presidency.

8. From mid-January through April 1996, the president's schedule included twenty-seven coffee hours, thirteen dinners, and eleven days of travel, along with other political events, according to a memorandum from Evelyn S. Lieberman, deputy White House chief of staff at the time. This memorandum was published in the *New York Times,* February 26, 1997, A18.

9. Gore was accused of violating an 1882 law that prohibits government employees from soliciting funds from federal property. The law was intended to protect government employees from being forced to engage in fundraising for the administration in power. Whether the legislation, which was rarely enforced, was intended to apply to the vice president and president is unclear. The Democratic National Committee paid for the installation of the telephone line for the calls, and Gore charged them to a Clinton-Gore campaign credit card. Taxpayer money was not involved, but use of the campaign credit card in effect meant that the campaign was paying for the solicitation of soft money. This technically violated the law, which allows only the parties, not the individual campaigns, to raise this money.

10. Tom Delay, Statement on Shays-Meehan Bill, August 3, 1998, <http://www.majoritywhip.house.gov/Reform/080398/cfrkillshaysmeehan.asp>.

11. According to the survey conducted by Princeton Survey Research Associates for the Center for Responsive Politics, 52 percent of the respondents believed that the use of money in elections determines whether a political candidate wins or loses an election "often"; 38 percent, "sometimes"; and only 7 percent, "hardly ever." Princeton Survey Research Associates, "Money and Politics: A National Survey of the Public's Views on How Money Impacts on the Political System" (Washington, DC: Center for Responsive Politics, 1997), question 20B.

12. Gary C. Jacobson, *The Politics of Congressional Elections* (Boston: Little, Brown, 1983), 42.

13. Princeton Survey Research Associates, "Money and Politics," part II, 1–2.

14. According to the "Money and Politics" survey, the following percentages of respondents said that the use of money to buy political influence occurs "often":

Leads elected officials to support policies they don't think are best for the country	45
Leads elected officials to spend too much time fundraising	63
Leads elected officials to vote against constituent interests	44
Keeps important legislation from being passed	48
Gets someone appointed to office who would not otherwise be considered	50
Gives one group more influence by keeping another from having its fair say	55

15. A poll of 1,347 adults in 1997 asked the question "Whose attempts to buy influence bother you the most?" The percentage of responses were as follows:

Wealthy people	21
Foreign governments	45
American special-interest groups	25
Don't know	8

"Financing Campaigns: Skepticism, and a Need for Change," *New York Times,* April 8, 1997, A14.

16. Annenberg Center for Public Policy, University of Pennsylvania, *Issue Advertising in the 1999–2000 Election Cycle,* February 1, 2001, 1–7.

17. Alliance for Better Campaigns, "Gouging Democracy."

18. Pew Research Center For The People & The Press, *Deconstructing Distrust*; and Center on Policy Attitudes, "Expecting More Say," 36.

19. Pew Research Center For The People & The Press, "Why Americans Aren't Stirred by Campaign Finance Reform," March 27, 2001.

20. Gallup Poll, "Poll Trends: Campaign Finance Reform," March 2001.

21. In the "Money and Politics" survey, only 15 percent rated campaign finance as the nation's top priority; 45 percent saw it as a high priority (question 25). A 1999 survey conducted by the Pew Research Center For The People & The Press found 28 percent citing campaign finance reform as a top priority. In contrast 23 percent said it was not too important. "Third Party Chances Limited," July 22, 1999, 26, question 14q. In October 1999, only 11 percent indicated campaign finance reform should be the top priority for Congress, while 28 percent thought it should be a high priority. Gallup Poll, "Social and Economic Indicators," <http://www.gallup.com/poll/indicators/indcamp_fin.asp>.

22. Even though many people say the system is broken and needs fixing, they have very limited knowledge of the current law, how it works, who has benefited, and what changes may be necessary. The "Money and Politics" survey conducted for the Center for Responsive Politics in April 1997 asked respondents to answer five multiple-choice questions about the current law and its impact. Fewer than 1 percent got them all right, 4 percent got four correct, and 8 percent got three correct. Even more disheartening, 30 to 40 percent didn't even try to *guess* the right answer to each question. Here are the questions and the percentage of the group that got each one correct. An asterisk indicates the right answer.

- Do you happen to know which political party's national committee raised more money during the 1996 election cycle: Was it the Democrats or the Republicans or did the two parties raise about the same amount of money?

Democrats	24%
Republicans*	21
About the same	12
Don't know	43

- As far as you know how much money does current law allow CORPORATIONS to give, as much as they want (1), only a limited amount (2), or are they not allowed to contribute any money(3)? Don't know (4)

	1	2	3	4
DIRECTLY to campaigns of candidates for president and Congress	17	43	4*	36
To national parties for party building activities such as get-out-the-vote efforts	24*	32	2	42

- As far as you know, how much money does current law allow PRIVATE CITIZENS to give . . . as much as they want (1), only a limited amount (2), or are they not allowed to contribute any money (3)? Don't know (4)

	1	2	3	4
DIRECTLY to campaigns of candidates for president and Congress	27	41*	2	30
To national parties, for party building activities such as get-out-the-vote efforts	32*	27	1	40

Princeton Survey Research Associates, "Money and Politics," questions 22–24.

23. For the first fifteen months of the 1997–1998 election cycle, the gambling industry was the largest contributor to the Senate Republican campaign committee, giving more than $750,000. Total contributions to federal candidates during the first eighteen months of the election cycle by the industry came to $2,865 million, with the Republicans receiving 65 percent and Democrats 35. Center for Responsive Politics, "Money Alert," July 13, 1998, <http://www.opensecrets.org/alerts/v4/alrtv4n27.htm>.

24. Jackie Koszcuk, "'Soft Money' Speaks Loudly on Capitol Hill This Season," *Congressional Quarterly* 56 (June 27, 1998): 1736–1742.

25. Annenberg Center for Public Policy, *Issue Advertising,* 13; and David B. Magleby, ed., *Getting Inside the Outside Campaign* (Provo, UT: Brigham Young University, 2000), 2.

26. A related concern is the practice of bundling. Pioneered by Emily's List, a PAC that supports women's candidates, the bundling procedure solicits individual contributions for candidates, collects them, bundles the checks for individual candidates together, and sends them to the candidates. In this way, the PAC's activities can result in much more money for a candidate than the $5,000 maximum a PAC can contribute.

By prohibiting this practice, Congress could reduce the influence of PACs that have perfected this procedure. But Congress would decrease neither the dependence of congressional candidates on special-interest money nor the desires of these groups to find ways to help the candidates of their choice. And, as we've discovered with the politics of campaign finance, where there's a will, there's a way.

27. Related to spending limits are loan limits. Candidates often are forced to borrow huge sums of money to finance campaigns. If they win, they may spend several years paying it back; if they lose, the loans may not be repaid. Sometimes, as a condition for support, the winning candidate in a nomination contest will help the losers to pay back their loans. Sometimes they won't.

28. CBS News Poll, July 13–14, 1999, as reported in "The Polling Report," <http://www.pollingreport.com/politics.htm>.

6

News Media:
Watchdog or Pit Bull?

Did you know that . . .

- there are more free and accessible sources of campaign information than in the past, yet public knowledge remains abysmally low?
- although Americans say they believe in freedom of the press, almost half the people believe that the media have too much freedom?
- a majority of the population want to prevent the broadcast media from projecting a winner in presidential elections while people are still voting?
- the voting-age group that is least informed about the campaign is the youngest: those between eighteen and twenty-nine?
- television is the primary source of election news in almost every advanced democratic nation?
- television news covers campaigns and elections as if they were sporting events?
- when the public has been asked to evaluate news media coverage of recent national campaigns, the average grade has been between C and C+?
- the "spin" put on campaign coverage today is more negative than positive?
- television anchors and correspondents received six times more airtime than the candidates on the major networks' evening news shows during the 2000 presidential campaign?
- the only professional group that rates lower than television and newspaper correspondents on Gallup's honesty and moral character scale is members of Congress?
- 1996 was the first presidential election in which all the major candidates for president and Congress had websites?
- the Internet is the fastest growing communications vehicle for the major news organizations?

- of the twenty-two presidential debates during the 2000 nominations, only two were carried by a major network and none during prime time?
- only one in four people between the ages of eighteen and twenty-nine reports that he or she pays close attention to the news?
- the television audience watching presidential debates has been steadily declining?

Is this any way to run a democratic election?

A FREE AND fair press is essential to a democratic electoral process. In theory, the news media expand the information available and reach more people than would a campaign conducted by word of mouth, printed literature distributed by parties, or an event-driven campaign. The press provides a more objective presentation and analysis of that information than could be expected from self-interested candidates and parties. It facilitates comparisons among those running for office and puts the campaign debate within a historical and contemporary context, which makes for a more informed judgment. For all these reasons, media coverage of election campaigns is important, more so as the electorate has expanded and the number of elections has increased.

Weakening party organizations and new communications technology, however, have placed additional burdens on the media, burdens that the press has had difficulty handling. The news media have become fair game for criticism from candidates, elected officials, parties, and the general public.

Why has the mass media's role in the electoral process become so crucial, and how well are the various news media playing that role? To answer these questions, we turn first to the reasons why elections have become so media driven. Then we'll explore the changes in communications technology that have thrust the news media front and center. Next, we'll look at the ways contemporary campaigns are communicated to voters and the impact of that communication on the electorate and the electoral process. The final part of the chapter discusses various proposals for improving the scope and content of communications, with the goal being a more informed and involved public.

MEDIA-DRIVEN DEMOCRATIC ELECTIONS: "THAT'S THE WAY IT IS"

With the words "That's the way it is," long-time television news anchor Walter Cronkite ended each broadcast of the CBS evening news. It was as if there could be no other news than what Walter and the network's correspondents reported, nor any other way to present it than in the pictures and words that came into living rooms across the country every weekday evening for half an hour.

Seeing is believing, and the three major networks made Americans believers. They also made the candidates into television personalities and their campaigns into made-for-TV productions. Radio and television became the principal vehicles through which campaigning was conducted and the electorate was informed. And that's the way it still is today. The mass media and their news outlets form the major link between the candidates, their parties, their campaigns, and the electorate, the prism through which the vast majority of people view the elections.

Not only do the news media report the election campaign in living color, they also interpret it. They "spin" it, shaping the news by what they choose to present and how they choose to present it. Moreover, they explain the meaning of the elections, help define the agenda for newly elected officials, and then become the watchdogs and assessors of their performance in office. These functions give the news media enormous power.

To the extent that the information presented is accurate, comprehensive, relevant, and impartial, the electorate is well served. To the extent that the information is incomplete, inaccurate, incomprehensible, truncated, skewed, biased, or unfair, then the electorate is shortchanged, and the democratic electoral process suffers as a result. In short, the scope, content, and spin of the news can enhance or warp the public's vision, facilitate or impede its electoral decisions, energize or turn off voters, and provide realistic or unrealistic policy expectations for the general public. All of this can affect attitudes toward politicians and government.

If partisan attitudes were stronger and more compelling influences on voting; if political parties were better organized at the grassroots level; if personal contacts were the main way voters got educated and mobilized; if party leaders were more directly responsible for the selection of nominees and for their campaigns; if the parties had clearer, more well-defined platforms on which they would, if elected, make their public policy decisions—then the role of the news media in democratic elections, though still important, wouldn't have become as central as it is today. But, as we noted in Chapter 4, partisan attitudes have weakened, party organizations have eroded, losing touch with their mass base, and elections have become more candidate centered and personality oriented, with more emphasis on the individuality of those running than on the team of which they are presumably a part.

Technology has also driven some of these changes. It has speeded up and expanded communication links, shortening the time frame in which news reaches people and making it easier, cheaper, and in some ways even better (in the sense of getting the big picture) to stay at home to watch the campaign unfold and to listen to the candidates.

For better or worse, the press has moved or been thrust into the roles that parties used to play when communicating with the voters. And, according to Thomas E. Patterson, in his very influential book *Out of Order,* the news media are not suited for this task.

> The job of parties is to aggregate society's interests and offer voters a choice between coherent competing alternatives. . . . The press is not equipped to play a comparable role. The media's incentive lies in attracting and holding the audience's attention,

and thus it endeavors to deliver the news in a form that will do so. . . . The press is necessarily guided by its own conventions and organizational imperatives, and these are certain to dominate its decisions. Hence, it cannot be expected to organize political choice in a coherent way.[1]

If members of the press were subject to the same type of scrutiny they give to the candidates and their campaigns, this enlarged role might not be so dangerous or dysfunctional for contemporary electoral politics. But, alas, they are not. The First Amendment guarantees a free press, and the news media are quick to bridle at any restrictions on their freedom to cover an election and report it as they see it.

Part of the problem stems from what they report and how they report it. Part stems from their "pack" tendencies, which magnify the coverage they emphasize and minimize other less reported or unreported news about the election. Part of it stems from the candidates' reaction to the coverage they expect. Candidates orchestrate and compartmentalize their newsworthy activities and statements into morsels that they hope the press will devour and regurgitate. Moreover, candidates also try to reinforce their good news and their opponents' bad news through paid advertising, which is *not* subject to the same standards for truthfulness and accuracy as is commercial advertising. And, to make matters worse, the media bombardment precedes and follows the campaign, drawing the news out over many months and, in the case of the presidential election, even years, thereby numbing the voters.

It's almost as if three interrelated campaigns are going on at once. In one, the candidates are appealing directly to the electorate for votes. In another, they're attempting to win the media campaign by controlling the agenda, spinning their news, leaking unfavorable stories about their opponents, and reacting quickly to controversies highlighted in the press. The third campaign is the one the media report to the electorate. It consists of entertaining news that will command the attention of their consumers rather than educate the polity in the exercise of its civic responsibilities.

How did we get to this state of affairs? Hasn't the press always had a perspective from which it reported political events, a perspective that wasn't exactly neutral?

THE EVOLUTION OF ELECTION NEWS

The American press has always been politicized. From the onset of the Revolutionary War, to the ratification debate, to the evaluation of the nation's new government, the press had a discernible political perspective that shaped what was reported as news. Early newspapers were opinionated and argumentative, but they weren't aimed at the general population. They were intended for the educated and business classes.

The audience for and content of newspapers began to change during the 1830s, as the parties expanded their popular base. Technological improvements, a growth in literacy, and the movement toward greater public involvement in political affairs all contributed to the rise of the "penny press"—newspapers that sold for a penny and were profitable by virtue of their advertising and mass circulation. To sell more papers, news stories had to be entertaining and exciting. Electoral campaigns fit this mold better than most other news about politics and government. As a consequence, campaigns have received extensive coverage through the years.

Technology has played its part. The invention of the telegraph helped make it possible for an emerging Washington press corps to communicate information about national political issues to the entire country. The first radio station began operating in 1920, and radio remained the principal electronic news medium from the 1920s to the 1950s. The 1924 presidential election was the first to be reported on radio; the conventions, major speeches, and election returns were broadcast to a national listening audience. During the 1928 election, both major presidential candidates (Herbert Hoover and Alfred E. Smith) spent campaign funds on radio advertising.

Television came into its own in the 1950s. Quickly the number of television sets and the hours that people watched grew. TV soon became the primary source of fast-breaking news events and the primary communication vehicle for people to acquire their knowledge of the candidates and issues. In contrast, newspaper readership declined, particularly among the younger generations. Table 6.1 indicates the primary sources on which people in the United States and other democratic nations depend for their campaign news.

The effect of television was felt as early as 1952, when Republican vice presidential candidate Richard Nixon denied allegations that he had obtained and used campaign gifts for himself and his family. The speech in which Nixon also

TABLE 6.1 Changing Sources of Campaign News (Percentages)

	1992	1996	2000
Television (Net)*	82	72	70
Network	55	36	22
Local	29	23	22
Cable	29	21	36
Newspapers	57	60	39
Radio	12	19	15
Magazines	9	11	4
Internet	n/a	3	11

*Numbers add to more than 100 percent because voters could list up to two primary sources.

Source: Pew Research Center For the People & The Press, "2000," figure 6, p. 4.

vowed not to give up the family dog, Checkers, who had been given to the Nixons by political supporters, generated favorable public reaction and testified to the power of television if used effectively by candidates. Forty years later, Bill Clinton turned to television first to deny accusations of extramarital affairs that threatened to derail his presidential campaign, later to repackage himself as a mainstream moderate, the protector of the people's popular health, education, and environmental programs, which, he claimed, the Republicans were threatening, and finally, as a hard-working and much traveled president doing the public's business as the Republican Congress unleashed its personal vendetta against him that culminated in his impeachment by the House of Representatives.

The marketing of candidates on television, through paid political advertising and newsworthy speeches and events, has revolutionized the electoral process, particularly the strategy and tactics of campaigning. It has enabled candidates to craft their own images and to challenge those of their opponents. Another example of the power of television came during the four debates held in 1960 between the two major presidential candidates, Senator John F. Kennedy and Vice President Richard M. Nixon. In their first debate, the vice president's pallid appearance, darting eyes, and unrehearsed responses damaged his image and contributed to Kennedy's narrow victory.

The growing importance of television affected the print media as well. Because television reported events at or close to the time they happened, newspapers and magazines had to supplement their coverage and commentary in order to provide an additional dimension and thereby maintain a product that people would want to buy. One way they did so was to "find" news by investigating activities that on the surface might not have appeared newsworthy.

The development and expansion of twenty-four-hour cable news left the major broadcast networks in a similar situation. Because they aren't usually the first to report fast-breaking events, they've had to find news and make that which has been aired more interesting. To do this, the broadcast networks have become more interpretive, investigative, and adversarial in their reporting of election news. Their news stories have also become shorter and more action oriented, in order to placate the short attention spans of viewers who sit with remote control devices at their fingertips, waiting to use them in anticipation of being bored. News from the broadcast networks has also become *softer,* "more sensational, more personality-centered, less time-bound, more practical, and more incident-based than other news."[2] Soft news is less concerned with policy matters, less concerned with political leadership, less concerned with major events and their consequences, and much less complex than the more traditional hard news. It is also consuming an increasing proportion of the content of network and cable news.[3]

To make matters worse, the major networks have cut back on their news staff, on their foreign news bureaus, and even on their coverage of electoral politics (see Table 6.2.) When the decreasing coverage of campaigns is combined with the increasing amount of soft news on news shows, the result is less detailed information made available to the general, viewing public by the major television networks.

In partial compensation, most of these networks, major magazines, and newspapers have also established websites on which they post information on fast-breaking events, present their regular news report and commentaries, and archive contemporary news stories. There has also been a growth of public interest websites on which more detailed policy discussions and candidate evaluations are provided, as well as campaign speeches and policy positions. Were the public to access these sites, they could gain a substantial resource for learning about the campaign.

People are increasingly going online for campaign news. About 18 percent of the population did so for the 2000 election.[4] However, most user surveys have found a demographic profile of users that reflects the best informed and most interested segments of the population, i.e. college-educated people in higher-income brackets.[5] The one exception is younger people, those in the eighteen-to-thirty age bracket, who came of age during the Internet revolution. Surveys have also found that people who use the Internet to obtain campaign information tend to access the popular news websites: CNN, America Online, and Yahoo. They do so primarily because those sites offer a quick and convenient way to stay informed.[6]

If the most informed individuals stay informed on the web, then the availability of more sites and more information may not be expanding the informed public as much as it is keeping that public up-to-date and reinforcing the political predilections they bring to a campaign. Because Internet users can bookmark

TABLE 6.2 Election News Coverage, 1988–2000

	2000	1996	1992	1988
Amount of Coverage				
Number of stories	462	483	728	589
Minutes per day	12.6	12.3	24.6	17
Average sound bite (seconds)	7.8	8.2	8.4	9.8
Focus of Coverage (percent of stories)				
Horserace	71	48	58	58
Policy issues	40	37	32	39
Tone of Coverage (percent good press)				
Dem. nominee	40	50	52	31
GOP nominee	37	33	29	38

Based on evaluations by nonpartisan sources in election stories on ABC, CBS, and NBC evening newscasts.

Source: From *Media Monitor,* Center for Media & Public Affairs, "Campaign 2000 Final: How TV News Covered the General Election," November/December 2000, pp. 1–3. Used by permission of the Center for Media & Public Affairs.

their favorite sites, they are more likely to choose sites that reflect their interests and attitudes rather than challenge them. The bottom line seems to be that there is more information out there but most of the general public is not using it to become more knowledgeable about campaigns and elections.

Moreover, because the major news networks now have to complete with hundreds of cable and satellite entertainment channels in addition to the mushrooming of websites, the information they provide has to be more captivating, more recent, and seemingly more oriented toward human interest. In short, there is more information, but it is not necessarily more newsworthy.

There is another problem, too. Not only has the diversity of programs available to the general population by cable and satellite increased, but so has the speed at which information travels. Rumors move so fast on the Internet that the establishment press has had to relax its two-source verification rule, often giving allegations as much attention as verifiable items in the news. This attention in turn lends credibility to the rumor, clouds the line between fact and fiction, and encourages others to engage in this type of destructive and self-serving behavior.

To make matters worse from the candidates' perspective, a credibility gap has also emerged: the news media no longer give politicians and public officials the benefit of the doubt. The press regularly imputes political motives to all statements and actions of candidates for office. In turn, candidates see the press as hostile and overly negative. In fact, they often point to that negativism when justifying their own attempts to put a favorable spin on the news. And they've taken to talk or entertainment radio and television to circumvent the national press corps and get their messages across.

THE ADEQUACY OF CONTEMPORARY CAMPAIGN COVERAGE

To what extent do the news media present information about elections fairly and accurately? To what extent do they skew the news toward the desires of their mass audience, presenting what they believe people want to know, not necessarily what some believe they need to know, in order to make an informed, rational judgment on election day? To what extent do they fulfill the informational needs of a democratic electoral process?

Journalistic Bias: Ideological or Professional?

In deciding what to report, the news media impose their bias. Some believe that it's an ideological bias. Conservatives and Republicans in particular see the national press as liberal, Democratic, and likely to favor candidates who share this political perspective. To support their contentions, these conservative critics often point to studies about the media that show the overwhelming majority of national news reporters and correspondents to be Democratic, liberal, and urban oriented.[7] Others, however, point to the influence of the conservative corporate executives who oversee the communications empires of newspapers, radio stations, and television networks; to the corporate interests that advertise on these media and contribute to their profits; and to the editorials that reflect the conservative views of the owners, the publishers, and corporate advertisers.[8]

Although some people perceive a press bias, most do not see that bias as partisan.[9] A majority of people in the last three presidential elections judged news coverage to be fair.[10] Nonetheless, there were evaluative differences among partisans, with Republicans being more critical than independents, who were more critical than Democrats.[11] Table 6.3 indicates public perceptions of media bias.

Academic observers perceive a professional bias that is reflected in the definition of what is newsworthy. All events, activities, and statements during elections are not equally newsworthy. The criterion of audience interest is the principal one the press uses to determine the newsworthiness of an item or event. From the perspective of the press, if an item is new, surprising, exciting, different, dramatic, or involving conflict, then it's more newsworthy than one that doesn't share any of these characteristics. The first utterance is more newsworthy than the second one, the unexpected development more newsworthy than the predicted outcome, the misstatement more newsworthy than the standard speech, and the contest more newsworthy than the substance of the issues.

The media's orientation also extends to the format in which news is reported. It must be direct and, above all, simple. Positions are presented and contrasted as black or white; gray areas get less attention. The story usually has a singular focus. There's a punch line or bottom line toward which the report is directed.

TABLE 6.3 Perceptions of News Media Accuracy, 1985–2000 (Percentages)

Question: In general, do you think news organizations get the facts straight or do you think news organizations' stories and reports are often inaccurate? (The question was rotated in all surveys listed except June 1985.)

	Facts straight	Often inaccurate	No opinion
2000 (December 2–4)	32	65	3
1998 (July 13–14)	50	45	5
1989 (August 9–28)	54	44	2
1988 (January 8–17)	44	48	8
1985 (June 22)	55	34	11

Source: Gallup Poll, "Media Use and Evaluation," <http://www.gallup.com>.

Sound Bite Campaigning

The concept of what's news and how news is reported creates incentives for candidates to come up with new angles, new policies, and new events to galvanize public attention. It also encourages them to play it safe, not think out loud, not take chances. Words, expressions, and ideas are pre-tested in focus groups to gauge how the public will react to them before candidates express them in public. To combat a press eager to highlight critical and unexpected reactions, candidates stage their events, recruit their audiences, and try to engineer a "spontaneous" response from them. They speak in sound bites designed to capture public attention and do so in an environment tailored to reinforce them. The size of the "bite" serves an additional need of the news media, particularly radio and television. It facilitates the compartmentalization of news, compressing it into proportions that the press believes the public can digest.

To the extent that the public gains its information about the campaign from these short, simple statements, the amount of knowledge and especially the depth of it will suffer. Newspapers, particularly national ones such as the *New York Times, Christian Science Monitor,* and *Wall Street Journal,* and comprehensive metropolitan dailies such as the *Chicago Tribune, Los Angeles Times,* and *Washington Post,* provide more extensive coverage. But only a small portion of the electorate regularly reads these papers, much less focuses on election news in them. As a result, what the bulk of the electorate receives is a snapshot, a partial and truncated piece of the campaign. Is it any wonder that people are poorly informed? Is it any wonder that they retain so little of the news they see on television?

Interpretive Reporting

There's another problem with contemporary campaign coverage in the mass media: it is highly mediated. People today see and hear more from the correspondents reporting the news than from the candidates making it. S. Robert Lichter and his associates reported that the average campaign story on the networks' evening news shows had correspondents and anchors on six times longer than the candidates.[12] In fact, the candidates are seen and heard only briefly. The average length of a quotation from a candidate on the evening news in 1988 was 9.8 seconds; in 1992 it was 8.3 seconds; in 1996 it was 8.2; in 2000 it was 7.8.[13] Compare this to 42.3 seconds in 1968. Is it any wonder that candidates seek alternative channels to get their message to voters—channels such as talk radio, entertainment television, and the Internet?[14]

A major part of the media's interpretation of campaign news is the story line into which most campaign events are fitted. According to Thomas Patterson, a dominant story emerges and then events within the campaign are explained in terms of it. In 1992 the story was the vulnerability of President Bush, first revealed by Pat Buchanan's surprising showing against him in the early caucuses and primaries, then by the "conservative takeover" of the Republican national convention, and finally by Bush's weak showing in the general election. The character issues that Bush raised about his opponents and his own plans for future policies weren't nearly as newsworthy in that election. Patterson describes this particular story line as the "likely-loser scenario."[15] It plagued George Bush in 1992 and Robert Dole in 1996.[16]

For Clinton, the story line, especially in 1996, was just the opposite. It was that of the "front-runner," who had a large lead and skillfully maneuvered to keep it. In this particular story, the press attributed Clinton's lead and inevitable success to a beneficial economic environment, superior resources, the perquisites of the presidency, and an extremely well-organized and well-run campaign. The news media's depiction of Ronald Reagan's 1984 presidential campaign had been presented in a similar manner, providing yet another illustration of the media's use of the front-runner script.[17]

A majority of the public believes that members of the news media often let their preferences influence the way they report the news. Interpretive reporting contributes to the perception of media bias. It has made voters more wary and less trusting of television correspondents. According to a poll conducted by the Gallup organization in 1999, only one-fifth of the public believes that television and newspaper reporters have high or very high honesty and ethical standards. Members of Congress, however, are rated even lower.[18]

The Election Game

The story about the election is almost always reported as if it were a sporting event. The candidates are the players, and their moves (words, activities, and images) are usually described as strategic and tactical devices to achieve the principal goal: winning the election. Even their policy positions are evaluated within this game schema, often described as calculated attempts to appeal to certain political constituencies.

The metaphor most frequently used in the election game is that of a horserace. A race—especially if it is close and if the result isn't readily predictable—generates excitement. Excitement holds interest, which sells newspapers and magazines and increases the size of radio and television audiences. So do surprise, drama, and human interest stories. When these elements are present, elections get more coverage than when they're lacking, although the differences were small between the 1996 and 2000 presidential elections (see Table 6.2).

In addition to conveying excitement and stimulating public interest, there's another reason why the media use the game format. It lends an aura of objectivity to reporting. It encourages the press to present quantitative data on the public's reaction to the campaign. Public opinion surveys, reported as news, are usually the dominant news item during the primaries and caucuses, often at the expense of substantive policy issues, and they share the spotlight with other campaign-related events during the general election.

Emphasizing the horserace isn't a new phenomenon, but it occurs at the expense of the policy debate. Table 6.2 on p. 129 indicates the amount of time given on the evening news to horserace, policy, and other campaign issues in the last four presidential elections. The table suggests that policy issues rise to public attention only when the race isn't close, as in the 1996 presidential election.

What's the consequence of this type of coverage on the electorate? Simply put, it results in people's remembering less about the policy issues and about the candidates' programs for dealing with them. Although the candidates' positions get attention in the news media, the costs and consequences of their proposed solutions don't get nearly as much. A few national newspapers and magazines do provide this type of coverage, and occasionally the major broadcast networks will have a special program on a particularly vexing economic or social issue, but for most people it's the horserace, the candidates themselves, and their strategies and tactics that get the most attention.

Bad News

Campaign news coverage also tends to be highly critical. Of course, criticism per se isn't harmful to a democratic electoral process; in fact, it's a necessary part of that process. But an overemphasis on the negative, particularly on negative personal, character issues, can disillusion voters, decrease turnout, and render the election a contest among lesser evils.[19]

Why all the negativism? Are the candidates less qualified now than they were in the past? Most scholarly observers don't think so. They offer three principal reasons for the contemporary press's negativism: underlying skepticism about the motives and interests of politicians and elected officials; increasing emphasis on character issues, combined with scrutiny of private behavior; and increased competition with tabloid journalism in the news and entertainment marketplace. Conflict is deemed more visible than consensus, hence the emphasis on it by the press.[20]

The Vietnam War and the Watergate scandal ushered in an era of investigative journalism in which the media adopted an attitude of distrust and disbelief in their coverage of politics and government. Public officials and candidates for office were no longer taken at their word, no longer given the benefit of doubt. The press assumed that their statements and actions were self-interested, not necessarily in the national interest, and that it was the job of the media to reveal hidden motives, strategies, and goals—to present the other side.

As we've mentioned, campaign coverage became more candidate centered as investigative journalism began to focus more on the people who were seeking office rather than on their partisan connection. Pretty soon, the line between public and private was obliterated, with the press trumpeting the importance of character as its rationale for reporting what used to be considered private (and therefore irrelevant) behavior.

With the tabloid press eager to highlight the personal foibles and relationships of prominent people, even if only rumored, the mainstream press found itself pressured by competition to follow suit. It often uses a report in the tabloid media or a news conference held by an individual as the pretext for reporting this type of information as news. Thus the allegations of Gennifer Flowers that she was Bill Clinton's lover for eleven years became front-page news and a relevant campaign story in 1992.

Opposition research by campaigns against each other regularly stimulates and supplements this type of media coverage. Leaks have become a common and accepted way to alert the press to negative facts and rumors about one's opponents. Because the negative is often surprising and unexpected, this type of news feeds into the media's addiction to information that grabs their audience.

From the candidates' perspective, the bad news is magnified by the fact that they don't get the opportunity to respond in kind, to explain their side of events in anywhere near the detail of the charges made against them. Moreover, if the charges prove to be inaccurate, any corrections made by the press don't get nearly the emphasis as the story that prompted them.

As a consequence, candidates are left with little alternative but to defend themselves against even the most reckless charges, thereby giving even more attention to those charges at the expense of substantive policy issues. Not only must they respond quickly to allegations against them, so as not to allow an unfavorable image to become part of the public's perception, but they also have an incentive to get the "dirt" on their opponents to leak it to the press. To make matters worse, candidates also have an incentive to reinforce negative personal news by running negative personal advertising against their opponents.

A number of unfortunate consequences for a democratic electoral process follow from this type of campaign behavior and media coverage. The electorate gets a jaundiced view of the campaign. It's described more as a personal contest between two or more gladiators than as an issue-oriented policy debate or a campaign between two parties with opposing philosophies and goals. It's presented by television anchors, correspondents, and star newspaper reporters, not by the candidates. It emphasizes the bad over the good.

PUBLIC CYNICISM ABOUT THE MEDIA

Not only does the news media coverage of campaigns focus on the contest and the contestants rather than on the consequences of their policy, not only does it lessen respect for the candidates of all parties, not only does it impute their motives, but it also contributes to cynicism about the press itself.

In theory, there is broad support for a free press. Although many people may not understand the protections that the First Amendment provides media in the United States today, they do believe that newspapers, radio, television, and news magazines are necessary for a democratic society to hold the government in check.[21] The belief that a free press is essential to a democratic society is shared by people in other democracies, as is the value that people place on keeping up with national affairs.[22]

But, despite the support for a free press, the desire to keep up with events, and the dependence on the media for election news, criticism of how the media do their job has been growing. Put simply, people find the press less believable, more inaccurate, and more biased than they did in the past (see Table 6.3).

Yet, despite the criticism of the press for what it reports and how it reports it, for its invasiveness, its inaccuracies, and its "gotcha" type of journalism, people are attracted to tabloid-like news and retain much information from it. They evidence greater knowledge of celebrities in the news than they do of public officials.[23]

The public's ambivalence toward the news media, the people's desire for gossip, scandal, and conflict, but also their criticism of the press for providing and emphasizing this type of information, create a situation in which the marketplace dictates the outcome. The mass media give their audience what they believe their audience wants. In this sense they're responding to their consumers' demands. The more specialized press serves the desires of more specialized groups, such as the governing elite who may have different, more policy-oriented demands. The interests of the public and the orientation of a profit-oriented media toward satisfying these often conflicting interests pose a real dilemma for a democratic society. How do we achieve an informed citizenry, involved in public affairs, in a free market economy, *if that citizenry doesn't want to be informed and involved in public affairs?* Before we address this vexing dilemma, though, we should explore two subsidiary issues. Is today's citizenry less informed by the news media than were citizens two or three decades ago? And, equally important, how much public information is necessary for people to make an informed voting decision?

The Dumbing of the Electorate: Does It Matter?

The time frame for our first question—about the level of information that the general public possesses—is relatively short if we wish to answer it with survey data. National polls of public knowledge, attitudes, and opinions weren't conducted with any regularity until after World War II. Moreover, to make comparisons, responses to similar questions have to be analyzed. Finally, the vast majority of public affairs surveys asked attitude and opinion questions rather than informational ones. In fact, information is frequently provided in the question or statement so that people can respond intelligently.

The anecdotal evidence isn't encouraging. Americans retain little information about specific issues. Many would be hard-pressed to name their congressional representatives, much less assess their performance in office—unless, of course, they were involved in a scandal or had abused their position. A national survey taken in January 2000 at the onset of the presidential campaign found that one-third of the people did not know which of the presidential candidates was currently governor of Texas, only 30 percent knew that Bill Bradley was a former senator from New Jersey, and only 17 percent correctly identified John McCain as a cosponsor of a campaign finance bill in Congress (73 percent did not know or refused to give an answer).[24] Similarly, in December 1995, when Senate Majority Leader Robert Dole was the leading candidate for the 1996 Republican presidential nomination, only 34 percent could correctly identify the person who served as majority leader of the Senate.[25] Vice President Al Gore did better in the same survey; 60 percent knew who he was.[26]

Presumably the campaign performs an educational function for those who have only a rudimentary knowledge of the candidates and issues. Those with the least knowledge are people under thirty. According to the researchers at the Pew Research Center, "Americans under 30 represented a generation that knew less, cared less, and read newspapers less than previous generations of young people." More than 40 percent of those under thirty indicate that they have little or no interest in politics, compared with about 25 percent of older adults. Perhaps this is why only one in five between the ages of eighteen and twenty-nine pay close attention to the news.[27]

Not only is the level of information low, but today's population is reading fewer major newspapers than people read in the past. People get their news primarily from television, and increasingly from a diverse set of television news sources—twenty-four-hour cable news, local news, and network evening news shows. Cable reports current national events over and over, throwing in a mixture of weather, sports, and financial news; local news is about crime, traffic, weather, schools, community issues and politics, with a small dose of national news occasionally included. To compete, the evening news on the broadcast networks has become more of a news magazine. And, as we noted earlier in this chapter, news stories have become shorter, more interpretive, more candidate centered, and less issue oriented than they used to be. All of these changes suggest that there's a connection between the acquisition and presentation of news, as well as between the primary media sources and their audience.

Yet, from the perspective of the electorate, voters still claim that they have sufficient information to make an informed judgment on election day. At least that's what they have told survey researchers who asked them after the last four presidential elections. Table 6.4 indicates the percentages of the voting electorate who said that they were satisfied or dissatisfied with the information they got from the last four presidential campaigns.

TABLE 6.4 Voters' Perceptions of Information Adequacy, 1988–2000 (Percentages)

	1988	1992	1996	2000
Learned enough to make an informed choice	59	77	75	83
Did not learn enough from the campaign	39	20	23	15
Don't know/refused	2	3	2	2

Source: Pew Research Center For The People & The Press, "Campaign 2000 Highly Rated," November 16, 2000.

It's interesting to note, however, that voters do not evaluate the press nearly as well as they evaluate the information they received from news media. On a scale of A to F, they have given the press a C for its coverage of the last four presidential elections, and they also believe that the media exercise too much influence on the results.[28]

Information and Democracy: Three Views

Our second issue has to do with how much public knowledge and activity are necessary to maintain the health and vitality of a democratic society. There are several schools of thought on this.

Those who subscribe to the **elitist model** of democracy believe that, as long as the leadership is informed, involved, and responsible to the people through the electoral process, the political system can function properly. This minimalist theory of public involvement maintains that democratic criteria are satisfied if the citizenry has the opportunity to participate in elections and enough basic information to do so. Citizens need to be able to minimally differentiate the candidates and their principal policy positions, factor in their own perceptions of reality, and make a voting decision. But everyone doesn't have to be informed and participate in civic affairs for the system to work.

The **pluralist model** sees the system as democratic if it permits the people to pursue their interests within the political arena. Elections are one of the political processes in which they can do so, but not the only one. Public demonstrations, letter-writing campaigns, and personal contacts are other means by which those outside of government can influence those in it. Again, the burden of being informed and involved rests primarily on the group leadership, on those in and out of power; the requirement for the populace is that its interests can be discerned, expressed, and pursued.

In both the elite and the pluralistic models, the process by which people express their views is the main criterion for claiming that the system is democratic. The **popular,** or **plebiscitary, model** demands more. It requires a higher level of public involvement in politics and government. Within the electoral arena, this translates into more public debate, more interaction between the candidates and the electorate, and more people voting.

Those who adopt this perspective see the decline in public trust and confidence in politics and government as dangerous because it can lead to a concentration of power in the hands of a few. It can also reduce support for governmental decisions and for the people who make them, and weaken the legitimacy of the rules and processes of the political system itself. One sign of alienation would be the growth of organized, armed vigilantes or militias, those who see it as their mission to take the law into their own hands. Another would be an increase in terrorist activities. A third might be the failure of a significant portion of the population to participate in elections and to vote.

It's difficult to answer the question of how informed and involved a citizenry must be in order to maintain a democratic political system. But there's little doubt that the more information, involvement, and active support the general population gives to the candidates who run for office, to the party platforms on which they run, and to their experience and performance in office the better. Of course, people don't get all their information about campaigns from the news media. Candidate advertisements are another source of information, as are personal contacts and experience, particularly when those experiences reinforce or refute the claims candidates make. However, news coverage is still a very important component of the process of gathering sufficient information to make an informed voting decision. Hence the issue addressed in the last part of this chapter: how to facilitate an attentive and involved public through the mass media.

WHAT CAN BE DONE?

Criticizing contemporary press coverage of elections is much easier than making constructive suggestions for changing it. The electorate may be getting what it wants but not necessarily what it needs. It's all well and good to berate the news media for not presenting a detailed discussion of the issues. But what good would it do to present such a discussion if the public weren't interested in it, didn't follow it, or got turned off by it? Besides, as we've noted, there's plenty of detailed and easily accessible information about the candidates and their campaigns, the parties and their platforms, and the voters and their interests and desires. All of this information is readily available in national newspapers and magazines, on public radio and television, and on the websites of the participants as well as interest group publications received by its members.

We can wring our hands and bemoan the fact that most people don't regularly consult these sources. We can say that they should, but we certainly aren't ready to reimpose literacy tests as a condition for voting. We can blame this state of affairs on the failure of civic education in the schools, a claim that probably has some merit, but shaking our heads sadly about underinformed, uninvolved, generally apathetic citizens won't change the situation, although it might enable some to rationalize it more satisfactorily.

We can blame the problem on the news media. Thomas Patterson believes that those who determine media markets have made a wrong-headed assumption that people interested in news want an endless diet of soft, tabloid-oriented pablum to consume. Not so, he says. In a study of the news preferences of television audiences, he found hard news to be more appealing to more people than soft news. Moreover, he also discovered that consumers of hard news were less tolerant of soft news than consumers of soft news were of hard news.[29] Patterson concludes that in an effort to compete with the increasing variety and number of news/entertainment shows, the national news networks have done themselves and our democracy a disservice by increasing their emphasis on soft news.[30] So we ask, what can be done to change contemporary media coverage of elections?

Redefine Election News

One suggestion is to induce those who control the scope and methods of electoral coverage to change their definition of news, their standards for reporting it, and their game-oriented emphasis. A Task Force on Campaign Reform, funded by the Pew Charitable Trusts, urges such an approach. It suggests that the press "use the campaign controversies as spring boards reporting on the real substance of politics and political careers, rather than treating them as self-contained episodes."[31] Similarly, instead of entertaining horserace stories, reporting polls of who's ahead and by how much, the task force recommends more analysis of *why* different groups seem to be supporting different candidates; more in-depth reporting, be it on character or substantive policy concerns; and more emphasis on the big issues that transcend day-to-day events. It also makes the observation that election news could be more repetitive, that news doesn't always have to be new, and that the test for including information be the level of public knowledge on a subject, not the level of the press's knowledge about it.[32] Too often, the catalyst for a story has been the desire to scoop other journalists for something new and different, rather than the importance of the issue to the voters and the country.

Thomas Patterson reaches much the same conclusion when he argues that the hard news component must be strengthened if people are to have the information they need to make an informed judgment on election day. "What is good for democracy is also good for the press," he writes.[33]

These are excellent suggestions, but they require the news media to change their journalistic orientation. Such changes tend to come slowly, if at all, and they're usually dictated by the marketplace. Citizens could vote for these reforms with their television dials, by tuning in to news programs that provide more in-depth, policy-oriented coverage, such as public radio and television, media outlets whose audience has increased over the last two decades.[34] But that opportunity currently exists, and we see the results. Without a massive, negative reaction to contemporary election coverage or a massive public relations campaign—much like campaigns for eating healthy foods, for not smoking, and for control of firearms—people are unlikely to change their reading, listening, and viewing habits quickly or easily.

Shorten the Campaign

A different type of suggestion was proposed by Thomas Patterson several years ago. In his perceptive study of coverage of media and elections *Out of Order,* Patterson recommends shortening election campaigns, particularly the long and arduous nomination contests, which now consume more time than the general election.[35] A more compact campaign, he believes, would of necessity focus the mass media on the more important issues, cut down their interpretations and negativity, and force the political parties to play a greater role in communicating with the voters.[36] But it would also provide less time for an inattentive public to learn about the candidates and issues. Moreover, national legislation would probably be required to impose the time period in which campaigning could occur, thereby increasing even more the regulatory role of the federal government in elections. Unless campaign finance laws were changed, candidates would still have to raise considerable sums of money and do so *before* the official campaign began. How would they obtain money without campaigning? If candidates were forbidden to raise early money, and if the current laws remained in place, incumbents and wealthy candidates would be even more advantaged than they are today. Besides, what guarantee would there be that the news media would become any less interpretive and negative?

Communicate More Directly

Another recommendation, made in some of the campaign finance proposals as well as by several bipartisan groups and commissions, is to conduct more of the campaign spontaneously and directly though the mass media. This would be done by extending the number of debates among the candidates, as well as providing them with free broadcast time. Most European democracies feature debates among the principal candidates or party leaders, and some, such as France, Germany, Sweden, and the United Kingdom, also require on-air time to be provided to the parties. But these countries also operate government-controlled networks on which to provide such time, and the United States doesn't.

If these suggestions were implemented in the United States, they might reduce but not eliminate the press's role as mediator between the candidates and the electorate. Depending on the format of the debates and the amount of free time to which candidates would be entitled, these changes would give those running for office greater opportunity to address the issues in their own words. They would also exercise more control over the agenda of the campaign.

Require More Debates

Debates are useful for several reasons. They enable the public to see, compare, and evaluate candidates in the same setting, at the same time, and on the same criteria: their knowledge of the problems, their priorities and issue positions, and their communicative skills. Debates attract relatively large audiences, larger than most other political events during the election cycle. They allow candidates to speak in their own words, uninterrupted for a specified time to which the participants have agreed. Coincidentally, certain debate formats reduce the press's role as intermediary.[37]

But not all candidates benefit equally from debates. Front-runners, particularly incumbents, see little advantage in debating their challengers; and, when they do, they're usually able to dictate the timing and format of the debate to their perceived advantage. Most candidates play it safe, anticipating their opponents' arguments and rehearsing lines in advance. Spontaneity is minimized.

Nor do the parties gain from debates particularly during the nomination phase. Candidates usually try to distinguish themselves from one another rather than indicate what good partisans they are and will continue to be if elected.

Nor would debates continue to maintain a large audience, particularly if there were a lot of them. The major networks might not carry most of them. In 2000 they aired only two of the twenty-two debates during the nomination period, neither of which appeared in prime time. The World Series regularly preempts a presidential debate on one of the networks. And even if the debates were easily available on television, it is likely that once their aura wore off, and having other news and entertainment options from which to choose, the principal audience would probably be composed of strong partisans who root for their candidate and inadvertent viewers who watch for a few minutes and then move on to other channels.

There's been a decline in the proportion of the viewing audience that has watched the presidential election debates since 1960. Table 6.5 shows the estimated debate audience in terms of numbers of voters.

There are other problems with having debates as the principal vehicle through which the candidates communicate with voters. Debates reward performance skills. They benefit telegenic candidates who are well prepared, well coached, and comfortable with television, those who can give quick and catchy responses to the questions of moderators or the comments of their opponents. Those who take longer to make a point, who agonize over the complexities of issues, who don't communicate easily or quickly in sound bites may be disadvantaged. Are debate

TABLE 6.5 Presidential Debate Television Audiences, 1960–2000

Year	Number of debates	Average estimated size (in millions)
1960	4	77
1976	4	65
1980	1	81
1984	3	66
1988	3	66
1992	4	66
1996	3	40
2000	4	38

Data include vice presidential debates, which were held in every year but 1960 and 1980.

Source: "How Many Watched," *New York Times,* October 6, 1996, A25; "Debates Ratings Beat Baseball," Associated Press, October 17, 1996; estimate for 2000 based on Nielsen media research as reported in the *New York Times,* October 19, 2000, A22.

skills important for elected officials? Should they be a major factor, potentially affecting the election outcome?[38]

If the networks didn't voluntarily air debates or provide free airtime, could they be forced to do so as a condition for obtaining their broadcast licenses? Would they be compensated for lost advertising revenue? If so, by whom—the taxpayers, the parties, the candidates, or perhaps commercial debate sponsors? Maybe the candidates could eat Ball Park hot dogs, drink Bud Light, wear Nike athletic shoes, or freshen their breath with Altoids.

Then there are the issues of how many debates should be held, for what offices, and which candidates should be invited to them: all who are running or just those of the major parties? The longer the invitation list, the more candidates who would be encouraged to run. In the nomination phase, a plethora of candidates would factionalize the parties even further and trivialize the debates. But having only the major party candidates would reinforce their built-in advantage under the current system, unleveling the playing field even more for third-party and independent candidates.

Take the case of H. Ross Perot. In 1992 he was invited by the commission sponsoring the presidential debates to participate in them. The members of the commission believed that Perot was a viable candidate and could win the election or at least deny one of the major party candidates an Electoral College victory. Perot wasn't invited in 1996 nor was Ralph Nader or Pat Buchanan in 2000 because the same commission believed they couldn't carry a single state, let alone win the national election. Thus, in the commission's view, these third-party candidacies wouldn't preclude a Democratic or Republican Electoral College majority from occurring.

The commission's decision became a self-fulfilling prophecy. Without the debate podium, with less public funding, none of these candidates could overcome the impression, reinforced by the media, that they weren't viable.

A shorter campaign combined with a required debate format could reduce the news media's role, although, if the past is any indication, the press would still analyze the debates, solicit and report public reactions, and declare winners and losers. Would voters benefit from this arrangement? Would they gain and retain more objective information about the candidates, their positions, and their intellectual, communicative, and political skills? Would they be better able to make a considered judgment on election day?

Give Candidates Free Airtime

Whatever your answer to those questions, it's clear that the candidates and their handlers wouldn't be satisfied if debates were the only way they could use the mass media to reach voters.[39] Candidates want to communicate on their own, in their own setting. And the Constitution protects their right to do so, much as it protects the press's right to cover the election as it sees fit.

Occasionally, some candidates have been given free time by a major network, as in the 1996 and 2000 presidential elections. However, it is not a lot of time. In 2000, the networks provided an average of 64 seconds of free time per night in the month before the elections and local stations only 45 seconds per night.[40] Only a small percentage of voters report that they have seen this type of candidate discourse, which may explain why the impact of free television time thus far has been negligible.[41]

Various free-time proposals have been advanced. One would simply depend on voluntary time made available by the networks and independent stations. Another would be to *require* the networks to provide a certain amount of time to meet their public interest obligations and as a condition for getting and renewing their broadcast licenses. Congress has also granted the major networks free access to digital technology. Free time could be regarded as a partial payback.

Naturally, the major corporations that control the communications industry oppose a free-time requirement imposed on them by government, particularly one that obligates them to give it during prime time. They fear that they would lose money. They point to the large number of candidates for national office who would want to take advantage of such time. Could minor party candidates be excluded? Who would decide? And how could the free time be monitored?

Although most candidates would probably use free time that was made available to them, it's unlikely that, when doing so, they would forgo other forms of communication, such as political advertising, or even deviate very much from the message of their ads. So would more free time really be more of the same political "propaganda"—advertising in another form?

Summary: News Media Dilemmas in a Nutshell

The press is a critical link between the candidates and the electorate. Since the 1830s, the mass media—first newspapers, then radio and television, and now the Internet—have brought the campaign to the voters. That function has become even more important in the last three decades, with the declining influence of the parties and their organizations on the electorate, with advances in communications technology, and with the resulting increased personalization of political campaigns.

Moreover, the news media themselves have changed. From a few major news networks to many media outlets, from radio to television to the Internet, from once-a-day reporting to constant and instantaneous news, the media have become both diverse and, at the same time, omnipresent. If these changes had contributed to a more attentive, informed, and involved electorate, then the democracy would have been well served, but, alas, they have not.

Part of the reason is the scope, content, and format of the election news that is reported; part is the spin and the public's reaction to it. A journalistic orientation toward making the election news as interesting and captivating as possible (in light of greater competition) has resulted in media coverage that lacks substance. The emphasis is on newness, controversy, and drama, rather than on partisan and policy debates. The coverage has become more compartmentalized, more interpretive, and, with the advent of investigative reporting, more negative. The candidates are presented as players in an unfolding drama. The campaign story is told with sports metaphors and analogies, is strewn with juicy personality tidbits, and features the contending forces, each trying to manipulate the electorate to its advantage.

Coverage affects the campaign. It forces the candidates to orchestrate their activities for television with irresistible sound bites in their speeches, captivating pictures at their events, and well-known talking heads to spin their message.

The public is informed primarily by this coverage. From the media's perspective, it is what their audience wants, although Patterson's research indicates that the media may be wrong. But from the perspective of democratic theory, it isn't enough of what an informed, intelligent electorate needs in order to make a meaningful decision on election day. The public, too, is critical of this coverage yet continues to consume it and claim that it has sufficient information to make intelligent voting decisions. Herein lies one of the press dilemmas: What good would it do to present more of the substantive policy debate if people were turned off by it or tuned out of it? A second dilemma relates to energizing the electorate and making people more positive about the electoral process. Is this the media's role?

Suggestions have been made to shorten the campaign and facilitate more direct communication between the candidates and voters, with more debates and free airtime. But whether these could or should be imposed on profit-making media and, if so, whether they would provide more of the substantive debate that is presently lacking, is unclear.

Now It's Your Turn

Discussion Questions

1. What is the connection between public interest in politics and news about politics?
2. How does journalistic bias affect the scope and content of information that people gain about elections?
3. Is sufficient information available for the electorate to make an informed judgment on election day? If not, who's at fault? If so, what's the problem and how can it be fixed?
4. Should government exercise more control over the scope and content of campaign coverage?
5. What inducements might encourage the news media to provide more substantive policy information about contemporary election issues and more in-depth studies of the qualifications of those who seek elective office?
6. Can campaigns for federal office be made less dependent on media coverage? Should they be?

7. Do you think that the press exercises too much influence on election outcomes?

Topics for Debate

Challenge or defend the following statements:

1. A free press cannot be a fair and objective press.
2. If voters lack the information they need to make an informed voting decision today, it's their own fault.
3. A democratic electoral process requires the electorate to be opinionated but not necessarily informed.
4. Government should require the principal broadcast and cable news networks to give all candidates for federal office adequate and free airtime.
5. The private personal behavior of candidates is irrelevant to their public performance in office and should not be reported as election news.
6. The news media have a liberal ideological bias.
7. The news media have an obligation to report substantive policy debate in depth, whether or not the people are interested in that debate.

Exercises

1. A major television network asks for your advice on how to improve its campaign coverage of the next election. It would like you to prepare a memo with three goals in mind: meeting the network's public responsibility to inform voters, satisfying the interests of the viewing audience, and gaining audience ratings higher than the competition's. Draft the memo. In your analysis, indicate the following:
   a. the aspects of the campaign that you'd cover and the proportion of coverage you'd give to each,
   b. the attention to be given to third-party and independent candidates versus major party candidates, to national versus local coverage, and to primaries versus the general election.

   In addition, the network would like to know whether it should

   • relax its two-source verification rule in the interest of competition,
   • air rumors and allegations about personal behavior if they appear credible,
   • include in the candidates' personality profiles information on their physical and mental health,
   • give attention to candidate misstatements, inconsistencies, and off-color remarks.
2. Critique the news coverage of a current campaign on one of the twenty-four-hour news networks, on public television, and on one of the broadcast networks on the basis of its adequacy, fairness, and information quality. In your critique, indicate the following:
   a. what you consider to be the most important issues of the campaign and the scope and emphasis given to each,

b. whether the reporting was objective and the analysis fair and helpful,

c. whether the candidates and parties were treated equally,

d. which medium provided the best coverage from the perspective of a democratic electoral process.

On the basis of the individual coverage provided, do you think voters would have enough accurate information to make an informed decision on election day?

Internet Resources

- Annenberg Public Policy Center <http://www.appcpenn.org>
  Part of the Annenberg School of Communications of the University of Pennsylvania, the public policy center conducts studies on the media, which it makes available on this website.
- Center for Media and Public Affairs <http://www.cmpa.com>
  Evaluates the amount and spin of television coverage of the news.
- The Freedom Forum <http://www.freedomforum.org>
  An organization sponsored by the Gannett Foundation that provides information on media issues, particularly as they relate to the First Amendment; links to other Gannett groups, Newseum, and Press Watch, that also contain useful information on coverage of elections.
- Newspaperlinks.com <http://www.newspaperlinks.com>
  Provides links to the online editions of local newspapers across the country.
- Politics Online <http://www.politicsonline.com>
  A good source for presidential campaigning on the Internet.
- Other media sources with campaign websites:
  ABC News Politics <http://abcnews.go.com>
  Associated Press <http://wire.ap.org>
  CBS News <http://www.cbsnews.com>
  CNN All Politics <http://cnn.com/ALLPOLITICS>
  CSPAN <http://www.cspan.org>
  Los Angeles Times <http://latimes.com>
  NBC News <http://www.msnbc.com>
  New York Times <http://www.nytimes.com>
  USA Today <http://www.usatoday.com>
  Washington Post <http://washingtonpost.com>

Selected Readings

Alvarez, Michael R. *Information and Elections.* Ann Arbor: University of Michigan Press, 1997.

Ansolabehere, Stephen, and Shanto Iyengar. *Going Negative: How Political Advertisements Shrink and Polarize the Electorate.* New York: Free Press, 1995.

Clark, Peter, and Susan H. Evans. *Covering Campaigns: Journalism in Congressional Elections.* Stanford, CA: Stanford University Press, 1983.

Davis, Richard, and Diana Owen. *New Media and American Politics*. New York: Oxford University Press, 1998.

Graber, Doris A. *Mass Media and American Politics*. 5th ed. Washington, DC: Congressional Quarterly Books, 1997.

———. *Processing the News*. New York: Longman, 1988.

Iyengar, Shanto. *Is Anyone Responsible?* Chicago: University of Chicago Press, 1991.

Iyengar, Shanto, and Donald Kinder. *News That Matters: Television and American Opinion*. Chicago: University of Chicago Press, 1987.

Jamieson, Kathleen Hall. *Everything You Think You Know About Politics and Why You're Wrong*. New York: Free Press, 2000.

Just, Marion, et al. *Crosstalk: Citizens, Candidates, and the Media in a Presidential Election*. Chicago: University of Chicago Press, 1996.

Kerbal, Matthew R. *If It Bleeds It Leads*. Boulder, Co.: Westview, 2000.

Lichter, S. Robert, Stanley Rothman, and Linda Lichter. *The Media Elite*. Bethesda, MD: Alder and Alder, 1986.

Patterson, Thomas E. *Out of Order*. New York: Knopf, 1993.

Notes

1. Thomas E. Patterson, *Out of Order* (New York: Knopf, 1993), 209.

2. Thomas E. Patterson, *Doing Well and Doing Good: How Soft News and Critical Journalism Are Shrinking the New Audience and Weakening Democracy—And What News Outlets Can Do About It* (Cambridge, MA: Harvard University Press, 2000), 4.

3. Ibid., 4–5.

4. Pew Research Center For The People & the Press, "Internet Election News Audience Seeks Convenience, Familiar Names," December 3, 2000, 1.

5. Ibid.

6. Ibid.

7. The study most often cited is S. Robert Lichter, Stanley Rothman, and Linda Lichter, *The Media Elite* (Bethesda, MD: Adler and Adler, 1986).

8. Republican candidates have traditionally enjoyed the backing of more newspaper editorials on the election than have Democratic candidates. Doris A. Graber, *Mass Media and American Politics*, 5th ed. (Washington, DC: Congressional Quarterly Books, 1997), 250.

9. Pew Research Center For The People & The Press, "The Tough Job of Communicating with Voters," February 5, 2000, 10.

10. Pew Research Center For The People & The Press, "Media Seen as Fair, but Tilting to Gore," October 15, 2000, 12.

11. Pew Research Center For The People & The Press, "The Tough Job of Communicating," 10–11, and "Media Seen as Fair," 1.

12. Why do reporters and correspondents dominate election coverage? From the producers' perspective, interpretive news is more interesting, more focused, more likely to hold an audience, and more likely to present the big picture than are one-sided extended remarks by candidates. From the reporters' perspective, explaining the story makes it more understandable to more people and at the same time contributes to their professional career, to their status, to the salary they can command, to lucrative speaking invitations, to book contracts, and to future opportunities for fame and fortune. From a candidate's perspective, this is very frustrating.

13. "Take This Campaign—Please," *Media Monitor* (September–October 1996): 2; "Campaign 2000 Final," *Media Monitor* (November/December): 2.

14. The use of the talk/entertainment format has several advantages for candidates. They're treated more like celebrities than like politicians. Their hosts tend to be more cordial and less adversarial than news commentators and reporters. Moreover, their audience is different. Those who watch these shows tend to be less oriented toward partisan politics and thus may be more amenable to influence by the candidates who appear on them.

15. Patterson, *Out of Order*, 119–120.

16. Senator Dole was portrayed as a weak candidate, hopelessly trailing the popular incumbent president. Moreover, his low rating in the polls, compared with President Clinton's ratings, was used as a basis for evaluating and assessing the status of his campaign and how his strategy and tactics were not working. The news media repeatedly referred to Dole's struggling campaign and to his attempts to "jump-start" it.

17. Two other narratives are about a "bandwagon" that attracts supporters and allows candidates to build a lead, and about "losing ground." In the first scenario, the image of strong and decisive leadership generates support; in the second, the image of weak and vacillating leadership contributes to erosion. Jimmy Carter's primary spurt in 1976 provides an illustration of the bandwagon; his decline in the general election exemplifies the losing-ground story. Patterson, *Out of Order*, 118–119.

18. Gallup Poll, "Nurses Displace Pharmacists at Top of Expanded Honesty and Ethics Poll," November 16, 1999, <http://www.gallup.com/poll/releases/pr991116.asp>.

19. Negativism has been particularly evident at the presidential level and has been directed against incumbents. In 1980 Jimmy Carter was treated more harshly than Ronald Reagan, and in 1984 Reagan was treated more harshly than Walter Mondale. Vice President George Bush, running for president in 1988, fared poorly as well, but so did his Democratic opponent, Michael Dukakis. Much the same pattern emerged in 1992. S. Robert Lichter and his associates at the Center for Media and Public Affairs found that 69 percent of the evaluations of Bush—his campaign, his positions, his performance, his general desirability—were negative, compared with 63 percent for Clinton and 54 percent for Perot. Bill Clinton did better in 1996, but Robert Dole did not. Only half of Clinton's coverage on the evening news was negative; two out of three comments about Dole were negative.

20. Jorgen Westerstahl and Folke Johansson, "New Ideologies as Molders of Domestic News," *European Journal of Communication* xx (1986): 146–147.

21. In a survey conducted by the Center for Survey Research and Analysis at the University of Connecticut in the spring of 2001, 82 percent of the respondents said that a

free press is necessary to hold the government in check. "American Attitudes About the First Amendment, 2001," p. 4.

22. Surveys conducted in Canada, France, Germany, Italy, Mexico, Spain, and the United Kingdom in 1994 reveal broad support for a free press. Times Mirror Center for the People and the Press, "Mixed Message About Press Freedom on Both Sides of Atlantic," March 16, 1994.

23. Pew Research Center For The People & The Press, "Press 'Unfair, Inaccurate and Pushy': Fewer Favor Media Scrutiny of Political Leaders," March 21, 1997, 1.

24. "Campaign 2000 Typology Survey," conducted August 24–September 10, 2000, for The Pew Research Center For The People & The Press, question 21.

25. Washington Post, Kaiser Family Foundation, and Harvard University Survey Project 1996, "Why Don't Americans Trust the Government?" 10.

26. Ibid.

27. Pew Research Center For The People & The Press, "The Times Mirror News Interest Index: 1989–1995," 7. See also Joan Shorenstein Center on the Press, Politics, and Public Policy, "Young Adults Largely Ignoring Presidential Campaign," December 28, 1999, 1, <http://www.vanishingvoter.org/releases/12-28-99.shtml>.

28. Pew Research Center For The People & The Press, November 16, 2000.

29. Patterson, *Doing Well and Doing Good,* 5–15.

30. Ibid., 7–9.

31. "Campaign Reform: Insights and Evidence," *Report of the Task Force on Campaign Reform,* Woodrow Wilson School of Public and International Affairs, Princeton University, September 1998, 23.

32. Ibid., 21–26.

33. Patterson, *Doing Well and Doing Good,* 15.

34. Ibid., 8.

35. Patterson, *Out of Order,* 207–242.

36. Ibid., 210.

37. A less intrusive format for the press could include a single moderator to start the debate and regulate time allotted the candidates, or a single moderator to serve as a master of ceremonies, who presides over a town meeting where people, not journalists, ask the questions.

38. There are also important procedural questions that could have an major impact on the electorate. When would debates occur? Who would set the dates? Who would be invited? Would candidates have to participate? What would the format be? Which institution would set the rules, choose the moderators, and oversee the debate? Would instant commentary by news media representatives be permitted? Such commentary may color public perceptions, as it did of the second Ford-Carter debate in 1976. That debate concerned foreign policy. Initial public reaction was favorable to President Ford. However, Ford made a misstatement in the debate, leading some to conclude that he was unaware of the Soviet Union's domination of countries in Eastern Europe. The media pointed out Ford's error in its commentary. The president's failure to correct himself for three days, combined with the media's emphasis on his mistake, changed

public perceptions about the debate and its winner, and about Ford's competence in foreign affairs.

39. In the 2000 Democratic nomination process, Vice President Al Gore challenged his rival Bill Bradley to forgo ads and just debate. Bradley refused, claiming that he needed to advertise because he was not as well known as Gore and did not have the vice presidential podium.

40. Alliance for Better Campaigns, "Gouging Democracy: How the Television Industry Profiteered on Campaign 2000," <http://www.bettercampaigns.org/Doldisc/gouging.htm>.

41. Christopher Adasiewicz, Douglas Rivlin, and Jeffrey Stronger, "Free Television for Presidential Candidates: The 1996 Experiment," Annenberg Public Policy Center, University of Pennsylvania, March 1997.

7 The Nomination Process: Whose Is It Anyway?

Did you know that . . .

- party reforms to increase rank-and-file influence over the presidential nomination have essentially shifted power from one party elite to another, from state leaders to ideological activists?
- the goal of improving representation at the national nominating conventions has resulted in the selection of delegates who are demographically more representative but ideologically less representative of mainstream partisans?
- the changes in party rules to open the nomination process to a variety of candidates continue to advantage those who are nationally known and well funded?
- despite the length of the nomination campaign and the extensive coverage of it by local and national news media, voter turnout has remained about one-third that of the general election, or about 15 percent of the voting-age population?
- aspirants to a party's presidential nomination usually take more extreme policy positions in their quest for the nomination than they do in their general election campaign?
- the last time a presidential nominee didn't personally select his running mate was in 1956, when the Democratic convention chose Estes Kefauver over John F. Kennedy?
- television coverage of the national nominating conventions has decreased as the parties' attempts to orchestrate them for television have increased?
- the incumbency advantage is greater in the nomination process than in the general election?

- the increasing front-loading of presidential primaries works to benefit front-running candidates?
- the race for money has become in effect the first primary?

Is this any way to run a democratic election?

N O ASPECT of the electoral process has changed more fundamentally and quickly since the 1970s than the way the major political parties choose their candidates for office. In the past, when party organizations were stronger, the leaders of those organizations controlled the process by which nominees were selected. Although the actual mechanisms varied from state to state, most nominations were controlled by party organizations whose leadership dictated the results.

In exercising that control, the leadership had three goals in mind in addition to its primary objective of winning the election. First, party leaders wanted to reward the faithful who had worked for their candidates in previous elections. Next, they sought to choose experienced people who had worked their way up the ladder of elective office, who understood the rules and practices, and who, above all, were willing to abide by them. And, finally, party leaders wanted to select partisans whose primary loyalty was to the party, its positions, its programs, and especially its leadership.

The merit of such a nomination system was that it fostered and maintained strong party organizations and loyalties. The organizations provided continuity in programs, policies, and personnel. The loyalties gave the party a cadre of workers and voters on whom it could depend.

The main disadvantage of such a system was that it was a top-down rather than a bottom-up system. It was less participatory, less democratic. It kept party bosses, even corrupt ones, in power. It facilitated an old-boys' network. People had to play by the rules in order to get ahead. Rank-and-file partisans had little influence on the nominees and their policy positions.

THE MOVEMENT FROM AN ELITE TO A MORE POPULAR SYSTEM

The Progressive movement at the beginning of the twentieth century was a reaction to the closed and seemingly elitist character of American political parties. Progressives wanted to reform the political system in order to encourage greater public participation in the nomination and election processes. Conducting primary elections in which partisans could select the candidates they preferred for public office was one of their most touted political reforms.

The Progressive movement prospered for almost three decades. From 1900 to 1916, twenty-five states enacted laws to permit or require primary elections.

After World War I, however, low turnout, higher election costs, and unhappy party leaders persuaded state officials to return to the older ways of selecting nominees.

Not until after World War II did democratizing tendencies begin to reemerge, along with a communication technology—television—that could bring candidates into full public view in American living rooms. The rapid expansion of television programming, the purchase of television sets, and people's addiction to this new entertainment/news medium provided incentives for candidates—particularly those who were unable or unwilling to obtain positions of power within the traditional party hierarchy—to take to the airways to gain public support. A new era in democratic political activity was about to begin.

The catalyst behind the shift from a party leadership–dominated nomination system to a more publicly based one was the rule changes that first occurred in the Democratic party after its raucous 1968 presidential nominating convention. At that time, the successful nominee, Vice President Hubert H. Humphrey, won without campaigning in any of the party's primary elections. As a unifying gesture to those who had participated in the primaries and were frustrated by their failure to effect the choice of nominees, the Democratic convention approved the establishment of a commission to review and suggest changes in its presidential nominating procedures.

In making its recommendations, the commission had one primary charge: to make the selection process more open to rank-and-file partisans and in this way more democratic. A set of rules designed to facilitate rank-and-file involvement in the nomination process and greater diversity in the composition of convention delegates was enacted. The rules established selection criteria that state parties had to meet to ensure that their delegates would be certified as official delegates to the national convention. Delegates not chosen in conformity with party rules could be challenged and even prevented from representing their state parties at the convention.[1]

The Democratic party in the 1970s and early 1980s was in a strong position to impose its new rules on the states. As the plurality party, the Democrats controlled about three quarters of the state legislatures, and they were able to convince their elected officials in the states to enact laws that put them in compliance with the new party rules.

The changes affected the Republican selection process as well. Although the GOP didn't initially mandate rule changes for its state parties in the presidential nomination process, as the Democrats did, the new laws enacted by the states were applicable to them as well, forcing or giving their state affiliates the option of conducting primary elections.[2] Most of them did so, not wanting to be seen as opposing popular reforms.[3]

The new system rapidly took hold. Today, all states conduct primaries for nominations. More than half use them exclusively; others employ a combination of primaries, state caucuses, and conventions.[4]

In effect, the parties opened up their nomination process. They decentralized power that had already been decentralized by virtue of the federal system of government. Power flowed to those who participated. The parties hoped that increased participation would broaden their base of support, energize their electorate, increase their representative character, and make them more responsive to the interests of their partisans. It seemed like a win-win situation for the party organization and its partisans. In practice, however, it was not.

THE DEMOCRATIZATION OF NOMINATIONS: REPRESENTATIVE OR UNREPRESENTATIVE?

The Good News

The rules changes have contributed to the democratization of the nomination processes in both parties. By opening up their nomination process, the parties have involved more people in the selection of their nominees. Table 7.1 indicates the number of primaries and voters and the percentage of delegates selected in primaries from 1912 to the present.

A second consequence of more open nominations has been broader representation of the party's electoral coalition at its national conventions. Delegates who attend these conventions are demographically more representative of rank-and-file party voters than they were prior to the rule changes. There are more women, more minorities, and more young people.

A third result, which has also improved the democratic character of the system, has been to tie candidates closer to the desires and interests of their electoral supporters. To gain the nomination, candidates have to take positions on salient issues, and keep them if elected, because their renomination is always open to challenge.

A fourth consequence has been to increase the pool of potential candidates. The number of people vying for their party's nomination at all levels of government has increased, especially when incumbents decide not to run for reelection.[5] The range of challengers is also greater. Anyone with access to the mass media, by virtue of his or her own career or financial base, can mount a campaign and, in some cases, even win. George McGovern, Jimmy Carter, Michael Dukakis, and Bill Clinton wouldn't have been likely presidential nominees under the old system in which state party leaders chose the candidate. Al Gore and George W. Bush might have been, however.

Another more democratic aspect of the new nomination process is that it enlarges the arena of debate by allowing candidates to use the process as a vehicle for promoting their ideas—be they the liberal economic and social programs that Jesse Jackson trumpeted in his quest for the 1984 and 1988 Democratic presidential nomination or the traditional, more conservative Christian values that Pat Robertson (1988), Pat Buchanan (1992 and 2000), and Alan Keyes and

TABLE 7.1 Participation in Presidential Primaries, 1912–2000

Year	Democratic Party			Republican Party			Total	
	No. of primaries	Votes cast	Delegates selected through primaries (%)	No. of primaries	Votes cast	Delegates selected through primaries (%)	Votes cast	Delegates selected through primaries (%)
1912	12	974,775	32.9	13	2,261,240	41.7	3,236,015	37.3
1916	20	1,187,691	53.5	20	1,923,374	58.9	3,111,065	56.2
1920	16	571,671	44.6	20	3,186,248	57.8	3,757,919	51.2
1924	14	763,858	35.5	17	3,525,185	45.3	4,289,043	40.4
1928	16	1,264,220	42.2	15	4,110,288	44.9	5,374,508	43.5
1932	16	2,952,933	40.0	14	2,346,996	37.7	5,299,929	38.8
1936	14	5,181,808	36.5	12	3,319,810	37.5	8,501,618	37.0
1940	13	4,468,631	35.8	13	3,227,875	38.8	7,696,506	37.3
1944	14	1,867,609	36.7	13	2,271,605	38.7	4,139,214	37.7
1948	14	2,151,865	36.3	12	2,653,255	36.0	4,805,120	36.1
1952	16	4,928,006	38.7	13	7,801,413	39.0	12,729,419	38.8
1956	19	5,832,592	42.7	19	5,828,272	44.8	11,660,864	43.7
1960	16	5,686,664	38.3	15	5,537,967	38.6	11,224,631	38.5
1964	16	6,247,435	45.7	16	5,935,339	45.6	12,182,774	45.6
1968	15	7,535,069	40.2	15	4,473,551	38.1	12,008,620	39.1
1972	21	15,993,965	65.3	20	6,188,281	56.8	22,182,246	61.0
1976	27	16,052,652	76.0	26	10,374,125	71.0	26,426,777	73.5
1980	35	18,747,825	71.8	35	12,690,451	76.0	31,438,276	73.7
1984	30	18,009,217	52.4	25	6,575,651	71.0	24,584,868	59.6
1988	37	22,961,936	66.6	37	12,165,115	76.9	35,127,051	70.2
1992	40	20,239,385	66.9	39	12,696,547	83.9	32,935,932	72.7
1996	35	10,947,364	67.0	43	13,991,649	90.0	24,939,013	78.5
2000	40	14,659,481	85.7	43	20,707,157	93.1	35,366,638	89.4

Source: 1912–1992: Michael Nelson, *Congressional Quarterly's Guide to the Presidency,* p. 201; copyright © 1996. Used by permission of CQ Press. 1996–2000: Federal Election Commission.

Gary Bauer (1996 and 2000) advocated when they ran for the Republican presidential nomination. Millionaire Steve Forbes's campaign for the 1996 and 2000 Republican nominations on the promise of a flat income tax and socially conservative policy positions is but another example. Needless to add, in the process of running for the nomination, the candidates also promote themselves, thereby fostering their own political ambitions and satisfying their own psychological needs.

The number of candidates seeking their party's nomination, the range of issues, and the diversity of their public appeals have sensitized the parties to their heterogeneous base. Lauding their diversity, the parties have given economic and social groups within them a chance to be heard, to pursue their interests, and even to put forth candidates who can win the nominations. All of this has put the parties more in touch with themselves. But it has also given those who can effectively mobilize their supporters much more influence. Therein lies the potential for all and the problem for some.

The Bad News

The reforms in the nomination process have also had a number of unintended consequences that aren't nearly as beneficial to the representative character of the political system. The partisans who do participate, though more numerous than in the postprimary period, still aren't reflective of "average" Republicans and Democrats. Even more than voters in the general election, primary voters and caucus participants overrepresent those in higher income and education groups. Older people who have more information, time, and incentive also tend to be more involved than the under-thirty age cohort.

The open system has also given party activists—people who tend to be more issue and ideology oriented than the average partisan and much more so than the average voter—more influence because of their activism, their organizational skills, and the resources available to them. The more extreme the activists' beliefs, the more likely they are to find candidates who do not share their beliefs, which in turn provides these activists with greater motivation to get involved. If activists are successful in winning the nomination for their candidate, they are likely to encourage those with the most strongly held opposing views to get involved as well in their party's primary or in the general election. Ideological zeal begets ideological zeal.[6] The growth of media advertising, specifically issue advocacy, during the nomination phase of the electoral cycle has also contributed to the mobilization of more ideologically driven partisans (for a discussion of issue advocacy in the 2000 election, see Chapter 8, pages 184–186).

The need to mobilize increasingly apathetic partisans has also given groups within the parties, which have and are willing to commit their resources to educating the public and to mobilizing their supporters on behalf of particular candidates, much greater impact on the primary elections. This impact is often reinforced by the lobbying of these groups during and after elections, lobbying that keeps party candidates and elected officials tied to their core supporters. By emphasizing the policy positions that these groups advocate, the candidates have become more issue and ideologically oriented themselves. They believe they have to do so in order to get nominated, elected, and reelected.

We see this trend in the presidential selection process, particularly at the beginning of the nomination quest. Aspirants for the Republican nomination move to the ideological right of their party, Democrats to the ideological left of theirs. Later on, they may find that these early positions alienate mainstream supporters whose perspectives are more moderate and whose policy orientation is less well defined.

We also see this ideological trend in the delegates who are selected to attend the national party conventions. They, too, tend to be more ideological in their thinking and beliefs than do rank-and-file party identifiers.[7] Thus, even though demographic representation at conventions has improved, attitudinal representation hasn't.

What an irony! Here the parties have reformed their nomination processes to better reflect the attitudes, opinions, and candidate choices of their rank-and-file supporters. In doing so, they've adopted rules to tie the eventual selection of nominees more closely to the party's electorate. However, that electorate has been disproportionately influenced by activists who tend to hold (and are probably motivated by) more strongly held and ideologically consistent beliefs than is the typical voter or even the typical partisan voter. Thus, as a consequence of opening the process to achieve better representation, the parties may not represent the moderate, mainstream electorate nearly as well as they did when their leaders picked the nominees. A democratic process has led to undemocratic consequences.

And that isn't all. Not only have the parties' elected officials become less representative of their rank and file, they also seem less capable of governing. Ideologues are not good compromisers.

THE IMPACT OF NOMINATIONS ON GOVERNMENT

Taking more consistent ideological stands is just the first step toward pursuing these policy positions if elected. The growing ideologicalization of American parties has resulted in sharper partisan divisions within Congress and, parenthetically, less civility among its members. The old-boys' club, which operated according to informal folkways and mores, has given way to the new activist politics replete with ideologically laced rhetoric and partisan confrontation, which closed down the government in the winter of 1995–1996 for almost a month, two years later led to a presidential impeachment, and has impeded the enactment of legislation. One of the principal promises that George W. Bush made during the 2000 campaign and claimed to have achieved as president was to end the partisan rhetoric and return civility to Washington politics.[8]

The bitterness of contemporary politics has energized the institutional rivalry that normally exists between president and Congress. The fact that divided government—one party controlling the executive branch and the other controlling one or both houses of Congress—has become the rule, not the exception, exaggerates the divisions within government and thereby prevents one side from imposing its policy agenda on the other. Congressional investigations of the executive branch have increased while legislative output has decreased.

Friction within government has contributed to skepticism about government, how well it is functioning. People are also less trusting of those who represent them than they were two or three decades ago.

Obviously, all of the factors that have contributed to the deterioration of America's political culture and to its governing problems can't be blamed on the nomination process alone. The causes are deep-seated and varied. They've taken place over a longer period of time than have nomination reforms. Moreover, they've been exacerbated by social, technological, and political change. Nonetheless, the democratization of the nomination process has had a discernible impact, which many evaluate as negative.

IMPROVING THE NOMINATION SYSTEM

What can be done about this representational problem and its impact on government? A return to the good old days, when party bosses controlled the selection of party candidates and influenced the policy positions they took, seems both unlikely and undesirable. There would be little public support for making the selection process more elitist and for reducing the input of rank-and-file voters, despite the fact that so many party identifiers don't choose to take part in the nomination process.

Nor would there be support for taking the party's internal politics out of the public arena or limiting media access to it. Some might desire the press to exercise more self-control, particularly when reporting and assessing the personal traits and private behavior of candidates, but there is far from unanimity on this point.

Should Nominations Be Made More Democratic?

If going back to the old system isn't a viable option, then what is? Perhaps the parties could level the playing field by getting a greater cross-section of their partisans to participate. Because activists gain disproportionate influence from their political involvement, getting more people aware, interested, and involved in primaries could lessen this influence. Presumably, if a broader cross-section of the party participated in nomination politics, the candidates would have more incentive to appeal to a wider range of interests and views. But how could more people be encouraged to get involved, particularly given the cynicism and apathy so apparent at the end of the twentieth and beginning of the twenty-first century?

As we noted in Chapter 5, spending more money hasn't resulted in higher proportions of the population voting. The average turnout in primaries remains at only about 15 percent of the voting-age population although in highly competitive, early primaries the turnout tends to be higher.[9] Presumably, candidates seeking their party's nomination are doing all they can to bring out as many of their supporters as possible.

And even if it were possible to motivate more people to participate, there's another danger. Energizing more partisans could polarize the party, making a divisive nomination struggle difficult to overcome in the general election campaign.

From the perspective of party leaders, divisive nominations are a problem. The more divisive the nomination, they believe, the higher the odds against winning the general election, because the nominee's image has been damaged by his or her opponents in the primaries.[10] As a consequence, party leaders would like to reduce the negative effects that bitter internecine warfare produces, not exacerbate them.

Can Divisive Nominations Be Avoided?

Reducing divisive primaries and their impact, however, isn't achieved by leveling the playing field. It's achieved by "unleveling" it even more, by giving advantage to the advantaged—to well-known, well-financed candidates and, frequently, to incumbents. In short, the parties are faced with a situation in which they can encourage more candidates and voters to participate, possibly factionalizing themselves more in the process, or they can discourage participation, possibly making the nominees less representative of those with strong views. But they can't seem to do both.

The Democrats adjusted some of the rules in their presidential nominating process to give their national leaders with national reputations an advantage. They made two adjustments. First, they created the position of unpledged superdelegate, which they bestow on state and national party leaders and elected officials. Theoretically, superdelegates can exercise a dominant influence at a divided convention by voting in favor of the most electable candidate. In practice, however, nominations have been decided well before the conventions, leaving the superdelegates with little to do other than try to enhance their own visibility and image by speaking before live television cameras.

Second, to tighten the nomination schedule to decrease the odds that outside candidates could parlay early caucus and primary victories into a bandwagon for the nomination, the Democrats created a window of time during which caucuses and primaries can be held. It extends from the first Tuesday in March to the second Tuesday in June. Iowa and New Hampshire, states whose tradition and law require them to be the first caucus and primary states, respectively, are given exceptions to hold their contests before the window opens. However, imposing these rules on recalcitrant states that move their nominating selection process earlier than allowed by the official schedule has proved difficult for the Democrats, even though the Supreme Court has held that parties can enforce rules for the selection of delegates at their national nominating conventions.

Although the Republicans haven't imposed a schedule on their state parties, beginning with the 2000 nomination they introduced an incentive system that gives states extra convention delegates if they hold their nomination contest after April 15. But what good is such an incentive if the nominee has effectively been determined *before* a state votes? As a consequence, the incentive has had little appeal, and the front-loading has continued and even accelerated in 2000 with California and New York, along with nine other states, scheduling their primaries on the first Tuesday in March. Many of the southern states hold their contests on the second Tuesday. By the end of the third Tuesday, an estimated 80 percent of the each party's delegates in 2000 were selected.

Front-loading creates inequities. It gives greater influence to states that hold their contests first. To the extent that partisans in these states are not representative of the party's rank and file, their selection can skew the outcome. The winning candidate may not be the first choice of most party voters or even the most acceptable compromise candidate.

Front-loading also moves the campaign forward into the year preceding the election. It lengthens the nomination period but shortens its competitive phase. In 2000, both nominations were settled in six weeks from the first caucus at the end of January through Super Tuesday in early March. From a democratic perspective, perhaps the most serious consequence of having the early caucuses and primaries determine the outcome is that the nomination is decided before most people are paying attention to it. By the time the party's electorate tunes in, many of the candidates may have dropped out. Six of the twelve Republican contenders for the 2000 nomination withdrew before the first state voted.

Finally, front-loading creates a down period of three to four months after a winner has emerged but before the conventions are held. Naturally public interest declines during this period, forcing the parties and candidates to engage in expensive advertising in order to remain in the public spotlight.

Inequitable state representation, reduced rank-and-file participation, and the need to raise more money to keep their preemptive nominee on television encouraged both major parties to reexamine their nomination process and its impact. The Democrats initially decided to stick to their rules that imposed a three-month period during which states could schedule their caucuses or primaries, but revisited the issue at the request of national party chairman, Terry McAuliffe. The Republicans had no such rules. An advisory commission proposed a far-reaching change that would have grouped states according to size and forced them to hold their caucuses and primaries on the same day over a three-month period with the smallest states going first. The large states strongly objected to this plan, and George W. Bush, not wanting to create a divisive issue at the 2000 Republican convention, urged members of the party's rules committee to defeat the proposal, and they did.

In addition to the front-loading effect, there has also been a regionalization of the presidential nomination contests, with states in similar regions of the country agreeing to hold their primaries and caucuses around the same time, often on the same day. This movement, which began in 1988 with a southern regional primary, continued and expanded in each subsequent nomination cycle. The incentive for states in a region to hold their contests on the same day is that they have a better chance of luring candidates into their area to address regional concerns and spend campaign dollars when doing so.

Together, the front-loading and regionalization of the primary process has advantaged candidates with established national reputations—those who are well known, well funded, and well organized. It has disadvantaged those without such reputations and resources, those who need to use the early contests in the small states to establish their credibility, gain national recognition, and build a financial and organizational base. Engaging in multistate campaigning and using extensive media require substantial resources, which front-runners usually have and outsiders usually lack.

Giving advantage to nationally recognized candidates isn't necessarily undesirable or undemocratic. Political experience is normally considered a valuable prerequisite for higher office. However, when national recognition and political experience combine to create unequal campaign resources, then outsiders without these resources are penalized. Even personal wealth won't suffice. Ross Perot and Steve Forbes could buy the recognition they needed in 1992, 1996, and 2000 by spending millions of their own money on advertisements, but they couldn't buy experience or obtain the votes required to win.

Should the Parties Institute a National Primary?

The hodgepodge of primaries, scheduling issues, low turnout, and dissatisfaction with the candidates who have won their party's nomination have led some to recommend a national primary in which both major parties would choose their nominees in a direct popular vote. The simplicity of this suggestion, the promise of bringing out more people to vote, and the expectation that the prospective nominees would have to address national issues like those they would encounter in office have generated support for such a proposal. Gallup polls taken over the last two decades indicate that about two-thirds of the electorate prefer a national primary over the present system.[11]

Although proposals for a national primary vary, most would have the election in the early summer, preceding the national nominating conventions, which would continue to be held. Candidates who could demonstrate their popularity and electability, perhaps by obtaining a certain number of signatures on petitions or receiving a minimum percentage of support in the public opinion polls conducted in the months before the primary, could enter. Anyone who received a majority would automatically be the nominee. In some plans, a plurality would be sufficient, provided it was at least 40 percent. In the event that no one received 40 percent, a runoff election could be held several weeks later between the top two finishers, or the convention could choose the nominee from among the top vote getters.

Obviously, a national primary would be consistent with the democratic principle of one person–one vote. Moreover, the attention that such an election would receive from the press and the candidates should provide greater incentives for a higher voter turnout than currently exists, particularly in states that hold their nomination contests after the apparent winner has emerged. If more people participated, the electorate would probably be more representative than the current electorate that chooses the parties' nominees. And finally, the outcome of the vote should be clear; no longer could the press interpret winners and losers as it saw fit.

The flip side of a national primary, however, is that it would exacerbate the advantages that front-runners already have, particularly Washington-based insiders and large-state governors, people who can raise the money for an expensive and only partially subsidized national campaign. Lesser-known candidates, unless independently wealthy and willing to spend their own fortunes on a presidential nomination race, would have little chance.

Another potential problem is that a national primary could increase divisiveness within the parties, contribute to the personification of politics, and weaken the organizational base of the parties. State leaders would have less influence on the presidential nomination process, and national party leaders might find themselves challenged by the national organization that helped elect the successful candidate. Moreover, a postprimary convention couldn't be expected to tie the nominee to the party, although it might tie the party to the nominee, at least through the general election.

The cumulative impact of a national primary, followed by national party conventions, followed by a national election might be too much campaign and election, more than the electorate was willing or able to absorb. Imagine the same themes and appeals, statements and advertisements, debates and more debates echoing across the land for a period of time lasting six months to a year. Voters might tune out; they might become even more cynical and distrustful of politicians, particularly if such a long national campaign produced a long list of promises that the winning candidate would be expected to fulfill and on which that candidate's presidency would be evaluated. Certainly, governing might prove to be more difficult if party leaders and members of Congress had little to do with the nominees' victory and thus lacked an incentive to follow the new president's lead.

Whether a national primary winner would be the party's strongest candidate is also open to question. With a large field of contenders, those with the most devoted or ideological supporters might do best. Candidates who don't arouse the passions of the die-hards, but who are more acceptable to the party's mainstream, might not do as well. Everybody's second choice might not even finish second unless a system of approval or of cumulative voting were used, each of which is likely to be very complex.[12] These potential negative consequences on the major parties is the reason why they haven't supported such a plan, despite its general public appeal. And if there's little support within the parties for a national primary, then it's very unlikely that Congress would impose it on them.

NATIONAL NOMINATING CONVENTIONS: ANACHRONISM OR STILL RELEVANT?

At the presidential level, the changes in party rules have rendered national nominating conventions obsolete, at least as far as the selection of nominees is concerned. The identity of the likely candidate is known well in advance of the convention, as a result of the presidential primaries. Even the vice presidential selection isn't the convention's to make. By tradition, the nominee chooses a running mate, and the convention ratifies the choice. Why wouldn't it do so when a majority of the delegates are supporters of the presidential nominee?

So what's left for the convention to decide? Sometimes, national nominating conventions debate and resolve platform disputes. Most of the time they don't. They ratify the document, a combination of principles and policies, which a party committee, again most likely controlled by the candidate who has won the primaries and caucuses, has drafted.

If disputes do emerge, they often reveal real and deep-seated differences among rank-and-file partisans, but they come to light primarily because the mass media highlight them. In other words, news coverage is an incentive for the minority to publicize its disagreement, taking its fight to the convention floor even though the prospects for victory appear to be slight. Under the circumstances, what a dissident group gains is national visibility for its position. Even the threat of embarrassing the nominee by taking an oppositional position to the floor may be enough for the leading candidate to concede some platform points in an effort to avoid the appearance of disunity.

Why hold conventions? If the delegates are chosen in accordance with party rules and are unlikely to change the pledges they have made to support particular candidates, if the convention rules are decided in advance, if the successful candidate for the presidential nomination is preordained by the primaries and caucuses, if that candidate can choose a running mate, if the platform is hammered out in advance, then why hold conventions at all? This is a question that the news media are asking with increasing frequency.

From the press's perspective, there's little news. In fact, correspondents and commentators often have to manufacture news by highlighting disagreements, no matter how small; by engaging in seemingly endless and often trivial commentary; and by suggesting potential conflicts, which may or may not come to pass.

Why cover political conventions if they aren't newsworthy? The major networks are doing less and less of it, leaving the proceedings to C-SPAN and continuous coverage to the twenty-four-hour cable news channels.

From the candidates', parties', and interest groups' perspectives, however, the conventions remain an important political tradition that they wish to continue. The assembled delegates constitute an anointing body that legitimizes the nominees' selection and a responsive audience that demonstrates enthusiasm for what their party has to offer. The convention provides a national podium from which the candidates can launch their campaign and from which other leaders can gain recognition.

From the party's perspective, conventions provide a unifying mechanism, one that can help heal the divisions of the nomination process. They're a reward to the delegates for their past participation and an inducement for them to continue to work in the party's political campaigns, particularly the one that is just beginning. And, finally, they are publicity for the party, its positions, its candidates, and its supporters. There's the rub.

The party wishes to present itself in the best possible light: unified, enthusiastic, optimistic, with a clear sense of purpose, direction, and demonstrated governing abilities. Its leaders orchestrate the proceedings so that they will have this desired impact. The news media, in contrast, are interested in news (naturally, as they define it—new, unexpected, dramatic, of human interest). They're also concerned with their public responsibility and their profitability, their bottom line measured in terms of audience, readers, subscribers, and ratings—the number who read, watch, or listen.

The objectives of the party and the news media are often in conflict. Parties need media coverage of their conventions far more than the news media need to report them, particularly if conventions are boring and predictable, as most of them in the last three decades were. Presented with this dilemma, the parties stage their meetings to be as interesting and informative as possible. There are daily themes, scripts, films, celebrities, and politicians—all made available to live cameras and microphones. But the parties' elaborate public relations extravaganzas seem to reinforce the news media's contention that the conventions have become almost all pomp and ceremony, with little or no substance. Broadcast network coverage of the major party conventions, which has declined substantially, may soon be relegated entirely to the cable news and public affairs networks.

Third-party conventions presently receive practically no live coverage on the major broadcast networks. Ross Perot's acceptance speech at his Reform party convention in 1996 and Ralph Nader's at the Green party convention in 2000 were aired only by cable networks, such as CNN and C-SPAN.

If the major networks no longer cover convention proceedings live, then are conventions still necessary? Will they survive? The parties hope so and, in 2000, launched interactive websites to provide information to and gain input from those who accessed the sites. The major networks also provided updated convention news on their web pages. However, the number of "hits" these sites received during this period was substantially less than what they usually receive, suggesting a lower level of interest among the Internet-oriented electorate.[13]

If conventions are abolished then how will parties unify themselves after a divisive nomination struggle? How will they decide on and approve a platform on the critical issues? How will they be able to engage and energize the public, particularly independent voters who tend to be less interested, less informed, and less involved? When will the general election campaign officially begin, or will it be an endless campaign from precandidacy to nomination to election and then to precandidacy again?

Previously in this chapter (and also in Chapter 2), we discussed two other possible nomination scenarios: a regional primary system that seems to be evolving or a national presidential primary that receives support from some proponents of further democratizing the process. Either system would affect the rationale for continuing national nominating conventions. If regional primaries were to be established, by voluntary agreements among states, by national rules mandated by the parties, or by act of Congress, a national nominating convention could still serve as a potential decision maker in the event that the primaries were not decisive. It could act as a body that chose or ratified the vice presidential nominee and as a platform maker for the candidates in the general election. The cheerleader and launchpad functions would also be important for the convention. Similarly, if a national primary were instituted and the leading candidate didn't receive the required percentage of the vote, the convention could then choose the nominee from among the top candidates. It could also serve as the decisive body to approve a platform for the winning candidate.

THE INCUMBENCY ADVANTAGE

For all the hoopla about how open the nomination process has become, incumbents who run for reelection usually win. The deck is stacked even more against challengers in nominations than it is in general elections. Take Congress, for example. Since the end of World War II, 190 House incumbents out of 11,131 were defeated in their quest for renomination (less than 2 percent), and 40 senators lost renomination out of 806 who sought it (5 percent). Table 7.2 indicates incumbency success in renomination for Congress since 1946.

Why do incumbents do so well? The system gives them important built-in benefits. These include greater name recognition, superior fund-raising skills, more campaign experience coupled with access to more experienced campaign aides, frequently a grassroots organization, along with the ability to give help to and get help from other party leaders. These benefits translate into great odds for most incumbents seeking renomination.

The incumbency advantage is enhanced by the absence of competition. For the obvious reason that it is so difficult to defeat them, incumbents face fewer challengers than do candidates who run for open seats (seats for which an incumbent isn't running).

TABLE 7.2 Congressional Incumbents Seeking Renomination, 1946–2000

Year	Senate Total seeking renomination	Number defeated	Percentage defeated	House of Representatives Total seeking renomination	Number defeated	Percentage defeated
1946	30	6	20	398	18	5
1948	25	2	8	400	15	4
1950	32	5	16	400	6	2
1952	31	2	6	389	9	2
1954	32	2	6	407	6	1
1956	29	0	0	411	6	1
1958	28	0	0	396	3	1
1960	29	0	0	405	5	1
1962	35	1	3	402	12	3
1964	33	1	3	397	8	2
1966	32	3	9	411	8	2
1968	28	4	14	409	4	1
1970	31	1	3	401	10	2
1972	27	2	7	393	11	3
1974	27	2	7	391	8	2
1976	25	0	0	384	3	1
1978	25	3	12	382	5	1
1980	29	4	14	398	6	2
1982	30	0	0	393	10	3
1984	29	0	0	411	3	1
1986	28	0	0	394	3	1
1988	27	0	0	409	1	—
1990	32	0	0	406	1	—
1992	28	1	4	368	19	5
1994	26	0	0	387	4	1
1996	21	1*	5	384	2	1
1998	29	0	0	402	1	—
2000	28	0	0	403	3	1

*Sheila Frahm, appointed to fill Robert Dole's term, is counted as an incumbent seat.

Source: Norman J. Ornstein, Thomas E. Mann, and Michael J. Malbin, eds., *Vital Statistics on Congress, 1997–1998*, pp. 61–62; updated by author. Copyright © 1998. Used by permission of CQ Press.

Is the incumbency advantage good or bad? On the positive side, it provides the party with continuity in its candidacies. Because incumbents also have an advantage in the general election, it enables the party to maintain its elective positions, and constituents to keep their representative. The more senior a representative is, the greater is that person's influence within the legislative body likely to be and the more will that representative be able to do for his or her constituents.

On the negative side, however, the incumbent's renomination advantage translates into more independence from the party. There's little a party's leadership can do to a popular incumbent who chooses to deviate from the party's position on the issues.

Summary: Nomination Dilemmas in a Nutshell

In summary, the movement to a nomination process in which more people can easily participate has opened the parties and theoretically expanded their base. From a democratic perspective, that's good. However, in practice, only a portion of the rank and file participate. From a democratic perspective, that's bad. That the participants tend disproportionately to be those with strong ideological orientations and issue positions has contributed to more ideologically oriented parties, which has in turn alienated some of their rank and file and contributed to cynicism in the populace—certainly not a great result for the parties, their partisans, or the electorate as a whole, although as noted in Chapter 4, the major parties are still favorably evaluated by the population as well as by their own partisans.

Various proposals for reforming the nomination process at the presidential level have been advanced, and at least one, regional primaries, seems to be evolving from the present system. The goal of these proposals—democratizing the presidential selection process even more by getting more of the party's rank and file to participate—is laudable. The end result, however, may be to further advantage front-runners (particularly incumbents), to create more division within the parties, and to make the parties more subject to the influence of those who win their nominations rather than the other way around. We're left with a dilemma. Can the parties simultaneously be representative of their diverse base and also provide strong partisan, national leadership?

Now It's Your Turn

Discussion Questions

1. Why did the major political parties reform their nomination processes in the 1970s, and did the reforms achieve their desired goals?
2. From the perspectives of the parties, candidates, and partisan supporters what are the main advantages and disadvantages of the nomination processes today for president and members of Congress?
3. How would you reform the parties' current nomination rules to mitigate the disadvantages to the parties, candidates, and partisan supporters?
4. Does the advantage that incumbents have in renomination undercut a democratic electoral system?
5. What impact, if any, does the process of nomination have on the structure of the parties and their ability to govern if elected?

Topics for Debate

Challenge or defend the following statements:

1. The reforms in the major parties' presidential nominating processes should be reversed.
2. Congress should enact a national primary for selecting the major parties' presidential nominees.
3. Because Iowa and New Hampshire are not representative of the entire country, they should be prevented from holding the first caucus and primary election.
4. The vice presidential candidate of each party should be the candidate with the second most votes for the presidential nomination at the national nominating conventions.
5. Aspirants for their party's presidential nomination should not be allowed to campaign before the year of the election.
6. National nominating conventions are irrelevant and should be abolished.

Exercises

1. You've been asked to head a committee to reform the way your party chooses its nominees. The primary goals that the party wants you to consider when you propose your reforms are, in order of importance, to
   a. select the strongest and most qualified candidate to run in the general election,
   b. give all partisans an opportunity to participate in some way in the nominating process,
   c. increase the likelihood that the views of the winning candidate will reflect the views of the rank and file,
   d. have a nominating process that is open to all well-qualified candidates.
   In your plan, indicate
   a. when and how the nominees for national office will be selected,
   b. the rules for determining who can run and who can vote,
   c. the penalties, if any, that you would impose on recalcitrant state parties,
   d. the method for approving or amending your reforms,
   e. a conclusion explaining how and why your proposed reforms will be an improvement on the present system.
2. Critique the following proposal, submitted by the author to the Democratic and Republican Committees, which were reexamining their presidential nominating processes in 2000.

A Proposal to Reform the Presidential Nomination Process

Introduction

The major parties have lost control of their presidential nomination process. Candidates now compete for the nomination with their own organizations, fundraisers, media handlers, and policy advisors. Other than designing rules for allocating the delegates per state, and in the case of the Democrats, the period during which nomination contests presumably can occur; choosing the time and place of the nominating convention; and trying to work with the successful candidate on scripting the meeting, drafting the platform, and launching the presidential campaign, the national party organization has little formal role in its own process, unless of course, the successful aspirant is out of money after effectively winning the nomination but before the convention, in which case, that candidate will turn to the party for help for generic advertising and other public activities.

Moreover, state legislatures, with relatively little or no concern for the national party, set primary and caucus dates with two primary goals in mind: to maximize their influence on the nomination including on the policy positions of the candidates, and if possible, to benefit from the financial largesse that candidate advertising, media coverage, and other forms of campaign activity provide. The increasing front-loading of the process has resulted in a long and seemingly endless campaign that cannot help but affect the government's policymaking process during the time in which it is conducted, as the impact of Campaign 2000 on relations between Congress and the presidency and within the 106th Congress in its *first* sessions suggests. The longer the process and the greater the front-loading, the more likely that candidates with access to money will be greatly advantaged and that the inequalities within the system among states, voters, and candidates will be a continuing problem and source of discontent.

The states that hold their contests early gain more attention, money, and presumably influence—hence the reason for the front-loading. Turnout declines as a candidate builds what becomes an insurmountable lead. Voters lose interest; they tune out if they had ever tuned in.

The money race is probably the most egregious aspect of the front-loading problem. It overshadows the issues debate as the news media gravitate toward the more entertaining aspect of the nomination process, the "horse race." The amount of money raised or available to a candidate has become the criterion that the press uses prior to the early contests for evaluating who is ahead. As such, it undoubtedly contributes to public cynicism about politicians and "who owns them." Additionally, it produces candidate inequalities that can and probably should discourage quality people from running if they have do not access to the financial base they will need or if they find continuous fundraising unpleasant and a digression from the real business of the campaign.

Moreover, money begets money. Most people do not wish to bankroll a loser, a candidate who has little chance of winning the nomination. Stepping stones to the nomination are all but a historic footnote today.

Finally, the front-loading has created an interim period in which the party is given a Hobson's choice—either raise soft money and use it for generic advertising or do nothing, in which case the likely nominee, who has spent the maximum amount (assuming that candidate accepts federal matching grants), will be in a state of limbo with free media the only option to maintaining a public posture. Robert Dole was in this position in 1996.

What to Do?

The clock cannot be turned back. Primaries and multistaged caucuses cannot be replaced by backroom politics. Nor can the parties impose specific dates or deals on the states. The regional primary proposal advanced by various secretaries of state is a good idea. If it receives state support, I think the party should back it.

I would also favor exceptions for a few states (perhaps Iowa and New Hampshire or others if the early few are to be rotated) to hold their contests earlier. Face-to-face interaction between candidates and voters brings the campaign to the average partisan in a way that mass media advertising, computerized mailings, and professional phone banks cannot.

But the parties need to regain control of *their* process. Here's what I recommend:

1. Hold a two-day convention in the early months of the election year. The purpose of the convention would be to present a set of party principles to which candidates for the nomination would have to agree before they could officially run for the party's nomination. This would not be a detailed platform but a set of basic values and positions to which each aspirant would have to subscribe. The national committee should choose the drafters of these principles. The principles would have to be accepted by the delegates as the first order of business of the convention.

2. The delegates to this convention would be selected by virtue of the positions they hold in government or in the party. All elected party officials at the national level (members of Congress, president and vice president, if applicable), all state governors, big city mayors, and state legislative leaders, plus the members of the national committee, the chair and vice chair of the national party, all state party chairs, and past presidential candidates would make up the delegations.

3. Once the convention accepted the party's principles, the convention would then choose the candidates who could run for the party's presidential nomination in the state caucuses and primaries. Potential candidates would need to obtain the signatures of 10 percent of the delegates to be placed in nomination by a delegate whose speech could not exceed 15 minutes. After the nominations were completed, the convention would then vote on the list of candidates placed in nomination. Any candidate who received a certain percentage of the vote (somewhere between 20 and 25 percent) would be an official nominee of the party, eligible to run in its states' caucuses and primaries.

4. The second day of the convention would be a forum for the nominees. Each of the successful aspirants for the nomination would be invited to address the convention (and the American people via news media coverage) and explain why they want to be president, what they stand for in terms of policy, and what they would do in office.

5. After the nominees made their appeal at the convention, the nomination campaign would begin and would be conducted in much the same manner

as it is today. The national parties could set up their own rules for allocating the vote to the delegates selected, as the Democrats currently do, or leave the rules up to the states, as the Republicans do. Scheduling would still be up to the states, except that no contest could be held until at least one month after the opening convention was completed. The only nominees who could run would be those chosen by the convention, although the party might want to consider a petition process by which a candidate could demonstrate sufficient public support to enter the contest at a later time.

6. Nominees would be expected to remit to the party one quarter of all soft money raised and a smaller percentage of all hard money received from the time they officially declared their candidacy and filed with the FEC. The purpose of such payment would be threefold: to help pay for the costs of the initial convention in which the candidates launched their nomination campaign; to give the party money for the generic advertising it would be expected to air after the nomination had been effectively settled but before the summer nominating convention; to equalize fundraising a little more than the current system does.

7. The party would hold its regular nominating convention during the summer but would compress the meeting into two or three days, during which the platform would be spelled out in accordance with the party's principles, the candidate would be officially designated as the party's presidential nominee, a vice presidential nominee would be chosen, and the acceptance speeches of the party's candidates would launch the presidential campaign.

Internet Resources

- Congressional Quarterly <http://www.cq.com>
  An excellent source of information on strategy and tactics. Publishes a variety of journals on politics and government, including *Campaigns and Elections,* which can be accessed through the general site or directly at <http://www.camelect.com>

- National Journal <http://www.nationaljournal.com>
  Another excellent magazine for studying politics and government, with numerous links to its own and other publications.

- 2000 Election Calendar <http://www.fvap.gov>
  Provides scheduling information on the primaries and general election from the Federal Voting Assistance Program.

- White House 2000 and 2004: The Campaign
  <http://www.niu.edu/newsplace/whitehouse.html>
  Comprehensive site for information about campaigns.

- Yahoo! Full Coverage: Presidential Election 2000
  <http://headlines.yahoo.com/Full_Coverage/US/Presidential_Elections_2000>
  Provides links to news sources, audio, video, magazine articles, and editorials on the ongoing campaigns.

Selected Readings

Atkeson, Lonna Rae. "Divisive Primaries and General Election Outcomes: Another Look at Presidential Campaigns." *American Journal of Political Science* 42 (1998): 256–271.

Bartels, Larry M. *Presidential Primaries and the Dynamics of Public Choice.* Princeton, NJ: Princeton University Press, 1988.

Davis, James W. *National Conventions in an Age of Party Reform.* Westport, CT: Greenwood Press, 1983.

Greer, John G. *Nominating Presidents: An Evaluation of Voters and Primaries.* Westport, CT: Greenwood Press, 1989.

Mayer, William G., ed. *In Pursuit of the White House 2000.* Chatham, NJ: Chatham House, 1999.

Norrander, Barbara. "Ideological Representativeness of Presidential Primary Voters." *American Journal of Political Science* 33 (1989): 570–587.

Polsby, Nelson W. *The Consequences of Party Reform.* New York: Oxford University Press, 1983.

Shafer, Byron E. *Bifurcated Politics: Evolution and Reform in the National Party Convention.* Cambridge, MA: Harvard University Press, 1988.

———. *Quiet Revolution: The Struggle for the Democratic Party and the Shaping of Post Reform Politics.* New York: Russell Sage Foundation, 1983.

Smith, Larry David, and Dan Nimmo. *Cordial Concurrence: Orchestrating National Party Conventions in the Telepolitical Age.* New York: Praeger, 1991.

Task Force on Campaign Reform. *Campaign Reform: Insights and Evidence.* Princeton, NJ: Princeton University Press, 1998.

Notes

1. The Supreme Court gave the parties this power in its 1975 landmark decision in *Cousins* v. *Wigoda* (419 U.S. 477). The Court held that political parties were private organizations with rights of association protected by the Constitution. They could compel state affiliates to abide by their rules of delegate selection for the national nominating convention unless there were compelling constitutional reasons for not doing so. The burden of proving these reasons was placed on the state that deviated from the party's rules.

 Although in theory the party has the power to enforce its national rules, in practice it is usually difficult to do so. State parties are subject to the election laws of the state. For the state party to conduct its own primary would be very difficult and costly.

2. Although the Republicans profess the same broad goals, they mandated only one national rule for their state parties: that they not discriminate in the selection of delegates on the basis of race, creed, color, national origin, or gender. In other aspects of delegate selection, the GOP enforces whatever rules its state party observes.

3. The principal difference is that the Republicans permit winner-take-all voting on a district or statewide basis, and the Democrats do not.

4. Paul Allen Beck and Frank J. Sorauf, *Party Politics in America,* 7th ed. (New York: HarperCollins, 1992), 234–235.

5. There are more challengers in a nomination contest to run against an incumbent of the opposition party in the general election than there are in the incumbent's party when that incumbent is seeking renomination. The more open system, however, keeps incumbents more attuned to their constituents' interests and needs, in part because of the threat of a challenger.

6. David C. King, "The Polarization of American Political Parties and Mistrust of Government," in *Why Americans Mistrust Government,* ed. Joseph S. Nye, Philip Zelikow, and David C. King (Cambridge, MA: Harvard University Press, 1997), 155–178, and David C. King, "Party Competition, Primaries, and Representation in the U.S. Congress," paper presented at MIT Conference on Parties and Congress, October 2, 1999.

7. This phenomenon was first identified by Herbert McCloskey, "Consensus and Ideology in American Politics," *American Political Science Review* 58 (1964), 361–82, and Jeane S. Kirkpatrick, *The New Presidential Elite* (New York: Russell Sage, 1976), and appears in the surveys of delegates since then. For a summary of these surveys see Stephen J. Wayne, *The Road to the White House 2000,* Postelection edition (New York: Bedford/St. Martins, 2001), 115.

8. Frank Bruni, "At 6 Months, Bush Says, He's Doing Well," *New York Times,* August 4, 2001, A10.

9. In states in which there were both Republican and Democratic primaries, turnout averaged almost 18 percent according to an analysis by the Committee for the Study of the American Electorate. Steven A. Holmes, "Many Stayed at Home," *New York Times,* September 1, 2000, A18.

10. Divisive primaries, however, if they encourage turnout can have the beneficial effect of mobilizing the party's electorate for the general election and subsequent contests. See Walter J. Stone, Lonna Rae Atkeson, and Ronald B. Rapoport, "Turning On or Turning Off? Mobilization and Demobilization Effects of Participation in Presidential Nomination Campaigns," *American Journal of Political Science* 36 (August 1992): 665–691.

11. Gallup Poll, "Electoral Reforms," April 10, 1988, as reported in *The Gallup Poll: Public Opinion 1988* (Wilmington, DE: Scholarly Resources, 1989), 60–61.

12. Approval voting allows the electorate to vote to approve or disapprove each candidate who is running. The candidate with the most approval votes is elected. In a system of cumulative voting, candidates are rank-ordered, and the ranks may be averaged to determine the winner.

13. PC Date Online, a firm that monitors traffic on news sites, reported a 14 percent drop in the number of people who accessed these sites during the 2000 political conventions. Howard Kurtz, "Web Coverage Does Not Spark Convention Interest," *Washington Post,* August 14, 2001, C1.

8

Campaign Communications: How Much Do They Matter?

Did you know that . . .

- the Republican stereotype of Democrats as big-government, liberal do-gooders and the Democratic stereotype of Republicans as big-business, mean-spirited conservatives have existed for more than fifty years?
- most people believe that personality issues are relevant and important, even though they also believe that too much emphasis is placed on them?
- political advertising in presidential elections began in 1952, and the first negative presidential ad was run in 1964?
- political consultants believe that they perform an essential role in the democratic electoral process? Over 80 percent of them find attack or negative advertising perfectly acceptable.
- a majority of people (58 percent) but only a very small percentage of journalists believe that criticism of public officials in the news media keeps officials from doing their job.
- political advertisers spent five times more on broadcast ads on television in 2000 than they did in 1980, even after adjusting for inflation?
- despite a law that requires television stations to charge candidates their lowest available rate, most candidates paid much more and their rates increased over the course of the campaign?
- political parties outspent their own presidential candidates in advertising designed to benefit their presidential campaign?
- about half of the almost one billion dollars spent on political advertising in 2000 was devoted to issue advocacy?

Is this any way to run a democratic election?

C AMPAIGNS MATTER! They determine who wins. They highlight the principal issues with which the public is concerned and that newly elected officials must address. They influence the electorate: who votes, for whom, and why. They test the major components of a democratic political system: free speech, public participation, group advocacy, meaningful choice, and ultimately, responsive and accountable government. Although political campaigns aren't the only factor that determines the election outcome, the salient issues, the information the electorate has at its disposal, voter turnout and behavior, and responsive government, they are a principal one. That's why they're so important.

However, campaigns can and do fall short of achieving their democratic goals. Instead of clarifying the issues for much of the voting public, they often obscure them; instead of turning out voters, they can turn them off; and instead of providing a realistic agenda for the new government, they frequently create unrealistic public expectations that newly elected officials may not be able to meet. And, as we've previously argued, they can also be a vehicle by which the advantaged, those with superior resources in the form of money, organization, and leadership, maintain or expand their political influence. In short, campaigns can strengthen or weaken the democratic system, depending on how they're conducted and what impact they have.

In this chapter we focus on campaign communications, on how well they inform and motivate voters. We begin by discussing the kinds of information that should be most helpful to the electorate in making an informed voting decision. Then we turn to the type of information that candidates usually convey in their basic appeals and to their modes of communication, which can intentionally or unintentionally distort the message the electorate receives. Finally, we look at the impact of campaigning and suggest ways in which communications between candidates and the voting public could be improved.

WHY CAMPAIGNS ARE NECESSARY: THE NEED TO BE INFORMED

Campaigning is obviously an integral part of the electoral process. Candidates need campaigns to accomplish their principal objective: winning elective office. They need them to learn about public concerns and to convince voters of the merits of their candidacy. The electorate needs campaigns for the same reasons: to voice their concerns, espouse their interests, and gain the information necessary to decide which of the candidates (and parties) are more likely to meet their needs and those of the country in the years ahead.

What does the electorate need to know? At the very least, voters need to be able to identify the candidates, make a judgment about what they will try to do if elected, and figure out how successful they're likely to be in comparison to the others who are running. The promises candidates make, the positions they take, and the priorities they enunciate should be a reasonable guide to their performance in office. If they aren't, then voters can hold incumbents and, to a lesser extent, their party accountable in the next election. If they are, then voters can evaluate the performance of public officials who seek reelection on the basis of how their policies worked and what the consequences were for society.

Knowing what candidates say, however, is only part of the information needed to make an intelligent voting decision. People also need to know facts about the candidates themselves: their experience, their qualifications, and their personal strengths and weaknesses. This is where character comes in.

Elected officials may not be in a position to fulfill their promises even if they try to do so. New issues may arise; unexpected events can and probably will occur; the economic, social, and political environment may change. Thus it's important to anticipate how candidates will adapt to change. Character provides an insight into work style, adaptability, and the capacity to handle new challenges.[1]

In addition to knowing about the candidates, their philosophy, policy positions, and character, the electorate also needs to know whether the candidates stand a good, fair, or poor chance of being elected. It would be nice to vote for a person who thinks as we do and in whom we have confidence, but it might also prove to be meaningless if that individual has little or no chance of winning. An intelligent voting decision may also include the component of not wasting your vote.[2] For the vast majority of people, voting for someone with little or no chance to win isn't a smart vote unless such a vote is intended to defeat one of the major candidates or simply to be a protest vote.

THE INFORMATION GAME: FINDING THE RIGHT BALANCE

The Policy Perspective: Generalities Versus Details

Given the importance of information to make an informed voting decision, how much detail should candidates provide? Should they present only a general map of the policy directions they hope to pursue, or should they fill in the specifics?

If the amount of information that people have or are interested in knowing is any indication, candidates should be more general than specific. They should talk about their philosophies, their basic goals, and their priorities. But being too general can also be a disadvantage if a candidate is perceived as being purposely vague or simply unknowledgeable about the issues. Take Republican Thomas E. Dewey in the 1948 presidential election, for example. With a large lead in the polls, not wanting to alienate a Democratic electorate, Dewey spoke in platitudes and generalities that seemed empty and directionless when compared to President Harry S Truman's straight talk, specific promises, and Democratic imagery. Truman sufficiently energized the faithful by the time of the election to win a surprising victory. The same criticism of being vague and talking in generalities was directed at George W. Bush by his Republican opponents at the beginning of the 2000 nomination campaign and subsequently by his Democratic rival. Bush used policy-oriented speeches and debate answers to counter this criticism, obviously to the satisfaction of many voters.

Being too specific, however, can turn off voters who don't understand or care about the details and alienate those who disagree with them. It can also put the candidate and, if successful, the elected official in a position from which compromise on public policy is made more difficult—not a desirable outcome (except perhaps to true believers) in a political system that divides power and requires compromise most of the time.

The Republicans' Contract with America, the platform on which House Republicans ran in 1994, is a case in point. The contract listed ten proposals that Republican candidates pledged to support if elected. The congressional party's refusal to compromise on these issues, particularly those that pertained to tax cuts and domestic spending, was a principal cause of the government shutdown in the winter of 1995–1996, a shutdown that reverberated to the Republicans' political detriment. Bill Clinton's promise to end discrimination against gays in the military is yet another illustration of a specific policy proposal that got the newly elected president into trouble at the very beginning of his administration.

The issue of generality versus specificity often puts candidates in a "damned if you do, damned if you don't" position. To win their party's nomination and build their electoral coalitions, they need to make specific promises to specific groups. The members of these groups are frequently the most ideologically oriented party identifiers. Then, in the general election, candidates usually have to broaden their appeal, moving toward the center of the political spectrum in order to attract others—independents, partisans of other parties, even those who are apolitical and whose needs and desires are quite diverse. It's a tough juggling act, made even tougher by the fact that it has to be pulled off in full public view. Promises will be recorded by the news media; inconsistencies will be highlighted; contrasting emphases will be noted by "gotcha" journalists.

From the perspective of the electorate, needs and desires for information vary. Within their own areas of interest and expertise, people demand and digest much more information than they do in most other areas, in which they have less knowledge and interest. Business executives, for instance, may want detailed information on tax policy, investment incentives, and labor-management issues. But they may be much less interested in policy with no discernible professional impact on them—say, a program to put 100,000 more teachers into classrooms or one that extends health insurance coverage to minors from low-income families. In contrast, homemakers with young children are probably more interested in these educational and social benefits and less interested in tax and management issues.

But even if the public weren't all that interested in policy, there's still reason to demand that candidates discuss their proposals in some detail. Such a discussion tells the electorate a lot about the candidates themselves: their intellectual competence and understanding, their consistency and logic, their communication skills, and, to some extent, their candor. These attributes have become increasingly important in candidate-centered elections. Here are two examples. In his 1972 presidential campaign, George McGovern proposed a $1,000 grant to all poor Americans, those whose income was below $12,000. But McGovern's inability to tell how much his plan would cost the taxpayers led many to question his understanding of these matters, much less the viability of his specific proposal. In 2000, after George W. Bush was unable to correctly identify the leaders of four countries whose conflicts put them in the news, he then had to demonstrate his understanding of foreign affairs to overcome the perception that he lacked the experience, knowledge, and skills to be an effective foreign policy leader—a qualification for the modern presidency. The promises candidates make, the answers they give, and the arguments they use to support their positions indicate their potential for making good policy judgments, for governing successfully.

The Character Issue: Public Versus Private Behavior

In recent elections, character issues have received much more attention, in some cases even dominating election coverage. In the 1996 presidential election, for example, only two policy issues, the economy and taxation, were mentioned on the major networks' evening news more than was Clinton's character.[3] In the 2000 presidential election, Gore's penchant for exaggeration and Bush's admitted drinking problem as a young man also raised important character questions with which both campaigns had to deal.

Electing the right people and having confidence in them is nothing new. What's different today is the emphasis on personal behavior outside the public arena. In the past such information was considered private and irrelevant and hence wasn't reported as news.

Are character and personal behavior legitimate issues? Most observers think that they are. They can point to numerous contemporary examples in which character affected performance. Richard Nixon's cover-up of the Watergate break-in and his disregard for the civil rights of others, Ronald Reagan's penchant for delegation and unwillingness or inability to closely supervise his aides, Jimmy Carter's reluctance to deal with the Washington political establishment or even to call members of Congress to ask them to vote for his programs, and Bill Clinton's lack of integrity and candor about his Arkansas political dealings and sexual improprieties were all character-based problems that adversely affected these presidents' performance in office.

Assessing candidates' character is important for several reasons. It provides an indication of how they may react to unforeseen events and situations, how flexible they are, how they make decisions, how they interact with their aides, and to whom they will turn for advice. It tells the electorate something about their work style, energy, confidence, empathy, honesty, candor, strength, and leadership skills.[4]

Overemphasizing character, however, can be harmful. It draws attention away from policy issues. It leads people to make inferences about behavior that may have little or nothing to do with job performance. It attributes too much influence to personality as a driving force and not enough to other factors that can affect what candidates say and do—from the information they have, to the goals they wish to attain, to the procedures and precedents they're expected to follow in office. It has also encouraged flippant, often superficial judgments by those not trained in psychological analysis and even by those who are.[5]

A preoccupation with personality can also lead to unrealistic expectations, both good and bad, of what a single person can do in a political system designed to prevent dominance by an individual or group, a system that decentralizes power and responsibility. Liberals feared that Ronald Reagan's strong anticommunist views and shoot-from-the-hip speaking style could plunge the country into war with the Soviet Union. Conservatives feared that Bill Clinton's penchant to please, combined with his promises to end discrimination against homosexuals in the military, support affirmative action, provide a comprehensive health care program with universal coverage for all Americans, and stimulate the economy with more federal spending, would result in an even bigger, more intrusive national government. Neither of these fears was realized, in part because institutional and political checks within the system prevented these presidents from dominating the government so as to impose their policy preferences on others.

Spin: Positivity Versus Negativity

Candidates obviously need to make their own cases. They have to provide reasons for voting *for* them and *against* their opponents. To do so, they must state their positions and qualifications and somehow get their opponents' negatives onto the public record. They may do so by leaking them to the news media, mentioning them in their own campaign advertising, or referring to them in speeches, press conferences, and debates.

The electorate needs to know some of this information. People have to evaluate the strengths and shortcomings of candidates in order to make an informed judgment about their suitability for the job. And, as we know, the candidates themselves aren't the best source of information about their own shortcomings. Most campaigns maintain an active opposition research operation on the belief that, if they don't find the dirt on their opponent, no one may. They also justify this research on the grounds that their opponents are engaging in it, as well as the public's need to know.

But how much negativism is desirable? Too much can lead to public cynicism about all the candidates. It can lead to a perception that the voting choice is about the lesser of two (or more) evils. Too much negativism can also have a boomerang effect on those who resort to it too heavily. Steve Forbes and Robert Dole both saw their poll numbers decline in 1996 as they began to air negative ads against their opponents. Finding the right balance, which appropriately trumpets one's own strengths and one's opponent's weaknesses, is a proper campaign objective. An avalanche of criticism focusing on negative personality traits is not, nor does that criticism always or usually work to the advantage of the campaign that uses it.

CAMPAIGN IMAGERY

Partisan Stereotyping

Campaign appeals can distort or clarify. In articulating their messages, candidates usually use partisan imagery. They do so to rouse the faithful, their core supporters. They also do so to stereotype negatively their opponent, particularly when they can find no other policy or character issues that resonate with the electorate.

Sounding a partisan refrain conjures up familiar images about the parties past and present, images that are both positive and negative. For Democratic candidates, the positive images are economic; they stem from the roots of the Roosevelt realignment. This is why Democratic candidates tend to emphasize bread-and-butter economic issues, such as jobs, wages, education, and social benefits for the working and middle classes, when they campaign for office. They contrast their empathy for the plight of the average American with Republicans' ties to the rich and their indifference, even hostility, toward the less fortunate.

From the Republicans' perspective, however, the economic images are very different. Republicans see themselves as defenders of the free enterprise capitalist system against their Democratic opponents, "tax and spend" liberals who favor big government and its "giveaway" programs that perpetuate dependency.

Social images are more complex. Democrats stress equal opportunity, whereas Republicans point to individual initiative. In the national security area, the stereotypes are less distinctive, although Republicans have been associated with a procapitalist ideology, a strong defense posture, and a Eurocentric orientation combined with a suspicion about becoming too involved in international organizations, whereas the Democrats have been linked to internationalism, aid to developing nations, and the promotion of human rights and democratic elections.

Partisan stereotyping can be dangerous and misleading because it puts everyone in the same boxes. All Democrats become liberal do-gooders and all Republicans, wealthy, law-and-order, mean-spirited conservatives. Such images cloud significant differences among candidates of both parties.

Stereotyping is also used to explain current positions and past actions. In 1988 partisan opponents presented Democratic presidential candidate Michael Dukakis as a knee-jerk liberal who released hardened criminals from jail. To support this accusation, a group opposing Dukakis aired a commercial about a Massachusetts prisoner, Willie Horton, who committed rape and murder while on parole. The Bush campaign then reinforced the distinction between Bush's tough approach to crime and Dukakis's leniency.[6]

To offset being stereotyped as a liberal in 1992, Bill Clinton called himself a "New Democrat" and took pains to differentiate his moderate policy orientation from the more liberal views of his Democratic predecessors and some of his competitors. In 1996 Clinton was highly successful in placing his opponent, Robert Dole, beside House Speaker Newt Gingrich, the philosopher of right-wing, extreme Republican politics. In 2000 George W. Bush tried to soften the image of Republicans as uncaring by pointing out that his conservatism was compassionate, while Al Gore reenforced the Democrats' popularist image and their propensity to using government as a vehicle for redistributing wealth from the rich to the poor.

Partisan stereotyping can get in the way of meaningful debate. It can cloud the issues; it often substitutes for a lack of information; and it can unfairly typecast individuals in a manner that doesn't accurately reflect their values, priorities, positions, or what they would do if elected to office.

Experience and Incumbency

Experience is the best teacher—at least that's what incumbents would like voters to believe. Incumbents use their office imagery to compare their qualifications with those of their opponents, reminding voters about what they've done for them and how they can use their influence to work on their constituents' behalf.

As we noted in Chapter 7, being an incumbent is usually a great advantage, almost as great in the general elections as in the nominations. What incumbency imagery does is to reinforce and extend the advantages that incumbents already have in running for reelection. The numbers speak for themselves. Table 8.1 notes reelection rates for members of Congress since 1946.

Although incumbent presidents haven't fared as well in reelections because they're subjected to closer and more critical press scrutiny, they've still won more than they've lost. Of the eighteen presidents who sought reelection in the twentieth century, only five (Taft in 1912, Hoover in 1932, Ford in 1976, Carter in 1980, and Bush in 1992) were defeated. It should also be noted that several avoided possible defeat by choosing not to run again.

Why are incumbents so advantaged? A lot has to do with their name recognition and the relatively low level of public knowledge about those who seek political office. Name recognition conveys a "known" quality. In general, people would rather vote for someone they've heard of than for someone about whom they know little or nothing. Incumbents tend to be disadvantaged in only two types of situations: when bad times or multiple grievances hurt those in power and when incumbents say or do something that their constituents find very objectionable. Although Al Gore blamed Clinton's personal behavior for his defeat, Clinton remained popular, with high approval ratings, throughout the 2000 election campaign.[7]

The purposive drawing of legislative districts within the states to create as many safe seats as possible for the party in power has also contributed to incumbency success in the House of Representatives. States as a whole, however,

TABLE 8.1 Congressional Reelection Rates, 1946–2000

Year	House of Representatives			Senate		
	Total seeking reelection who were renominated	Defeated in general election	Percentage reelected	Total seeking reelection who were renominated	Defeated in general election	Percentage reelected
1946	370	52	88.6	24	7	70.1
1948	385	68	82.3	23	8	65.2
1950	394	32	91.9	27	5	81.5
1952	380	26	93.2	29	9	69.0
1954	401	22	94.5	30	6	80.0
1956	405	16	96.0	29	4	86.2
1958	393	37	90.6	28	10	64.3
1960	400	25	93.8	29	1	96.6
1962	390	22	94.4	34	5	85.3
1964	389	45	88.4	32	4	87.5
1966	403	41	89.8	29	1	96.6
1968	405	9	97.8	24	4	83.3
1970	391	12	96.9	30	6	80.0
1972	382	13	95.5	25	5	80.0
1974	383	40	89.6	25	2	92.0
1976	381	13	96.6	25	9	64.0
1978	377	19	95.0	22	7	68.2
1980	392	31	92.1	25	9	64.0
1982	383	29	92.4	30	2	93.3
1984	408	16	96.1	29	3	89.7
1986	391	6	98.5	28	7	75.0
1988	408	6	98.5	27	4	85.2
1990	405	15	96.3	32	1	96.9
1992	349	24	93.1	27	4	85.2
1994	383	34	91.2	26	2	92.3
1996	382	21	94.5	20	1	95.0
1998	400	6	98.5	29	3	89.7
2000	400	7	98.3	28	6	78.6

Source: Basic data from Norman J. Ornstein, Thomas E. Mann, and Michael J. Malbin, eds., *Vital Statistics on Congress, 1997–1998*, pp. 61–62; copyright © 1998. Used by permission of CQ Press. Updated by author; percentages determined by author.

tend to be more competitive, hence the lower reelection rates for Senate incumbents. Moreover, Senate races tend to attract stronger candidates than House races do, candidates who are better known and better funded. According to political scientist Gary C. Jacobson, these factors help explain why Senate incumbents have been three times more likely to lose than their House counterparts.[8]

The incumbency advantage "unlevels" the playing field. It puts the burden on challengers to make the case for change. Unless they do so, they're unlikely to win. To defeat an incumbent requires resources. But, as we've noted, unless challengers are independently wealthy or have considerable backing from their party or wealthy contributors, they're usually unable to raise as much as their incumbent opponents. This is why those who desire elective office will try to wait until a seat is open before seeking it, unless they calculate that the recognition they gain by running against an incumbent (and losing) will put them in real contention the next time around.

COMMUNICATION DISTORTIONS

Accentuating the Positive

Political advertising has become part and parcel of contemporary electoral campaigns. And the ads are a big part of the distortion problem, in part because they're so effective. Candidates and their political consultants believe they need to advertise to reach voters. And they may be right. If political parties aren't as strong a link to the electorate as they once were, if the public is less interested, informed, and involved in electoral politics than in the past, if the broadcast networks carry less television news and if they give little free time to the candidates, if people spend more time tuned into mass media entertainment programming, then advertising in the mass media would seem to be an appropriate response.

Candidates for national office spend the bulk of their money on political advertising. At the presidential level, about two-thirds of the public funds given to the principal nominees go into media spots, campaign biographies, and speeches or town meetings sponsored by the candidates' organizations. For members of Congress, the proportions and media may vary, but the need for and use of political advertising doesn't. And that's not all.

The political parties have used their increasing amounts of soft money to engage in candidate-centered issue advocacy. In fact, in the 2000 presidential election, the major parties for the first time actually spent more on television advertising ($79.9 million) than did the candidates themselves ($67.1 million). Most of these expenditures came from their soft money accounts.[9]

Nonparty groups have also gotten into issue advocacy during election campaigns in a big way. They do so to advance their policy agenda, build their contribution base, enlarge their membership, demonstrate their political muscle, educate the public, and elect candidates who will promote and support their cause. And they spend millions of dollars in the process.

The Annenberg Center for Public Policy at the University of Pennsylvania researched the amount and cost of issue advocacy advertising in the seventy-five principal media markets during the 2000 election campaign. Researchers calculated that 339,000 issue advocacy political ads were aired in these markets from March 8 to November 7, 2000, at a cost of $509 million. About two-thirds of this amount was spent by the political parties using their soft money accounts. Nonparty groups accounted for the rest, with the bulk of expenditures coming from nine groups. Of those, Citizens for Better Medicare, sponsored and funded by the large pharmaceutical companies, spent the most ($25.4 million), followed by the AFL-CIO ($9.5 million).[10]

The Annenberg study also found that most of the issue advocacy was candidate centered—that is, the ads evaluated the candidates on the basis of their orientation toward the issues the groups were advocating. The report states, "[I]n the last two months of the campaign, almost all (94%) of the TV issue ads airing in the top 75 media markets made the case for or against a candidate."[11] Naturally, candidates whose positions had been criticized felt compelled to respond with ads of their own. Their responses increased the amount of political advertising and inflated its costs.[12] Since television stations can air only a limited number of ads and also have to meet the needs of their commercial sponsors, demand exceeded supply in the markets in which the election contests were most competitive. Candidates with the deepest war chests were advantaged, thereby further exacerbating the equity issue posed by unequal financial resources.

Total expenditures for political advertising on television in 2000 were between $771 million and $1 billion according to a joint study by the Alliance for Better Campaigns, a public interest group specializing in media, and the Norman Lear Center at the University of Southern California.[13] Approximately 1.2 million ads were aired, primarily on local stations. But the major networks still profited from the ads—they made about $234 million—because most of the local stations were affiliated with one of them.[14]

If the candidates had unlimited or equal amounts of money, if the parties and nonparty groups apportioned their expenditures equitably among the candidates running for office, if voters could distinguish between express advocacy, in which a vote for a specific candidate is recommended and issue advocacy, in which candidates and their policy positions are discussed but no recommendation to vote for a candidate is made, if voters could even tell the difference between ads paid for by the candidates and those paid for by party and nonparty groups, the rise in issue advocacy advertising would not pose such a problem for a democratic electoral process. But alas, these conditions and distinctions are not applicable in most elections.[15] They certainly were not in 2000.

Moreover, ads are not systematically evaluated by a neutral party for their truthfulness; people are often unaware of the sponsors of the ads and their political orientation, and candidates tend to pay premium rates. As a consequence, the growth of issue advocacy has distorted campaign communications.

Other factors contribute to the enhanced effect of political advertising on the electorate: the decreasing amount of election news coverage by the major broadcast networks, the availability of twenty-four-hour entertainment programming on cable and satellite television systems, and, especially, the inattention and distinterest in politics, campaigns, and elections within a large and growing proportion of the population. The size of the country, the limited number of pubic events attended by the candidates, the difficulty of actually seeing or meeting candidates in person (except for those in the early primary and caucus states), and the media orientation of contemporary campaigning have made the public more rather than less dependent on television for news about the election.

Because television remains the principal source of news for most Americans, political advertising provides much of the information people obtain and recall about the candidates and the issues. Although the public does not admit to being influenced by political commercials, studies by political scientists, beginning in the 1970s, indicate that people actually retain more information from the ads they see than from the news they watch. Why is this so? Ads are repeated frequently, whereas news stories aren't, except on the twenty-four-hour-news stations. Ads are dramatic; news reports may not be. Most advertising scripts have been pretested to find out the most effective words and pictures for getting a particular message across to a particular group. And ads target their audience more than broadcast journalists can. Most ads are straightforward, with little subtlety; the point is hammered home. The impact of advertising is often reinforced because the advertising directs attention to items that may already be in the news. And the ads themselves can *become* news if they're controversial enough, thereby repeating and reinforcing the message they present.

Studies have shown that people actually obtain and recall more substantive information about the candidates and their policy stands from advertisements than they do from news reports.[16] However, and not surprisingly, the public doesn't admit to finding political advertising helpful in making voting decisions.[17]

All advertising is obviously not beneficial to a democratic electoral process. Ads often make their point by exaggeration and inference. Many tread lightly on the truth. In a study of the accuracy of political advertising aired during the 1996 presidential election, Kathleen Hall Jamieson and her colleagues at the Annenberg Center for Public Policy found misleading statements or inferences in *half* of the political commercials they examined.[18]

Ads have become very controversial, in part because they're so slick and one-sided, in part because they may be deceptive and inaccurate. Moreover, advertising is thought to have contributed to people's negative feelings about politicians and politics.[19]

Excessive Negativity

One criticism of contemporary campaign commercials is that they've become increasingly personalized and negative. The conventional wisdom is that negative advertising is increasing with each election, that voters do not like it, but that it works.

Analysis of the political advertisements in the 2000 election campaign lends support to the proposition that the negative content of the ads remains very high. The Annenberg study of issue advocacy ads in 2000 found that "almost all the televised party ads after Super Tuesday, which were two-thirds of all the total number of issue ads shown, . . . mentioned a candidate and had an attack component."[20] In the last two months of the campaign, 84 percent of the televised ads for the campaign contained an attack. Parties attacked more than nonparty groups. Almost all the party ads on television criticized the opposition candidate.[21] Nor were the commercials designed by the candidates far behind. Darrell West found that 91 percent of Bush's prominent ads and 100 percent of Gore's had a negative component.[22] He also reported that 60 percent of the outside group ads during the fall campaign were negative in tone.[23]

What was different in 2000 was the tone of these ads. To avoid the perception of excessive negativity and an unfavorable public reaction to it, particularly during the nomination period, the candidates muted their critical commentary. However, as the contest heated up, during both the primaries and the general election, the advertising did as well. Nonetheless, from the public perspective, campaign 2000 was not as negative as previous presidential elections (see Table 8.2). Whether this public reaction was a consequence of more subtle advertising, less sensitivity to advertising, or more satisfaction with the candidates is unclear.

From the perspective of media consultants—the people who design, market, and profit from the ads—there are more negative ads because they are so effective. Political consultants generally subscribe to the belief that the more negatives a candidate has, the less likely that candidate is to win.[24]

Negative advertising can have a boomerang effect, however. Bush campaign officials were reluctant to use negative advertising early in the 1992 campaign because they feared a "there you go again" response from the press and public after Bush's successful negative advertising campaign four years earlier. And they were right; voters were more leery of the negative ads in 1992.[25] When Robert Dole raised character issues about Clinton in his 1996 election advertising,

TABLE 8.2 Public Perceptions of Negativity in Presidential Elections

Question: Compared to past presidential elections, would you say there was MORE mudslinging or negative campaigning in this campaign or LESS mudslinging or negative campaigning in this campaign?

	1992	1996	2000
More	69	49	34
Less	16	36	46
Same (volunteered response)	14	12	16
Don't Know/Refused	2	3	4

Source: Pew Research Center For The People & The Press, "Campaign 2000 Highly Rated," November 16, 2000, 17.

Dole's poll ratings actually declined. The public reacted negatively to his negativism. However, President Clinton's negative ads in 1996 failed to produce a similar reaction. The difference seemed to be that Clinton used contrast in his ads, mixing the positive with the negative. He focused on policy positions. Moreover, Clinton's ads didn't accuse Dole of personal failings, as Dole's did Clinton.

What is the impact of negative advertising on voters? The conventional wisdom is that negative ads are more effective, more disliked, and more harmful to the democratic electoral system than are positive ads. But the evidence supporting these propositions is mixed at best. An examination of the "effects" literature by four political scientists who statistically integrated 117 empirically based findings from 52 separate research projects on the subject concluded that "the literature finds no significant support for the suppositions that negative political ads are especially disliked, are especially effective, or substantially undermine public support for and participation in the electoral process."[26]

Evaluating Political Advertising

If advertisements mislead the public, as many scholars claim, should they be monitored and, if so, by whom? Some countries don't allow political advertising. Whether such a prohibition is good or bad is probably immaterial in the United States, because the First Amendment to the U.S. Constitution protects a candidate's right to advertise. But it doesn't necessarily follow that candidates should be free to say or claim anything they want under the banner of free speech. Just as obscenity isn't protected by the First Amendment, neither is libel or slander. However, the Supreme Court, in its efforts to protect and promote a free marketplace of ideas, has made it extremely difficult for public officials to prove that they've been libeled or slandered by the news media. Falsehood alone isn't sufficient evidence. Malice also has to be proved.[27]

Short of suing for libel and slander, what else can be done to promote and police truth in political advertising? Perhaps the regulations for commercial advertising, which make advertisers liable for the false claims of their products and give an independent regulatory body, the Federal Trade Commission, authority to prescribe penalties, could be applied to politics. However, it might be very difficult to prove an ad false if it presents only one aspect of a candidate's record or identifies only some of the positions that candidate has taken. Another problem would be the policing body itself, the Federal Election Commission. Given its composition of three Democrats and three Republicans, could it ever resolve a partisan issue over advertising?

What about the private sector? Should the news media monitor political advertising? They do when they consider political advertising newsworthy. Increasingly, such advertising has been covered by the news media as part of the campaign. The objective of this coverage is different from the advertising objective. Although the press may be interested in the ad's content and message, it usually is more interested in the ad's strategic impact on the contest, to whom the commercial is targeted, and how it may affect voters in the targeted group.[28]

The media's interest in the strategic impact of the advertising has a number of implications. More coverage is given to advertising in the more competitive races, that is, to the most controversial ads, which also tend to be the most negative ones or the ones that make the most outlandish claims. Because reporting on ads normally involves showing, printing, or describing them, the distinction between the content of an ad and the media's commentary is often lost on the general public. Darrell West notes that people tend to remember the ad more than they remember the criticism about it.[29]

Moreover, media coverage of advertising is not uniform. Most of the critical coverage comes from the national television networks and major newspapers. Yet most of the ads are carried on local stations. News about a particular ad is a one-time story, but the ad may be continually shown in major media markets. In recent elections, several of the larger regional and national newspapers have conducted "ad watches" in which the audio of the ad is printed, the video briefly described, and the content assessed for accuracy. Television news networks also air such watches but not with as much regularity as do the print media.

When done systematically and fairly, ad watches serve a useful purpose by calling attention to false claims and charges and by helping to correct perceptions that the public may develop about the candidates and their issue positions. The knowledge that the ads may come under press scrutiny also encourages those who design the ads to be more careful about what they say and show in their ads.

Other checks on advertising come from opposition candidates, public interest organizations, even prominent people. Nancy Reagan strongly objected to footage from the assassination attempt on her husband that was included in a 1996 Clinton ad on gun control. The ad featured James Brady, Reagan's press secretary, who was also seriously injured in the attack. After Mrs. Reagan's complaint, the Clinton campaign removed the objectionable footage, but not before the ad had been shown many times and had become a news item and point of controversy. Similarly, in 2000, when an interest group affiliated with the Republican party in Texas ran a version of an infamous 1964 negative ad that had prompted a strong protest at the time, the Bush campaign requested that the group sponsoring the ad withdraw it so as not to allow the ad to become a diversionary issue in the campaign.

How the press brings attention to deceptive and inaccurate campaign ads can have as much of an impact as the monitoring itself. Deceptive ads that are replayed in their entirety or only partially critiqued can reinforce the message of the ad rather than challenge it. Excessive press criticism of campaign advertising can also contribute to more rather than less public cynicism.

Another proposal, this one designed to rectify the balance between positive and negative ads, is to have the media charge more for ads that are primarily negative. But how would the emphasis be measured in ads that convey both positive and negative information? The advertising problem is a difficult one for a country that values free speech. There are no easy solutions.

THE NEW TECHNOLOGY: BETTER COMMUNICATION OR MORE EFFECTIVE MANIPULATION?

One of the major changes in political campaigns today is their professionalization. They are now run by individuals who are experts at discerning public attitudes, designing public appeals, and directing appeals to the most receptive audience. These political consultants and their profit-making businesses have replaced the party pros and their precinct captains as the new handlers of contemporary political campaigns.

Today, every aspect of the campaign—from public opinion poll to focus group reaction, from the orchestrated events to the guests invited to them, from the cameras that record the action to the spin masters who echo the theme and fax the sound bite—has been planned, staged, and recorded by and for the mass media. Campaigns have become made-for-TV productions. It's all a big show, with the candidates front and center and their aides working hard behind the scenes to make sure everything comes out all right or, if it doesn't, to fix it as soon as possible. *Nothing is left to chance.*

The beginning and ending points of the campaign are frequently public opinion polls. These surveys are used to find out what's on the public's mind; the initial perceptions of the candidates, parties, and issues by the electorate; and what the groups within and outside of the party's electoral coalition are concerned about. Armed with this knowledge, consultants can develop the broad outlines of a campaign: the strategic approach, the issue appeals, and the references to candidate traits, both positive and negative.

The basic rule is to be careful. Winging it is viewed as dumb and dangerous. Spontaneity is out of the question. Every major idea, every promise, and most words are pretested in focus groups to gauge the public's reaction and ultimately gain the most positive response. Once the message is designed and tested, it is targeted to specific groups of voters. There are four principal targeting mechanisms: telephone solicitation, direct mail, radio, and cable and local television. Broadcasting campaign appeals on the major networks is no longer viewed as the most cost-effective way to reach most voters. The rates are too high, the message is usually too broad, and the audience is too diffuse.

The targeting mechanism is used in conjunction with large databases that the parties and various political consultants have assembled over the years. Without knowing it, people become part of these mammoth databases if they ever make a contribution to a candidate running for office or to a group supporting a particular issue, or even if they subscribe to a particular publication.

Armed with the list and the language or special code words that turn on particular groups, the campaign targets its message that it tailors to specific groups on their preferred TV and radio stations in areas where their votes could make a difference. This way, people get their issues front and center and receive the positions of the candidate that most closely accord with their own views. What they don't get is the rest of that candidate's positions, because the campaign handlers believe that they wouldn't be interested in them or, worse yet, that they'd be opposed to them.

People may not realize the limited scope and content of the information they receive. As previous noted, the press doesn't cover the advertising campaigns with the same scrutiny that it reports on "real events." Take the Clinton ads that appeared in major media markets beginning in the summer of 1995 and continuing through the nomination process. The ads were purposely not run in two of the largest media markets—New York and Washington, DC—and were only occasionally run in a third, Los Angeles, the areas in which most of the national press corps lives and works. In the words of Clinton's political adviser Dick Morris, the person who designed the ad campaign:

> If the ads had run there [New York, Washington, and Los Angeles], the press would have grasped the magnitude of what we were doing. But if these cities remained "dark," the national press would not make an issue of our ads—of this we felt sure.
> . . . As the ads were shaping voters' attitudes . . . few newspapers ran articles, much less front-page articles, on the ads. Television—the very medium we were using—rarely mentioned the ads.[30]

The use of the Internet as a communication tool has also expanded candidates' outreach, but primarily to their own partisans. Having a website to solicit contributions, gain volunteers, educate supporters, and turn out voters has become a standard practice for most candidates seeking national office. In 2000 all the major party presidential hopefuls, most of the third-party presidential candidates, and a majority of congressional candidates had websites.[31] Some were very basic, presenting the candidate's biography and listing issue positions. Others actively solicited contributions and volunteers. Some had archives, advertisements, and even an interactive component to answer questions and involve those who accessed the site in some dimension of the campaign.

Internet campaigning has increased and undoubtedly will continue to do so, but to date it consumes only a very small part of the resources that candidates, parties, and interest groups devote to electoral politics. According to political scientist Darrell West, only $50 million out of about $3 billion was spent on these activities in 2000 by candidates for the presidency and Congress.[32]

Another computer-based technique used with increasing frequency is automated telephoning in which prominent individuals record a message that is sent to millions of voters. Pat Robertson, Barbara Bush, Bill Clinton, and Rev. Jesse Jackson all recorded political messages to energize their supporters in 2000. Phone banks in which volunteers make the calls to determine the intentions of likely voters and encourage their supporters to vote have been used with regularity for some time. A relatively new and controversial technique known as push polls was used in the 1996 and 2000 Republican primaries. Under the guise of conducting a survey, callers provide information designed to turn would-be voters against a particular candidate.

How have these new techniques affected the information voters receive about the candidates? Have they contributed to or detracted from a democratic dialogue? The fear is that the new technology has turned the image of an informed electorate groping with the issues as presented by the candidates into one of nearly inert objects of opportunity that candidates try to manipulate with their slick communications. The technology has also made candidates into composites of their consultants' professional imagery and, with their negative advertising, converted their opponents into caricatures of themselves. It has transformed a broad range of ideological and issue appeals into a narrow set of compartmentalized messages targeted to those most likely to approve and be energized by them.

Has the new communications technology undermined our democratic electoral process? Has it encouraged manipulation rather than persuasion? Does it create unrealistic expectations within the electorate? If so, then the technology has contributed to the rise in cynicism about politics and politicians that has been evident since the 1970s. An overwhelming percentage of the population believes that "politicians will tell voters what they want to hear, not what they will actually try to do if elected."[33] Obviously, the new technology isn't the sole cause and may not even be the principal cause of this political cynicism and mistrust, but it seems to be a contributor.

What can be done about the problem of misleading or incomplete information? The answer is, not much. The campaigns are unlikely to discard the new technology, but the media could cover its impact more thoroughly. Moreover, the new technology may change the electorate's appetite for information and the sources from which voters acquire it. Campaigning on the Internet has already become the next phase of the communications revolution in American electoral politics.

Summary: Campaign Communications Dilemmas in a Nutshell

Political campaigns are part and parcel of a democratic election process. They're important for several reasons. They enable candidates to interact with the electorate and hear voters' concerns. They also give candidates a podium from which to express their views, demonstrate their knowledge, respond to policy and personal inquiries, and make their appeal for votes. For the voters, campaigns are equally important as a source of information and an opportunity to question the candidates or at least evaluate their views and their qualifications for office.

The communication dilemma stems from conflicting candidate and voter needs and goals. The candidate's primary goal of winning creates an incentive to shape the scope, content, and spin of the information provided to voters. Candidates stress their best issues, not necessarily the country's most important ones. They present a partial perspective, not a comprehensive one. The voters are left with an incomplete picture in which the negatives often dominate. Is it any wonder people are suspicious of politicians and disappointed with elected officials?

There are other information distortions in campaigns as well. Partisan appeals conjure up familiar stereotypes by which individuals and parties are categorized, sometimes unfairly and almost always too simplistically. Incumbency imagery is used to buttress the resources and recognition that already give those in office an immense advantage in being reelected. Symbols, code words, and sound bites have substituted for argumentation and debate. Messages are more effectively designed, packaged, and targeted with modern computer-based communications technology, to rally the faithful and convince undecided and frequently under-informed voters that a particular candidate trumpets their views, promotes their issues, and will be responsive to their interests and needs if elected.

Personality issues are stressed; character traits are highlighted. Whether these traits are relevant depends on varying conceptions of the job. For those who see high public office as a position of trust, respect, and great moral and ethical responsibility, having the proper virtues and leading an exemplary life are essential qualifications. For those who have a results-oriented view of public service, who are more interested in policymaking than in personal modeling, then political skills, such as flexibility, persuasiveness, pragmatism, communication, and leadership abilities, are the most relevant traits for the job.

All of this hype and hoopla, all of these promises and images, can create unrealistic expectations that, if not met, can contribute to mistrust of politicians, apathy in the elective process, and cynicism about government.

Now It's Your Turn

Discussion Questions

1. Is information about personal behavior outside of office a relevant consideration for election to public office?
2. Does stereotyping add to or detract from an informed voting decision, particularly for voters who are less attentive to the candidates, their parties, and their policy positions?
3. Has the growth of issue advocacy contributed to a better informed electorate?
4. Should the federal government regulate truth in political advertising as it does in commercial advertising?
5. Is the incumbency advantage undemocratic? Does it facilitate or impede the operation of government?
6. Has the revolution in communications technology enhanced the democratic character of elections in the United States?

Topics for Debate

Challenge or defend the following statements:

1. Candidates should be held accountable for the accuracy of their political advertisements and be disqualified if their ads contain misleading or untrue accusations.

2. The government should establish a nonpartisan, independent regulatory agency to monitor and regulate all political communications.
3. Candidates who are the object of negative ads should be allowed to respond to them *at the expense of the campaign that sponsored the original negative ads.*
4. Candidates should be required to appear in all television ads that their campaigns sponsor.
5. Telephone campaigns sponsored by candidates that seek to identify voter preferences should be prevented by law from representing themselves as public opinion researchers.
6. The incumbency advantage is harmful to a democratic electoral process and should be modified in some way.

Exercises

1. A new federal agency has been established to monitor and regulate political advertising. You've been asked to develop the mission statement for this agency. In your statement, indicate the principal goals of the agency, the methods you suggest for monitoring advertising, the kinds of activities that should be regulated, and the penalties that should be imposed on violators.

   Alternatively, assume that your local newspaper has just assigned you to be its ad monitor. Monitor the advertising on local television and in the local newspaper for one week during one campaign. In the story you write for the paper, indicate the scope and content of the ads, the relevance and veracity of claims they made, the groups to whom the advertisements were targeted, and your general evaluation of the effectiveness of this advertising on the electorate. Do you think the advertising made a difference?
2. Analyze the content of one of the presidential debates in 2000 on the basis of the candidates' thematic emphases, policy specificity, general tone (positive or negative), and personal style. Which candidate do you think won the debate, and which acted in a more presidential manner? You can find a transcript of the debates on the website of the National Commission on Presidential Debates, <http://www.debates.org>.

Internet Resources

Most of the sites for chapter 7 are applicable to campaign communications as well. In addition, the offices of incumbents running for reelection should be useful for monitoring their activities or linking to their campaign website. For federal officials, begin with their institution:

- House of Representatives <http://www.house.gov>
- Senate <http://www.senate.gov>
- White House <http:www.whitehouse.gov>

All candidates and their campaigns should be accessible through their parties:

- Democrats <http://www.democrats.org>
- Republicans <http://www.rnc.org>
- Reform Party <http://www.reformparty.org>

Here are a few additional sites:

- CNN All Politics: Elections 2000 <http://CNN.com/allpolitics>
- PBS Online <http://www.pbs.org/election>
- Web White & Blue <http://www.webwhiteblue.org/campaign>

Selected Readings

Benoit, William L., Joseph R. Blaney, and P. M. Pier. *Campaign '96: A Functional Analysis of Acclaiming, Attacking, and Defending.* Westport, CT: Praeger, 1998.

Cox, Gary W., and Jonathan N. Katz. "Why Did the Incumbency Advantage in the U.S. House Elections Grow?" *American Journal of Political Science* 40 (1996): 478–497.

Dalager, Jon K. "Voters, Issues, and Elections: Are the Candidates' Messages Getting Through?" *Journal of Politics* 58 (1996): 486–515.

Devlin, L. Patrick. "Contrasts in Presidential Campaign Commercials of 1992." *American Behavioral Scientist* 37 (1993): 272–290.

———. "Contrasts in Presidential Campaign Commercials of 1996." *American Behavioral Scientist* 41 (1997): 1058–1084.

Diamond, Edwin, and Stephen Bates. *The Spot.* 3rd ed. Cambridge, MA: MIT Press, 1992.

Friedenberg, Robert V., ed. *Rhetorical Studies of National Political Debates, 1960–1992.* Westport, CT: Praeger, 1994.

Greer, John G. "Campaigns, Party Competition, and Political Advertising." In *Politicians and Party Politics,* edited by John G. Greer. Baltimore, MD: Johns Hopkins University Press, 1998.

Jamieson, Kathleen Hall. *Dirty Politics: Deception, Distraction, and Democracy.* New York: Oxford University Press, 1996.

———. *Packaging the Presidency: A History and Criticism of Presidential Campaign Advertising.* New York: Oxford University Press, 1996.

Kaid, Lynda Lee, and Anne Johnston. "Negative Versus Positive Television Advertising in U.S. Presidential Campaigns, 1960–1988." *Journal of Communications* 41 (1991): 53–64.

Kurtz, Howard. *Spin Cycle.* New York: Free Press, 1998.

Magleby, David, ed., *Getting Inside the Outside Campaign.* Provo, UT: Brigham Young University Press, 2000.

McCubbins, Mathew D., ed. *Under the Watchful Eye: Managing Presidential Campaigns in the Television Era.* Washington, DC: Congressional Quarterly Books, 1992.

Morris, Dick. *Behind the Oval Office.* New York: Random House, 1997.

Troy, Gil. *See How They Ran: The Changing Role of the Presidential Candidate.* New York: Free Press, 1991.

Wayne, Stephen J. *The Road to the White House, 2000, The Politics of Presidential Elections, The Post Election Edition.* 1st ed. New York: Bedford/St. Martin's, 2001.

West, Darrell M. *Air Wars.* 3rd ed. Washington, DC: Congressional Quarterly Books, 2001.

Woodward, Bob. *The Choice.* New York: Simon & Schuster, 1997.

Notes

1. There is no one right way to adapt to change. From the perspective of those who hold certain policy positions paramount, the candidates' consistency and their determination to pursue their policy goals despite situational changes may be critical criteria in their evaluation. Ronald Reagan's strong, conservative views and his determination to adhere to them throughout his presidency were seen by those of a similar persuasion as strengths. Others less happy with the policy direction and its impact saw it as a weakness, an inflexibility about adjusting to changing times. Bill Clinton's adaptability and willingness to compromise, given the opposition to many of his domestic policy proposals, were seen as strengths by those who wanted results but as weaknesses by those who didn't know where he stood, what he believed, and what he would do next. These critics found him unnervingly unprincipled.

2. For others, candidate viability is less important than registering discontent through the act of voting itself or sometimes by not voting. Some people wish to use their vote as a protest. Republicans in New Hampshire in 1992 were unhappy with President Bush. About one-third of them demonstrated their unhappiness by voting for Pat Buchanan in the Republican primary. Realistically, Buchanan had little chance of unseating the incumbent president, George Bush, for the Republican nomination, but angry New Hampshire voters didn't care. They were more interested in registering their unhappiness with Bush and his policies. Similarly, in 1996, 8.4 percent of those who voted cast ballots for H. Ross Perot, even though most of them must have known how unlikely it was that Perot would win. In fact, some people may have voted for Perot *because* he had little or no chance of winning. Thus there would be no danger in exercising this protest vote.

   Viability was an issue for supporters of the Reform and Green parties' candidates in 2000, although Nader voters faced another problem—the very tight race between the major party candidates. Since most Nader voters preferred Gore to Bush, their vote for Nader might contribute to Bush's victory, or so Gore argued in a campaign directed at Nader's supporters in the final weeks of election.

3. "Campaign '96 Final: How TV News Covered the General Election," *Media Monitor* 10 (November–December 1996): 3.

4. Which of these traits is most relevant to the voting decision may vary. Some may be endemic to the job, whereas others are important because of the times or the incumbent's obvious shortcomings.

5. Perhaps the most flagrant so-called personality analysis of a candidate occurred during the 1964 presidential election. A magazine, *Fact,* sent a letter and survey to the over-12,000 members of the American Psychiatric Association, asking them whether

they believed Republican candidate Barry Goldwater was psychologically fit to serve as president. Approximately 19 percent of the psychiatrists responded, and two out of three said "no." The magazine not only offered this data as evidence of Goldwater's unfitness for the presidency, but it also published comments, editing out some of the qualifying statements that the psychiatrists had included in their letters to the magazine. Groups such as the American Medical Association and journals such as the *American Journal of Psychiatry* quickly criticized the study as bogus medicine, lacking scientific credibility and validity. Warren Boroson, "What Psychiatrists Say About Goldwater," *Fact* 4 (September–October 1964): 24–64.

6. The most potent of the Bush crime ads was titled "Revolving Door." As prisoners were seen walking through a revolving door, an announcer said, "As governor, Michael Dukakis vetoed mandatory sentences for drug dealers. He vetoed the death penalty. His revolving-door policy gave weekend furloughs to first-degree murderers not eligible for parole. While out, many committed other crimes like kidnapping and rape. And many are still at large. Now Michael Dukakis says he wants to do for America what he's done for Massachusetts. America can't afford the risk." L. Patrick Devlin, "Contrasts in Presidential Campaign Commercials of 1988," *American Behavioral Scientist* 32 (March–April 1989): 389.

7. Gallup Poll, "Trends, 2000," <http://www.gallup.com/poll/trends/pt.jobapp_BC.asp>.

8. Gary C. Jacobson, "Congress: Elections and Stalemate," in *The Elections of 2000*, ed. Michael Nelson (Washington, DC: Congressional Quarterly Books, 2001), 198.

9. Brennan Center for Justice, press release, December 11, 2000, <http://www.brennancenter.org>.

10. Lorie Slass, "Spending on Issue Advocacy in the 2000 Cycle," in Annenberg Center for Public Policy, University of Pennsylvania, *Issue Advertising in the 1999–2000 Election Cycle*, February 1, 2000, 4–7, <http://www.appcpenn.org/issueads>.

11. Erika Falk, "Ad Content," ibid., 11.

12. Alliance for Better Campaigns, "Gouging Democracy: How the Television Industry Profiteered on Campaign 2000," 5, <http://www.bettercampaigns.org/Doldisc/gouging.htm>.

13. Ibid., 1.

14. Ibid.

15. In a study about various forms of campaign communication, David Magleby and his associates found that voters could not tell the difference among ads paid for by the candidates, their parties, and outside interest groups. People assumed that ads in which candidates were mentioned positively were sponsored by the candidates and ads in which candidates were mentioned negatively were sponsored by their opponents. David B. Magleby, ed., *Soft Money and Issue Advocacy in the 2000 Congressional Elections* (Provo, UT: Brigham Young University Press, 2001), 34–35. See also Magleby's "Dictum Without Data," at <http://www.byu.edu/outsidemoney/dictum>.

Researchers at the Annenberg Center for Public Policy came to much the same conclusion in *Issue Advocacy in the 1999–2000 Election Cycle*, 2.

16. Thomas E. Patterson and Robert McClure, *The Unseeing Eye* (New York: Putnam, 1976), 58; and Craig Leonard Brians and Martin P. Wattenberg, "Comparing Issue Knowledge and Salience: Comparing Reception from TV Commercials, TV News, and Newspapers," *American Journal of Political Science* (February 1996): 172–193.

17. Surveys conducted after the elections of 1992, 1996, and 2000 asked the following question: "How helpful were the candidates' commercials to you in deciding which candidate to vote for?" In each survey, a majority of voters found them not too helpful or not helpful at all. The percentages responding "not too helpful" or "not at all helpful" were 59 (1992), 73 (1996), and 66 (2000). Pew Research Center for The People & The Press, "Campaign 2000 Highly Rated," November 16, 2000.

18. Kathleen Hall Jamieson et al., "1966: Better or Worse?" Annenberg Center for Public Policy, University of Pennsylvania, November 1996.

19. See Stephen Ansolabehere and Shanto Iyengar, *Going Negative: How Political Advertisements Shrink and Polarize the Electorate* (New York: Free Press, 1995).

20. Falk, "Ad Content," 19.

21. Ibid., 17.

22. Darrell M. West, *Air Wars*, 3rd ed. (Washington, DC: Congressional Quarterly Books, 2001), 69.

23. Ibid.

24. The proposition that the more negatives, the less likely the win was pioneered by Republican strategist Lee Atwater, who directed the Bush campaign in 1988. See Thomas B. Edsall, "Why Bush Accentuates the Negative," *Washington Post,* October 2, 1988, C4.

As the consultants see it, people obtain more information from negative ads because these ads are more captivating. They are more confrontational, controversial, and therefore newsworthy. The Daisy Girl ad of 1964 and the Willie Horton ad of 1988 are cited as examples of controversial negative ads that became news in themselves.

25. Stephen J. Wayne, *The Road to the White House 1996: Post Election Edition* (New York: St. Martin's, 1997), 269.

26. Richard R. Lau, Lee Sigelman, Caroline Heldman, and Paul Babbitt, "The Effects of Negative Political Advertisements: A Meta-Analytic Assessment," *American Political Science Review* 93 (December 1999), 860.

27. See *New York Times* Co. v. *Sullivan,* 376 U.S. 254 (1964).

28. West, *Air Wars,* 78, 80.

29. Ibid., 86.

30. Dick Morris, *Behind the Oval Office* (New York; Random House, 1997), 139.

31. Annenberg Center for Public Policy, University of Pennsylvania, "Congressional Candidate Web Sites in Campaign 2000," 1, <http:/netelection.org/pressoffice/release01102001>.

32. West, *Air Wars,* 64.

33. According to "Why Don't Americans Trust the Government?"—a national survey conducted in 1996 by the *Washington Post,* Kaiser Family Foundation, and Harvard University—67 percent agreed strongly with this statement, 22 percent agreed somewhat, and only 10 percent disagreed.

9

Elections and Government: A Tenuous Connection

Did you know that . . .

- divided partisan control of the national government has been the rule, not the exception, since 1968?
- in almost half the states, the governor's party doesn't control both houses of the state legislature?
- in 2000 there was a total of 76 ballot issues in 14 states on which voters could register their preference?
- almost half of the policy initiatives in the 1990s were approved by state voters?
- by a two-to-one margin Americans in the 1990s indicated that they favored a smaller national government with fewer services than a larger one with more services? By a similarly large margin they also indicated that they opposed a decrease in government spending for social security, Medicare, education, the environment, health, and defense.
- Americans express more satisfaction with their democracy than do the citizens of most other democratic countries, despite the decline in the trust and confidence they have in their government?
- it's difficult to convert an electoral coalition into a governing coalition for an extended period of time?
- the distinctions between campaigning and governing have become blurred in recent years, as elected officials engage in "constant campaigning" to maintain their public support and to position themselves for the next election?
- election mandates rarely occur, even when one party dominates the outcome, as in 1994?
- the issue that mattered most to voters in 2000 was the economy, followed by education? Cutting taxes and putting social security on a strong financial foundation tied for the third most important.

- the interpretation of the election depends more on public opinion surveys taken after the vote than it does on the vote itself?

Is this any way to run a democratic election?

W HO GOVERNS, and how prepared are they to do so? What priorities and policy positions should newly elected officials pursue, and which party and candidates are more likely to be successful in pursuing them? How can those in power be kept attuned to popular sentiment, responsible to public needs, and accountable for their actions in office—all at the same time?

We hold elections to answer these questions. Elections determine the personnel for government and provide policy guidance for the new administration. They help forge and reinforce the coalitions that enable a government of shared powers and divided authority to make and implement public policy decisions. Finally, elections are the principal enforcement mechanism by which citizens keep those in power responsive to their needs and desires and accountable for their collective actions and individual behavior in office.

In this chapter, we explore how well American elections serve these purposes. Do they make governing easier or harder? Do they provide direction and legitimacy for the public policy that ensues, or do they present mixed signals, undefined mandates, and conflicting claims to those in positions of authority? Do they tie government decisions and actions more closely to the popular will, or do they, most of the time, reveal the absence of such a will? Do they encourage responsiveness in government or provide a nearly blank check for decision makers?

We begin this discussion by looking at the link between who wins and who governs, and how they govern. Then we move to the policy mandate—what the election means and how it affects the policy decisions of newly elected officials. From the mandate and its impact we turn to the tie between electoral and governing coalitions, the transference or maintenance of power by groups within the American polity. Finally, we end the chapter by completing the circle from public choice to government responsiveness, examining the extent to which elections hold public officials accountable for their decisions and behavior in office.

WHO GOVERNS: THE COMPATIBILITY OF THE WINNERS

The election determines the winners, but those winners aren't always compatible with one another. They may not know one another, may disagree on the priorities and issues, and may have different perceptions of how to do their job in government. Yet they all come with an electoral mandate to represent their constituency and act in its interests. One issue that directly affects government's ability to function efficiently is how to enhance the compatibility of newly elected officials in an electoral system designed to mirror the diversity of the population and the character of the federal system.

The compatibility problem is largely systemic, the product of a constitutional framework designed to brake rather than reflect the dominant mood of the moment by creating differing but overlapping electoral constituencies and terms of office. It's also rooted in the contemporary political environment, in more candidate-centered elections and weaker partisan ties. Given the roots of the problem—a political system that reflects the diversity of the society in its electoral processes—achieving compatibility in outlook, goals, and policy priorities requires stronger, more cohesive, policy-oriented parties, an overriding national threat, or some issue that unifies the population and helps produce a consensus for action, such as the September 2001 terrorist attack.

A related problem pertains to the compatibility of those elected with those who remain, the other elected and appointed officials and civil servants. Rarely does the personnel of an entire governmental body change. And even though a complete turnover is theoretically possible in the House of Representatives and in many state legislatures, turnover, in practice, tends to be very limited because of the incumbency advantages and the lack of competitive elections. The fewer new people chosen for government in any one election, the less likely is the election to redirect what government does or how it does it. The absence of turnover limits the impact of those who wanted and voted for change.

From the perspective of a participatory democracy, muting the latest expression of the popular will is an unfortunate consequence of overlapping terms of office. But the tradeoff is more experience, savvy, and continuity in government—all of which may produce better public policy over the long run and less legislative dependence on the executive branch for information and advice. With the limited knowledge that the public has on most issues, braking the emotion of the moment may actually result in a more considered public judgment later on, as more information becomes available and more people begin to understand the complexities of the issue.

Obtaining a considered judgment in the public interest but not becoming prisoner to the public passion of the moment was part of the original rationale for dividing powers and for overlapping constituencies and terms of office. Leery of an aroused majority, particularly if that majority acted to deny minorities their rights, the framers wanted to place hurdles on the road to policymaking. Their system of internal checks and balances requires sustained support over time, across electoral constituencies, and within and among institutions of government, in order to formulate new public policy.

That system, artfully designed in 1787, remains alive and well today. However, public expectations of the role of government have increased enormously. These expectations have been fueled in large part by the needs of an industrial and, later, technological society; by governmental responses to those needs, such as the New Deal and Great Society programs; and by politicians' promises made in their quest for elective office. How to overcome what the Constitution divides is *the* political challenge public officials face, a challenge made more difficult by the heterogeneity of the major parties and the growing autonomy of elections, such as those for president and Congress.

Voting for the best person regardless of party has reinforced the separation of powers. Add to this, Americans' distrust of big and distant government, and their more contemporary fear of ideologically driven party activists' trying to impose their policy agendas on the country, and one quickly arrives at a rationale for split-ticket voting. It's safer that way.

The point here is that the current electoral system, with its propensity to focus on the candidates at the expense of their partisan ties or even the principal policy issues, results in a government of strangers whose ties to their electoral constituency are stronger than their ties to one another.[1] In this sense, contemporary elections mirror America's diversity and facilitate divided government rather than reflect a national consensus that could serve as a guide for action as well as the foundation on which a governing coalition could be built.

Not only does the election determine those who will serve, it also influences those who will aid them in office. Except for professional campaign consultants, who continue to provide elected officials with for-profit services such as polling and media consulting, the people most likely to accompany the newly elected into public service are those who worked long and hard on their campaigns. These are the managers, field organizers, speech writers, researchers, press aides, and political strategists and tacticians. The lack of governing experience of many of these aides magnifies the initial adjustment problem for those elected to office for the first time.

There are several reasons why newly elected officials turn to their campaign aides when choosing their advisory and support staffs. They owe them a lot, and undoubtedly some of these aides have ambitions of their own, which may include moving to the capital and working with the person they helped elect. Moreover, campaign workers have demonstrated their loyalty and industry, two important qualifications for good staffing. That they aren't part of the previous team, which may have been rejected at the polls, is also seen as an advantage. And finally, those who have just won election to a new office for the first time won't usually have the contacts and acquaintances that incumbents possess, but they're familiar with their campaign staff. They know what they can do. So why not hire them?

Actually, there are plenty of reasons for not doing so. The principal ones are that campaigning differs from governing and that the skills and attitudes required for each also differ—although there's some overlap as well, especially between campaigning and the public dimension of government.[2]

THE RELATIONSHIP BETWEEN CAMPAIGNING AND GOVERNING

Do contemporary campaigns facilitate or impede governing? Do they provide the skills necessary for elected officials to perform representative and policy-making functions, or do they divert their focus, harden their positions, and convert governing into constant campaigning? They do both.

Similarities: The Constant Campaign

Governing is becoming more campaign oriented. It's increasingly conducted in the public arena; it has become poll driven. A principal motivation for elected officials making public policy decisions is how those decisions will affect their own reelection. Campaign skills are useful for these public aspects of governing.

In campaigns, the candidates and their entourage have to sell themselves and their policies to the electorate. They continue doing so once elected. Executive and legislative leaders in particular have to build support for their programs outside of government, in order to enhance support for their enactment in government. Governing officials, especially the president and state governors, must be concerned, like candidates, with their own popularity because it's thought to contribute to their political influence and subsequent policy successes.

Although both candidates and government officials appeal to the public, they do so in slightly different ways. In campaigns, the candidates try to lead the media, respond quickly to their opponents' charges and to press allegations, and continuously spin campaign-related issues. In government, elected officials announce policy, explain issues, and use the prestige of their office to enhance the credibility of their remarks. As public officials responsible for the formulation and execution of policy, they have to respond to critical media, which tend to highlight criticism of their decisions and actions. Moreover, they also have to contend with more investigative reporting than is possible within the limited time frame of a campaign and thus are frequently on the defensive. Candidates are moving targets; elected officials are sitting ducks.

In both campaigns and government, the press will impute the political motives of the subjects they cover. In the campaign, having a political motive is expected; political motives are what campaigns are all about. Not so in government, where political motives may be viewed as petty, partisan, and personal. Government officials have to defend the merits and motives of their actions in terms of the national interest. Thus candidate Bill Clinton could criticize Bob Dole's policy positions even though his motive was political, but the congressional Republicans' focus on Clinton's behavior in office and the impeachment trial itself were seen by many as partisan politics, not in the national interest.

Once elected, incumbents keep their eyes on the next election and do their best to ready themselves for it by raising money and performing services. The representative role—servicing constituency needs, representing constituency views, and satisfying constituency interests in the short run—has become more important; legislating longer-term national policy has become less important. Executive oversight has received more emphasis, particularly as it contributes to partisan positioning for the next election and spotlights the watchdog activities of particular representatives.

That more and more governing functions are subject to media scrutiny and take place within the public arena has both positive and negative consequences for democratic government. It benefits democracy, in that elected officials are motivated to stay closely tied to their electoral coalitions and more responsive to their needs. The cost of maintaining such ties, however, has been a growing public perception, fueled by the press, that elected officials follow, not lead, and do what's best for themselves (i.e., get reelected), not what's best for the country (i.e., doing what is right even if it hurts them politically).

A second problem that stems from the campaign-oriented environment in government is the hardening of policy positions. If candidates for office are increasingly defined by and held accountable for the promises they made and the positions they took during the campaign, it will be more difficult for them as elected officials to make the compromises necessary to govern. Strong ideological beliefs contribute to this problem.

The difficulties that a campaign-style atmosphere creates for government suggest that there are fundamental differences between campaigning and governing. Unless these differences are understood, contemporary election campaigns will continue to impede rather than facilitate the operation of democratic government.

Differences: Pace, Mentality, Orientation, and Experience

Pace—Hectic Versus Deliberative

A campaign has to keep up with events and presumably stay ahead of them, or face defeat on election day. It is frantic almost by definition. In a competitive electoral environment, a campaign exists in a state of perpetual motion; often, a crisis atmosphere prevails. But all of this motion and activity ends on a certain day, the same day that most of the campaign's personnel are out of jobs.

Not so with government. It can't operate in a perpetual crisis for extended periods without sacrificing the deliberation and cooperation needed to reach solutions to pending issues. Elected officials of the opposing parties still have to interact with one another after a major policy decision has been made. Whereas campaigns are a single battle with a definable end, government is a multiple set of skirmishes fought before and after elections with many of the same combatants. The relationships within government and the problems with which it deals persist over time, across institutions, even over the course of several administrations.

Mentality—Win at All Costs Versus Give and Take

A campaign is what political scientists like to call a "zero-sum game," at least until the next campaign begins. If one candidate wins, the other loses, and the game's over. The winners no longer have to consider the losers, who may fade quickly from the public spotlight. Government isn't a zero-sum game. For one thing, the losers on a particular issue don't disappear once a battle has been lost. They stay to fight another one. A case in point is the recent history of clashes between environmental and economic interests.

In 1977 Congress enacted far-reaching environmental legislation. Known as the Clean Air Act, it established standards for automobile as well as industrial emissions. Business interests, particularly automobile manufacturers, strongly opposed the legislation and tried to dilute and delay the emission standards. With Ronald Reagan's election in 1980, the advantage shifted from the environmentalists to business. The Reagan administration ordered the Environmental Protection Agency (EPA), the federal government's chief monitoring agency, to cut back its aggressive enforcement of the legislation, and Congress, led by the Republican-controlled Senate, resisted new and more stringent legislation. But once the Democrats gained a Senate majority in the 1986 midterm elections (they already had a majority in the House of Representatives) and George Bush succeeded Ronald Reagan as president, environmental interests gained the upper hand. They succeeded in getting Congress to strengthen the Clean Air Act by adding amendments that tightened controls on utilities burning soft coal and by raising the standards for acceptable levels of the automobile emissions. The business community, unhappy with the legislation and the president's support of it, put pressure on the administration not to implement the new standards. Fearful of losing business's support in the 1992 presidential election, the administration dragged its feet, leaving it to President Clinton to order the EPA to enforce the new standard. The victory was almost short-lived, as the Republican Congress selected in the 1994 midterm elections tried to cut the EPA budget by 25 percent and curtail its enforcement activities. Only the president's veto of the appropriations bill, the subsequent government shutdown, and the defection of a few moderate Republicans preserved the legislation and the EPA's enforcement of it. A status quo had been reached, but for how long?[3] The battle between economic and environmental interests soon broke out again, this time during the administration of George W. Bush over such issues as global warming, arsenic levels in water, carbon dioxide as a pollutant, higher emission standards for SUVs, drilling in the Arctic natural preserve, and the content and runoff of agricultural pesticides.

Campaigns need to be run efficiently. Their organization and operation are geared to one goal: winning the election. In government, although efficiency is desirable, there are other equally important goals. A legislative body has to deliberate on issues of public policy. In doing so, it must conduct hearings to permit outside groups to be heard, forge compromise among the contending parties, and then oversee the executive branch's implementation. All of this takes time, involving different people with different constituencies in different parts of the government. The legislative process may not be efficient, but it must be representative and should be deliberative.

Orientation—Consistency Versus Compromise

Candidates are judged by their potential for office. In demonstrating their qualifications, particularly if they aren't incumbents, they need to show that they have a grasp of the issues, have good ideas, and will keep their promises if elected. More often than not, keeping promises means adhering to the policy positions they articulated and highlighted during the campaign and trying to get them enacted into law.

Officeholders are judged by their performance as well as by conditions. They need to show results, or at least be in a position to claim responsibility for some achievements. Adhering to policy positions and not compromising on them could jeopardize a record of achievement. Moreover, elected officials are subject to myriad pressures from within and outside of the government: the bureaucracy, the media, interest groups, and the legislature. Not only do these groups have different agendas, different constituencies, and different time frames, they also may have the clout to thwart new initiatives. These political forces can't be ignored as a minority group can during a campaign.

Not only are campaigning and governing different, so are the permanence of the coalitions on which candidates and public officials depend. Electoral coalitions usually stay together for the duration of the political campaign. Governing alliances shift more with the issues. Today's opponent may be tomorrow's ally. Unlike those in campaigns, the losers and winners in government are not permanent enemies.

Experience—Outsiders Versus Insiders

The distinction between running and governing has been exacerbated of late by two developments: the changes within the electoral process that have provided greater opportunities for those with limited experience to run for office and the public's mistrust of those in power and its desire for new faces not connected to the current political establishment. In an increasing number of elections, lack of experience, in particular the absence of a connection to the "mess in government," is regarded as a virtue, not a liability.

Not only are many nonincumbent candidates neophytes to governing, but their campaign staffs may be as well. In the past, the political pros who ran the campaign had experience in electioneering and governing. Today, the political pros have been largely replaced by the professional campaign technocrats— pollsters, media consultants, political strategists, fundraisers, direct mailers, and grassroots organizers who sell their services to the highest bidders, some even without regard for partisanship.[4] These campaign technocrats usually have little if any governing experience and little desire to work *in* government; they do want to work *for* government, though, content to continue to sell their services to those in power, especially to incumbents getting ready to run again.

The others who work on campaigns are the trusted soldiers, the people who perform the day-to-day tasks, staging events, writing speeches, doing research, dealing with the press, setting up phone banks—all the nitty-gritty grunt work. They work long and hard for low salaries or for free; many are young, in or just out of college, with little government experience. They may be involved because they believe in the candidate, like the excitement of the campaign, or want a job once the campaign is over.[5] Whatever their motivation, they are not likely to have the inside information that a newly elected public official needs the most: knowing how things work and which people have the power to get things done.

The presidential transitions of Carter and Clinton suffered from many of these staffing inadequacies. The people they appointed to their White House staff came from their campaigns and had little or no experience in Washington politics, in dealing with the national press corps, the congressional leadership, and, in Clinton's case, the military establishment. Moreover, these newly appointed aides suffered from another malady that frequently afflicts the newly elected and their staffs: they came to power with chips on their shoulders. They assumed, probably correctly, that they won because people had grievances against those in power. Because Carter and Clinton were outsiders even within their own party, they were suspicious of all those in the establishment, Democrats and Republicans alike. Initially, they tried to have as little to do with them as possible.[6]

George W. Bush ran against the strident partisan tone of Washington politics, promising to return civility to political discourse and a bipartisan dimension to governing. Although Bush lacked Washington experience, he was a close observer of his father's presidency and surrounded himself with experienced Washington hands as he began transition planning. As a consequence, the Bush administration got off to a much better start than did the administrations of Carter and Clinton. Running against the Washington establishment may be an effective campaign strategy, particularly if the public is unhappy with the way it perceives the government to be working. But it's not an effective governing strategy, especially if the goal is to bridge institutional boundaries, to make and implement new public policy.

The Impact of Campaigning on Governing

Contemporary campaigning has made contemporary governing more difficult. Campaigns raise public expectations about public policy and public officials at the same time that they feed into distrust of politicians and the politics in which they engage. They emphasize personal accomplishments in a system designed to curb the exercise of institutional and political power. They harden policy positions in a government system that depends on compromise. They have increasingly brought partisan and ideological rhetoric into the policymaking arena where a pragmatic approach and quiet diplomacy used to get things done. And the candidates have developed a public persona that they continue to pursue once in office, a persona that can get in the way of behind-the-scenes compromises on major issues with which they have been associated.

A second impact of campaigning on governing, especially since the 1970s, has been the increasing number of winning candidates who haven't come up through the ranks and lack governing experience. These candidates may overestimate their ability to make a difference and underestimate the views and legitimacy of others who remain in the governing establishment. "Reinventing the wheel" wastes time and energy and increases the startup costs of government.

To make matters worse, candidates who aren't incumbents don't usually have access to the information and expertise that government officials have on issues of public policy. What they do have access to, however, are poll results that indicate political attitudes, salient issues, and public opinions on them. Armed with this information, it's relatively easy to craft a position that will be popular with a specific group. Campaigning by public opinion polls is just a short step away from governing by public opinion polls. An increasing number of public officials seem to have taken this step.

Directions for Reforms

If contemporary campaigning has contributed to the difficulty of governing, what changes might reverse this pattern and make governing easier? More party control over the electoral process might reduce the number of free agents elected to government and impose more discipline on those who are elected. But how can this be accomplished in light of the changes to the nomination process, weaker parties at the grassroots level, and candidate-centered campaigns?

If terms of office were longer, if voters were more nationally focused and less interested in the short-term impact, then elected officials would have more opportunity to make decisions in what they believed was the country's long-term interest, rather than their constituency's short-term one. But then ties between government and the governed would also be looser, responsiveness might suffer, and incumbents might be even more advantaged than they are today. Term limits could reduce this advantage, forcing greater turnover in office, but they would also result in the election of less experienced and knowledgeable public officials who would need time to acquire expertise or would be more dependent on civil servants and professional legislative staff for support. Besides, term limits are undemocratic.

THE ELECTION AND PUBLIC POLICY

In addition to choosing who will govern—which candidates, parties, and staffs—elections should provide policy guidance for government: what issues to address, what approaches to take, and even what specific proposals to make. Except for policy initiatives, which are increasingly appearing on state ballots, elections refract rather than reflect public opinion on most issues. The reason they do so is because they are primarily designed to choose people, not policies.

The Movement Toward Policy Initiatives

Ballot initiatives have become an increasingly popular vehicle for individuals, and especially for organized groups, to pursue their policy agendas when they are unable to do so successfully through the legislative process. Twenty-four states, mostly in the West and Midwest, provide for some type of policy referendum. Rooted in the Progressive era, these policy initiatives enable citizens to vote directly on an issue.[7] In this sense, they illustrate direct democracy at work.

However, to pursue a ballot initiative successfully costs money, lots of it, which the affluent can best afford. Just to get an initiative on the ballot, a certain percentage of the state's eligible voters must sign a petition within a specified period of time. The higher the percentage of signatures required and the shorter the time frame, the more difficult and expensive ballot access will be. If an organization lacks enough of its own volunteers, foot soldiers to gather these signatures, it will have to engage an outside firm to collect them and pay as much as three dollars per name. The total cost can run into the millions, and that's just the first step. A public relations campaign for the initiative must also be waged during the election period. If successful, it may still be challenged in the courts, as was California's Proposition 187, a ballot initiative approved by the voters that denied such state benefits as education and health care to illegal aliens and their families. The legal charges can also be substantial.[8]

Interest groups have become adept at using the initiative process to their own economic, ideological, or political advantage. The gambling industry, sports promoters, the Humane Society, and groups that want to impose legislative term limits, make English the official U.S. language, legalize the sale of marijuana for medical purposes, permit doctor-assisted suicides, issue school vouchers, and increase taxes for education all have used the initiative process to circumvent recalcitrant state legislatures. Even public officials have done so when they wish to apply pressure on them. Take the case of Governor Paul Cellucci of Massachusetts. Blocked by a Democratic legislature from lowering the state's tax rate, Cellucci threatened a ballot initiative to force the legislators to accede to his request.[9]

A few wealthy, public-interested individuals have also tried to use this process to achieve what they consider to be desirable public policy. Billionaire financier George Soros has spent millions in support of initiatives that would legalize the medical use of marijuana and would provide for forfeiture of assets and rehabilitation rather than lengthy jail terms for convicted drug offenders. Paul Allen, the cofounder of Microsoft, donated $3 million to supporters of an initiative to establish charter schools in the state of Washington. Businessman Tim Draper spent $23 million of his own money on an initiative to provide school vouchers to children in California. The list goes on.[10]

Others have also turned to initiatives to change policy, gain recognition, and even make money. Bill Sizemore has used the initiative process in Oregon probably more than any other state resident. He placed six initiatives on the 2000 ballot alone. He also runs a business that collects signatures for ballot initiatives, so he makes money and tries to affect public policy at the same time. Sizemore also used his visibility in the state to run for governor in 1998, but he was defeated.[11]

The amount of money that it takes to mount a successful initiative drive and the fact that much of the money and organization may come from outside the state have led some states to try to limit the number of ballot initiatives and the influence of outside groups. The state of Colorado enacted legislation that permitted only its registered voters to circulate initiative petitions. It required that they wear badges identifying themselves and their affiliation, and that the costs of initiative drives be made part of the public record. However, in 1999 the Supreme Court found that these restrictions violated the First Amendment by inhibiting communications with voters.[12]

In addition to the financial issue, there are other problems with the widespread use of these public referenda. Some are extremely complicated and difficult for the average person to understand, much less appreciate all the implications and costs. Reading them alone can take a considerable amount of time, which would hold up voting if everyone chose to do so. Moreover, initiatives circumvent the legislative process, thereby diminishing the role of those whose job it is to consider public policy issues, those who presumably have more qualifications to do so than the average person or voter.

According to political scientist Richard J. Ellis, an expert on the initiative process, there has been a steady increase in ballot initiatives since the 1970s. Whereas they averaged 35 per ballot in the 1970s and 50 in the 1980s, for the last two decades of the twentieth century the average number of state ballot initiatives was 76 per ballot, with the most (103) coming in 1996. Ellis reports that a little less than half of these initiatives have become law.[13]

Issue Voting in a Candidate-Oriented Environment

With the exception of policy initiatives, most elections are imperfect mechanisms for determining public policy. People vote for a variety of candidates, for a variety of reasons. Partisan affiliation, candidate qualifications, and candidates' issue positions are some of the factors that affect voting behavior. Of these, issues are least likely to be the primary one.[14]

People may also be voting against candidates because they're unhappy with the job they've done, the conditions that occurred while they were in power, their personal behavior while in office, or even their traits or policy positions that have come out during the campaign. Such a negative vote, if discernible, may indicate what the electorate does *not* want but not what it *does* want.

Another factor contributing to the difficulty of understanding the meaning of elections is that there are many candidates and many issues at many levels of government. People have different reasons for casting different votes. And they often split their ballot, voting for candidates from different parties. This type of voting behavior produces mixed results from which a clear message isn't easily discernible, despite political pundits' and exit pollsters' claims to the contrary.

If a voting pattern were to emerge, if one party were to win or maintain control of the legislative and executive branches, then there might be some reason for believing that the voters were sending a message—although the message itself wouldn't necessarily be clear. However, at the national level, such a pattern has been the exception, not the rule, since 1968. During this period, the same party has controlled the White House and both houses of Congress for a total of only six years and four months, muting whatever messages voters were sending. And even though there was one-party control at the beginning of George W. Bush's administration, the president could hardly claim an electoral mandate, having lost the popular vote. Under these circumstances, with mixed results in overlapping constituencies, what can the election returns tell us about the policy direction that newly elected officials should take? The answer is, usually, not very much.

The Absence of Policy Mandates

The national electoral system isn't structured in a way that facilitates policy voting. It has facilitated partisan voting by the people, but the weakening of partisan loyalties, the declining use of the party-column ballot, and the increasing candidate orientation of contemporary elections have made it more difficult to achieve partisan mandates today—although some claim that the 1994 midterm elections produced such a mandate for the Republicans, as did the elections of 1932, 1964, and 1976 for the Democrats.

In order to have a mandate for governing, a party's candidates must take discernible and compatible policy positions, distinguishable from the opposition's, and the electorate must vote for them because of those positions. Most elections don't meet these criteria. Candidates usually take a range of policy positions, often waffle on a few highly divisive and emotionally charged issues, and may differ from their party and its other candidates for national office in their priorities and their stands.

House Republican candidates did take consistent policy positions in 1994; all pledged to support the goals and proposals in their Contract with America. Other Republican candidates, however, didn't take such a pledge. Nonetheless, the results of the 1994 election, in which every Republican incumbent for Congress and governor won and the Republicans gained seats in most state legislatures, were interpreted as a partisan victory. But what did such a victory mean? What policy goals did it imply?

Newly elected Speaker of the House Newt Gingrich chose to interpret the vote as an affirmation of the ten basic goals and legislative proposals in the Contract with America. Such an interpretation provided Gingrich with a legislative agenda to pursue and promote in the House of Representatives. But Gingrich's interpretation also created performance expectations that the Republicans were unable to meet outside of the House.

Moreover, it was probably an incorrect interpretation. The vote in 1994 was a repudiation of the Clinton administration and the Democratic-controlled Congress; it was also a rejection of big government, big deficits, and big social programs such as health care. Indirectly, it could also be interpreted as a vote for less government, lower taxes, and a smaller deficit. But it was *not* a vote for the

Republicans' Contract with America. How do we know? Exit polls indicated that only 25 percent of the voters and 20 percent of the population had ever heard of the Contract with America, much less knew what was in it. How, then, could the 1994 election be a mandate for the policy proposals in that contract if such a small proportion of the population was aware of those proposals?

If newly elected officials are rarely given a clear mandate for governing, then how do they interpret the meaning of the election? How do they know what voters want and don't want them to do? Generally speaking, they assume that their constituency supports most of the policy positions they advocated, and they assume so because they won the election.

Although such an assumption is understandable on an individual level, it doesn't provide much collective guidance, much less the mandate that leaders of government desire to gain support for their policy goals. Where can these leaders turn in order to understand the meaning of the vote?

Exit Polls and the Meaning of the Vote

The results of the elections may not explain very much, other than who wins and who loses, but election-day surveys that probe voters to discern some of their opinions when they cast their ballots do. Such surveys enable analysts to correlate the opinions of voters with their votes and with their demographic and attitudinal characteristics. In this way, it's possible to interpret the meaning of the election. Exit polls provide one of the primary sources of data for this interpretation. The pre- and postelection surveys conducted by the Center for Political Studies at the University of Michigan, the National Election Studies, provide another valuable source.

Exit polls interview voters after they've cast ballots at randomly selected voting precincts across the country.[15] A large number of people are questioned: In 1996 it was 16,627, in 1998 it was 10,017, and in 2000 it was 13,130. On the basis of their answers, analysts are able to discern the attitudes, opinions, and choices of groups of voters.

The exit poll is usually very accurate because of its large size (compared to about 1,200 for other national surveys) and because it's conducted at so many different voting precincts across the country over the course of election day. Its principal limitation is that it provides only a snapshot of the electorate on that particular day. It can't show how the campaign affected the public's attitudes and opinions or the impact of other factors over the course of the election. But the National Election Studies, though much smaller, can because those surveys interview many of the same people before and after the election, making it possible to discern opinion change over the course of the campaign.

Although an exit poll of the 2000 election is not necessary to show that the electorate was evenly divided in the presidential election, the poll does reveal patterns that help explain why the election was so close (see Table 9.1). The principal factor was partisanship. In 2000 the parties were at rough parity with one another, and partisans voted overwhelmingly for their party's nominees. Core groups within each party's traditional electoral coalition also voted in record proportions along party lines: African Americans, Latinos, and organized labor for the Democratic candidates, the Christian Coalition for the Republicans. The independent vote was also closely divided, with Gore enjoying a slight edge. In the end he received 540,000 more popular votes than Bush.

There were significant demographic, geographic, and attitudinal divisions within the electorate in addition to party and race. The gender gap, evident since the 1980s, got larger in 2000. Not only did a majority of women vote Democratic and a majority of men Republican, but the difference in their partisan support was a whopping 22 percent.

The geographic divide was equally significant. Gore overwhelmed in the Northeast and mid-Atlantic states while Bush took the South. Gore won the Pacific Coast and Bush the traditional Republican mountain states, creating in effect a continental divide. Bush won the rural areas, Gore the cities, with the suburbs evenly divided.

Ideology and religion reinforced the partisan, gender, and geographic divisions. Liberals continued their embrace of the Democratic party, and conservatives were equally supportive of the Republicans. Moderates sided more with the Democrats, thereby counterbalancing the advantage that the larger number of conservatives than liberals gave the Republicans. Traditional voting patterns continued among religious groups, with Protestants supporting Bush and the Republicans, Catholics split, and Jews voting overwhelming for Gore and his Jewish running mate, Joseph Lieberman. A sectarian-nonsectarian division was also evident. The more regularly people attended religious services, the more likely they were to have voted Republican.

The economy was not an issue in 2000. However, Gore's decision to distance himself from the president and to emphasize his policies for the future not the achievements of the past, made it difficult for him to get credit for the economic prosperity of the Clinton years. Voters believed that either major party candidate was capable of managing the economy.

Social and cultural issues were more divisive. Bush voters decried the decline in morality and looked to the president to restore dignity to the Oval Office and promote traditional American values. They supported the right to bear arms, generally opposed abortion, and wanted less rather than more government. In contrast, Gore received the votes of those who felt the country was on the right track, who weren't as concerned about moral issues, who were more supportive of government programs to help the elderly and poor, and whose own financial situation had improved during the Clinton years. As expected, the way people evaluated the Clinton administration carried over to their presidential vote. Despite the distance that Gore tried to create between his own candidacy and Clinton's presidency, he did benefit from the president's high approval rating, which was 57 percent on election day according to the exit poll. Had Gore emphasized and embraced the policy successes of the Clinton years, he might have done even better.

TABLE 9.1 Portrait of the American Electorate, 1988–2000 (Percentages)

Percentage of 2000 Total		1988		1992			1996			2000		
		Bush	Dukakis	Clinton	Bush	Perot	Clinton	Dole	Perot	Bush	Gore	Nader
	Total vote	53	45	43	38	19	49	41	8	48	48	3
48	Men	57	41	41	38	21	43	44	10	53	42	3
52	Women	50	49	46	37	17	54	38	7	43	54	2
81	Whites	59	40	39	41	20	43	46	9	54	42	3
10	Blacks	12	86	82	11	7	84	12	4	9	90	1
7	Hispanics	30	69	62	25	14	72	21	6	35	62	2
2	Asians	—	—	29	55	16	43	48	8	41	55	3
65	Married	57	42	40	40	20	44	46	9	53	44	2
35	Unmarried	46	53	49	33	18	57	31	9	38	57	4
17	18–29 years old	52	47	44	34	22	53	34	10	46	48	5
33	30–44 years old	54	45	42	38	20	48	41	9	49	48	2
28	45–59 years old	57	42	41	40	19	48	41	9	49	48	2
22	60 and older	50	49	50	38	12	48	44	7	47	51	2
5	Not high school graduate	43	56	55	28	17	59	28	11	38	59	1
21	High school graduate	50	49	43	36	20	51	35	13	49	48	1
32	Some college education	57	42	42	37	21	48	40	10	51	45	3
24	College graduate	62	37	40	41	19	44	46	8	51	45	3
18	Postgraduate education	50	48	49	36	15	52	40	5	44	52	3
54	White Protestant	66	33	33	46	21	36	53	10	56	42	2
26	Catholic	52	47	44	36	20	53	37	9	47	50	2
4	Jewish	35	64	78	12	10	78	16	3	19	79	1
14	White born-again Christian	81	18	23	61	15	26	65	8	80	18	1
26	Union household	42	57	55	24	21	59	30	9	37	59	3
7	Family income under $15,000	37	62	59	23	18	59	28	11	37	57	4
16	$15,000–$29,999	49	50	45	35	20	53	36	9	41	54	3
24	$30,000–$49,999	56	44	41	38	21	48	40	10	48	49	2

TABLE 9.1 (continued)

Percentage of 2000 Total	1988 Bush	1988 Dukakis	1992 Clinton	1992 Bush	1992 Perot	1996 Clinton	1996 Dole	1996 Perot	2000 Bush	2000 Gore	2000 Nader
Family income (continued)											
25 Over $50,000	56	42	40	42	18	44	48	7	51	46	2
13 Over $75,000	62	37	36	48	16	41	51	7	52	45	2
15 Over $100,000	65	32	—	—	—	38	54	6	54	43	2
Family's financial situation is											
50 Better today	—	—	24	62	14	66	26	6	36	61	2
38 Same today	—	—	41	41	18	46	45	8	60	35	3
11 Worse today	—	—	61	14	25	27	57	13	63	33	4
23 From the North	50	49	47	35	18	55	34	9	39	56	3
26 From the Midwest	52	47	42	37	21	48	41	10	49	48	2
31 From the South	58	41	42	43	16	46	46	7	55	43	1
21 From the West	52	46	44	34	22	48	40	8	46	48	4
35 Republicans	91	8	10	73	17	13	80	6	91	8	1
27 Independents	55	43	38	32	30	43	35	17	47	45	6
39 Democrats	17	82	77	10	13	84	10	5	11	86	2
20 Liberals	18	81	68	14	18	78	11	7	13	80	6
50 Moderates	49	50	48	31	21	57	33	9	44	52	2
29 Conservatives	80	19	18	65	17	20	71	8	81	17	1
67 Employed*	56	43	42	38	20	48	40	9	48	49	2
33 Unemployed*	37	62	56	24	20	49	42	8	48	47	3
9 First-time voters	51	47	48	30	22	54	34	11	43	52	4

*In the 1996 poll the question was "Are you employed full time?" In 2000 it was "Do you work full-time for pay?" "Yes" answers were categorized as "employed," "no" answers as "unemployed."

Sources: 1988 data based on survey of voters conducted by the *New York Times*/CBS News; 1992–2000 data collected by Voter News Service.

The presidential elections of 1992 and 1996 had been referendums on the administration in power, but the 2000 election was not. It was more about the future than about the present, more about personal characteristics and leadership style than about policy issues, and perhaps more about how to govern than about exactly what government should do. Gleaning meaning from such an election, much less a mandate, has proven to be difficult.

In summary, it's very difficult to glean much meaning from the election just by looking at the results, at who wins and who loses. In order to identify the critical relationships that help explain voting behavior and the meaning of the vote, analysts need to know who voted for whom, what issues concerned voters, and what their opinions and attitudes were at the time they voted. Exit polls provide some of this information. To discern the effects of the campaign, to see how it influenced turnout and voting behavior, analysts need to know attitudes and opinions before and after the vote, data they can obtain from the National Election Studies.

Finally, it's important to note that, the more time that elapses after the election, the less important the election will be as a guide to policy and as an influence on those who make it.

POLICY AND PERFORMANCE: RESPONSIVENESS AND ACCOUNTABILITY

Government is based on the consent of the governed. That's the reason why public officials are so concerned about the meaning of the election and why they may even claim it to be a mandate from the voters. That meaning or claim ties elections to government in three ways:

- Elections should provide direction for public officials.
- Elections can help generate popular support for achieving election-based goals and more specific campaign promises.
- Elections reaffirm the legitimacy of government and, to a large extent, what it does.

Providing Direction

Campaigns are full of promises, both substantive and stylistic. They provide a broad and detailed blueprint for those in power. By doing so, they create expectations of performance. These expectations are often hyped by the emphasis the candidates themselves place on certain character skills and traits, which they claim they will employ if elected—strong and decisive leadership, moral and ethical behavior, open and honest government, "a kinder and gentler America," "never to tell a lie," "compassionate conservatism."

But here they have to be careful. If they set too high a bar for themselves, they may not be able to scale it, with the result that their popularity and probably also the public's confidence in them, their party, and their administration will decline. Reagan's high approval ratings before, during, and after his reelection indicated that most of the public believed that he had provided the strong leadership he had promised in his 1980 and 1984 campaigns, even though the electorate didn't always agree with the policy he enunciated. In contrast, Clinton's popularity in 1996 indicated that the public approved the work he was doing and the results he was achieving as president, even though they continued to have doubts about him personally, about his honesty, integrity, and moral character.

Bush's narrow victory in 2000 had the opposite effect. It lowered the bar, reducing public expectations. Perceptions of the president's performance in his first six months in office benefited from these lower expectations.

Multiple campaign promises, low levels of information among voters, and most people's preoccupation with current conditions give public officials considerable leverage in designing policy, as long as they stay within the broad parameters of acceptability and have a beneficial short-term result. In this sense and on a collective level, the electoral process provides both opportunities and flexibility for those in government.

What it doesn't often provide is the consensus required to make decisions on public policy happen. The task for legislative and executive leaders is to convert their election coalition into a governing coalition. And that task isn't easy.

Getting Results

The public quickly loses interest after an election. Some people are disappointed when their promises go unmet. Constituencies clash within as well as between parties. Well-financed interest groups exercise considerable power. The end result may be that the election determines the policymakers and provides broad guidelines and a plethora of specific proposals, few of which may have the backing of an electoral majority, much less a popular one. What many elections don't provide is the coalition across institutions of government that is necessary to get results. The principal task for elected leaders is to build this coalition and do so quickly, using their victory and the goodwill that ritually follows an election outcome to enhance their initial base of support.

George W. Bush employed bipartisan rhetoric and a partisan congressional majority to gain backing for his proposal to cut taxes. However, on other policy issues such as energy, health, and the environment, Republicans were less unified. Once control of the Senate shifted to the Democrats after James Jeffords's defection from the Republican party, the president had no choice but to convert his bipartisan rhetoric into a legislative strategy that involved consultation and eventually compromise with those who did not share his priorities or agree with all of his initial policy proposals.

There are other ways in which presidents try to get results: constant campaigning to mobilize supporters for their policies and for themselves, tying their policymaking proposals to the public polls so as to gain the maximum possible backing, and pointing to the next election as a support-building, action-forcing mechanism to keep their partisans in line.

In the absence of a partisan or ideological majority, it may be difficult for government to achieve sufficient consensus to act. The reasons for this difficulty are based in the political system itself, in which diverse constituencies produce and reflect diverse goals, interests, and needs to which public officials must be responsive. This diversity is reinforced by a constitutional system that requires policy majorities in both houses of Congress, a supportive president, and a hands-off judiciary to formulate and implement new public policy initiatives.

Ensuring Accountability

As a check on those in government, the electorate holds a trump card: rejection at the polls the next time around. The card isn't often played, however, for several reasons. The practical advantages of incumbency usually outweigh the theoretical option to vote someone out of office. With the exception of the president and other chief executives, it's difficult to assign individual responsibility for institutional action or inaction. It's even hard to assign individual responsibility for economic and social conditions, although executives do tend to receive more credit and blame than their influence over these conditions merits.

Another reason why it's difficult for the public to assess responsibility for what government does is that people generally aren't well informed about the actions of government. And they don't become well informed until the news media focus their attention on a particular issue for a sustained period, attention that may be reinforced by those who wish to take partisan advantage of the situation. A good example is press coverage of White House activities to raise money for the 1996 Democratic campaign, which was kept in the news mix by congressional hearings, expressions of Republican outrage, calls for investigation, and the 2000 election, particularly the campaign of John McCain.

Assigning collective responsibility is even more difficult than holding individuals accountable for their own actions. When control of the government is divided between the parties, credit and blame are shared. For example, which institution and party were to blame for the huge increase in the national debt that occurred during the Reagan years—the Republican president, the Republican Senate, or the Democratic House? And which institution should receive credit for the budget surpluses of the late 1990s—the Democratic president, the Republican Congress, or both? One of the most negative consequences of divided government is the inability to hold one party collectively accountable for public policy outcomes.

For individual behavior, however, responsibility can be pinpointed, even though it doesn't usually result in electoral defeat. There are some exceptions to the nonrejection rule by the voters. Outrageous personal behavior in office is one of them. Illegal acts, such as theft of government property, failure to pay income taxes or child support, even indulging on a regular basis in a prohibited substance like cocaine or marijuana, would probably produce sufficient negative media and public concern to force an official to resign from office or face the strong possibility of defeat in the next nomination or election. Similarly, immoral or unethical behavior, such as sexual improprieties, the flagrant misuse of public property, abusing the perquisites of office, or making serious false claims about one's military service or educational qualifications, would also endanger an official's reelection prospects, if only to encourage a quality challenger.

Accountability in government is enhanced by the potential for election defeat, even if that potential is rarely actualized. In the increasingly public arena of government, under the eye of an increasingly investigative press, and with the public relations campaigns that one's partisan or ideological opponents can wage to highlight behavior and actions that might be viewed as objectionable by a sizable electoral constituency, public officials tend to behave as if they were in the spotlight most of the time. They probably perceive themselves as more visible to their constituency than they actually are. As a result, responsiveness and accountability are fostered by the electorate's holding a trump card—even if it isn't used that often.

Summary: Elections and Government Dilemmas in a Nutshell

Elections provide a critical link between the people and their government. That is the very reason for having elections: to choose the people who will make the major public policy decisions, to provide them with policy direction and political support, to give their decisions legitimacy, and to keep them accountable.

Elections satisfy these democratic goals, but they do so imperfectly. They determine the winners, but the winners aren't always compatible with each other, much less with those already in power. Elections choose the most popular candidates (with the obvious exception of the 2000 presidential contest), but popularity and governing ability aren't synonymous and in some cases may not even be related.

The candidate orientation of contemporary elections, combined with the weakening of party ties and the growing autonomy of elections for different offices at different levels of government, more often than not yields a mixed verdict. It results in the election of candidates with varying perspectives, ideologies, partisan leanings, political experience, and policy interests.

Governing becomes more difficult when the differences among elected officials outweigh their commonalities. Adding to the problem is the perception of many successful candidates that they are and will remain primarily beholden to themselves, to their contributors, and to their constituents for election and reelection—not to their parties, to their president or other chief executive, or to some larger public interest.

Doing what makes political sense for the folks back home becomes a primary guide to government decision making. As a consequence, the electoral process seems to mirror the country's diversity much more effectively than it reflects majority sentiment across constituency lines. This is a problem for governing at the national level, a problem that can be magnified by electing inexperienced candidates and selecting inexperienced staff for advisory and administrative positions in government. To some extent, however, public opinion polls that reflect national popular sentiment counter the constituency orientation of legislative bodies.

The differences between campaigning and governing remain significant. Campaigns have definite winners and losers; government does not. Campaigns are replete with political and ideological rhetoric. Such rhetoric is an impediment to compromise in policymaking. Campaigns generate a crisis atmosphere; such an atmosphere is not conducive to the deliberation and adjustments that must accompany sound policymaking.

However, to the extent that governing is being conducted more and more in the public arena, the campaigning skills of going public, of tailoring and targeting messages to special groups to build support and achieve a favorable impression, are becoming an increasingly important component of governing.

Elections are supposed to guide public officials in what they do and in when and how they do it, but their outcomes often present mixed verdicts and messages. Unless the electorate is voting directly on a policy initiative, it's difficult to cull the meaning of an election, much less translate that meaning into a policy agenda for government. Exit polls and other national surveys provide some guidance about voters' attitudes, opinions, and the most salient issues, but they aren't exact measures, certainly not blueprints for governing. As a consequence, public officials usually have considerable discretion when making policy judgments, as long as they do so within the broad parameters of mainstream politics.

The potential for election defeat combined with negative publicity keeps elected officials responsive to their constituency, more so on an individual than on a collective basis. Accountability is enhanced by the increasingly public arena in which decision making occurs, by an attentive media, and by an opposition that wishes to gain political advantage. It is made more difficult by divided partisan control of government and, coincidentally, by the difficulties that national parties face in imposing discipline on their members.

Elections are also important for converting promises into performance. The key here is not only the composition of the majority, but also the ability of its elected leadership to convert their winning electoral coalition into a winning governing coalition. To be effective, that coalition has to cross constituency, institutional, and sometimes, even partisan lines, which is why its composition may shift on an issue-by-issue basis.

Do elections serve government? Yes, they do. They renew and reinforce the link between the elected and the electorate. They contribute to policy direction, coalition building, and legitimacy for and accountability in government. But they do so imperfectly and often indirectly, and they sometimes impede rather than enhance governing.

Now It's Your Turn

Discussion Questions

1. What constitutional changes would be necessary to elect public officials who are more ideologically and politically compatible with one another?
2. If the electorate were to vote on the basis of issues rather than candidates, would the meaning of elections be clearer and governing made easier?
3. Can the representative character of government and collective responsibility in government be enhanced at the same time?
4. How do elections affect the permanent government, what the bureaucracy does, and how it does it?
5. Now that you have completed this book, how would you answer the question posed by the title: "Is this any way to run a democratic election?"

Topics for Debate

Challenge or defend the following statements:

1. To enhance responsiveness and accountability in government, all elected public officials should stand for reelection every four years.
2. The electorate should be given the opportunity to express its opinion on the ten most salient national issues when voting on election day.
3. No congressional impeachment and conviction of the president should take effect unless it is approved in a special election of American voters.
4. All candidates for the presidency should be required to announce their cabinet choices at least one month before the election.
5. All new public officials should be required to take a course on the structure and operations of the institution to which they were elected or appointed.
6. All federal judges should be selected by popular vote for a fixed term of office.

Exercises

1. Upset by the gap between democratic theory and practice, a presidential commission has been studying ways to make American elections more compatible with the goals of a democratic political system. The commission has identified three objectives that it hopes any new electoral process will meet:
   a. Public preferences for individual candidates and the priorities they should pursue should be clearly identified.

    b. Public opinion on the most salient and controversial policy issues should be determined.

    c. The public's evaluation of how well those in power have performed in office should be indicated.

    With those objectives in mind, suggest changes to make American elections more compatible with democratic goals. In your proposal to the commission, anticipate and respond to likely criticisms. Also tell the commission how you would implement the changes you are suggesting and their likely impact on government.

2. List the campaign promises that George W. Bush made in his 2000 presidential campaign. You can find these promises on the website of a major news organization that provided extensive coverage of the 2000 election, such as CNN, <http://cnn.com/ELECTION/2000/resources/wheretheystand/index>. Determine, if you can,

    a. how Bush prioritized these promises,

    b. which of them he has tried to achieve and which of them he actually has achieved,

    c. which of his promises he has been forced to modify, reverse, or not pursue at this time.

    On the basis of your analysis, how would you rate Bush's success in converting his campaign agenda into a governing agenda and then into public policy?

Internet Resources

Most major media sources will report the large election exit poll in detail. The *New York Times* <http://www.nytimes.com> even allowed some manipulation of the data from that poll after the 1996 election. The Gallup Organization <http://www.gallup.com> as well as the Pew Research Center For The People & The Press <http://www.people-press.org> will likely conduct pre- and postelection surveys and make the results available on their websites. For a longitudinal analysis, the pre- and post–National Election Surveys conducted by the Center for Political Studies at the University of Michigan <http://www.umich.edu/nes> are the source of data for most political scientists. However, this data usually isn't available until about six months after the election. The Federal Election Commission will issue the official results of the national election on its website <http://www.fec.gov>; the fastest listing of unofficial results are the wire services such as the Associated Press <http://www.ap.org>.

Selected Readings

Abramson, Paul R., John H. Aldrich, Phil Paolino, and David W. Rohde. "Third-Party and Independent Candidates in American Politics: Wallace, Anderson, and Perot." *Political Science Quarterly* 110 (1995): 349–367.

Abramson, Paul R., John Aldrich, and David W. Rohde. *Change and Continuity in the 1996 Elections*. Washington, DC: Congressional Quarterly Books, 1998.

Dahl, Robert A. "Myth of the Presidential Mandate." *Political Science Quarterly* 105 (1990): 355–372.

Erikson, Robert S. "The 2000 Presidential Election in Historical Perspective," *Political Science Quarterly* 116 (2001): 29–52.

Fishel, Jeff. *Presidents and Promises*. Washington, DC: Congressional Quarterly Books, 1985.

Gaddie, Ronald Keith, and Charles S. Bullock III. *Elections to Open Seats in the U.S. House: Where the Action Is*. Lanham, MD: Rowman and Littlefield, 2000.

Ginsberg, Benjamin, and Alan Stone, eds. *Do Elections Matter?* Armonk, NY: M. E. Sharpe, 1996.

Herrnson, Paul S. *Congressional Elections: Campaigning at Home and in Washington*. Washington, DC: Congressional Quarterly Books, 2000.

Jacobson, Gary C. *The Electoral Origins of Divided Government: Competition in U.S. House Elections, 1946–1988*. Boulder, CO: Westview, 1990.

———. *The Politics of Congressional Elections*. New York: Longman, 2001.

Kelley, Stanley. *Interpreting Elections*. Princeton, NJ: Princeton University Press, 1983.

Miller, Arthur H., and Martin P. Wattenberg. "Throwing the Rascals Out: Policy and Performance Evaluations of Presidential Candidates, 1952–1980." *American Political Science Review* 79 (1985): 359–372.

Popkin, Samuel L. *The Reasoning Voter*. Chicago: University of Chicago Press, 1991.

Shienbaum, Kim Ezra. *Beyond the Electoral Connection*. Philadelphia: University of Pennsylvania Press, 1984.

Notes

1. The term "a government of strangers" was first suggested by Hugh Heclo in his book *A Government of Strangers* (Washington, DC: Brookings Institution, 1977).

2. For an excellent discussion of the differences between campaigning and governing for and in the presidency, see Charles O. Jones, *Passages to the Presidency* (Washington, DC: Brookings Institution, 1998).

3. Case study from Stephen J. Wayne, G. Calvin Mackenzie, David M. O'Brien, and Richard L. Cole, *The Politics of American Government*, 3rd ed. (New York: St. Martin's/Worth, 1999), 273–274.

4. A good example of the latter is Dick Morris, who came to President Clinton's aid after the Democrats' defeat in the 1994 midterm elections. Morris, who engineered Clinton's reelection victory, had previously worked as a political consultant for Clinton in his third campaign for the Arkansas governorship, as well as for conservative Republicans such as Trent Lott, the Senate Republican leader, and Jesse Helms, a senator from North Carolina.

5. Like the candidate they supported, they may also have little executive experience and be unfamiliar with the formal and informal procedures of the institution to which their candidate has been elected and with the people who work there.

6. Although senior members of the Reagan administration did not fall into this morass with the political establishment, they did with civil servants who staffed the federal bureaucracy. Reagan and his supporters distrusted the national government, particularly the bureaucracy, and they tried to circumvent the permanent government when putting their priority proposals in place. The problem was that Reagan's newly appointed department heads and their aides lacked the expertise to get things done. Over time, most of Reagan's political appointees grew to depend on and respect the civil servants who worked for them.

7. In addition to policy initiatives, some states also have a procedure known as a *referendum,* which allows a state legislature to place items directly before the voters on an election ballot.

8. A federal district court in San Francisco found that many of these restrictions were unconstitutional.

9. Richard J. Ellis, "The States: Direct Democracy," in *The Elections of 2000,* ed. Michael Nelson (Washington, DC: Congressional Quarterly Books, 2001), 141.

10. Ibid., 143–145.

11. Ibid., 137.

12. *Buckley* v. *American Constitutional Law Foundation,* U.S. 97-930 (1999).

13. Ellis, "The States," 134.

14. For issues to be the most important influence on voting behavior, voters must have an opinion on the issues, perceive differences in the candidates' positions, and then vote on the basis of these differences and in the direction of their own policy positions.

15. The random selection is made within states in such a way that principal geographic units (cities, suburbs, and rural areas), size of precincts, and precincts' past voting record are taken into account. Approximately 1,200 representatives of the polling organization administer the poll to voters who are chosen in a systematic way (for example, every fourth or fifth person) as they leave the voting booths. Voters are asked to complete a short questionnaire (thirty to forty items) designed to elicit information on voting choices, political attitudes, candidate evaluations and feelings, as well as the demographic characteristics of those who voted. Several times over the course of the day, the questionnaires are collected and tabulated, and the results are sent to a central computer bank. After most or all of the election polls in a state have been completed, the findings of the exit poll are broadcast. Over the course of the evening they are adjusted to reflect the actual results as they are tabulated.

Index